Parenting in the Screen Age

A Guide for Calm Conversations

Delaney Ruston, MD

From the maker of the acclaimed **SCREENAGERS** movies

STARHOUSE
MEDIA

ISBN: 978-1-7356396-0-4 (Paperback)
ISBN: 978-1-7356396-1-1 (eBook)

Front cover images © Shutterstock.com
Book cover and layout design by *the*BookDesigners

Printed in the United States of America.
First printing edition 2020.

Publisher:
Starhouse Media, LLC
121 San Anselmo Ave
Box 2832
San Anselmo, CA 94960
www.screenagersmovie.com
415-450-9585

Parenting
in the
Screen Age

Dedicated to Peter, Chase, and Tessa with immense love.

Contents

· · · ·

Introduction

. . .

It goes without saying

Well, it goes without saying, but let me say it anyway. Our tech revolution is incredible beyond words — the ability to get and share information is beyond anything I could ever have imagined, the ability to connect with others around the world is remarkable, and the list goes on and on and on. I would not go back, but I do think things can be improved upon. I often think that the new stresses of parenting and the new challenges we face are high prices we pay for all the millions of "goodies" the revolution has brought us. I see these parenting challenges as opportunities — reading this book will help you change the "price" of technology into "pay off" by exploring ways to raise kids in the digital age who will be better communicators, more emotionally aware, and more mindful and compassionate than if we weren't encouraged to parent more intentionally in this world of screen supremacy.

It also goes without saying, but I will say it anyway, screen time is not "ruining a generation," a phrase I have heard and read repeatedly across news outlets. Dooming a generation is unfair, untrue and downright mean. Our kids are wonderful and doing the best they can with the inner and outer resources they have at any given time.

This book is relevant during and post Covid-19

When Covid-19 hit, we all became more grateful than ever about the upsides of our tech revolution. In a matter of weeks, screen time became our lifeline, allowing for ongoing learning, the ability to connect with others, entertainment, news and much more. Tech often allowed for classrooms to go online and for work for us parents to continue.

At the same time, the challenges of screen time balance became even more pronounced. This book is all about how we, as parents, can feel as empowered as possible to help our kids maintain healthy screen time — whether during summer vacation, a busy school year, or stuck quarantined through a pandemic. The skills and strategies parents need around screen time endure. I wrote the vast majority of this book from the perspective of not being in a "shelter-in-place" situation, but there are suggestions woven throughout that are useful if you are sheltering in place. The book is full of hundreds of ideas around how to approach tech-themed conversations with your child and these themes are timeless.

How it all started

My stress around screen time issues and my kids began to form in 2011 when my son Chase was 12 and my daughter Tessa was 10. They started asking for more and more screen time. We had struggles when it was time to get off a screen. I felt at a loss of what to say or do.

I would think to myself, "If only there was a book like 'What To Expect When You're Expecting' that included a chapter called 'Expect a technology revolution and here are all the solutions you need.'" But alas, no such book existed.

Tensions could flare suddenly around all of this screen time conflict. It caused me to feel so many emotions — sadness, frustration, anger and then guilt for being angry. And, of course, worry.

At the time, Facebook was just starting and Chase, in seventh grade, was using it to interact with friends. At that time, I was worried about how it was such a time suck, as well as the crude and often offensive things he was seeing on the site, such as things being shared from a site called 9GAG.

This was the early period of "social media," and I was not yet thinking of the deeper issues to come.

Meanwhile, screen time in general made me worry about all the things my kids could be exposed to — all sorts of things in the media like violence, harsh words, intense shows, the risk of seeing pornography and more. What if they put up a little YouTube video that was not well-received? Would they feel left out of things others were doing? Would exposure to violent video games change them? Would video gaming overtake their free time?

Between my husband, Peter, and myself, there was mounting tension because we saw things differently when it came to screen time. Peter would say, "They just need to learn how to manage screen time themselves." Allowing our kids to learn from experience, with guardrails, of course, has always been something my husband and I greatly value. So, I understood his logic, but I would respond, "Wait, the pull towards screens is so strong, aren't we just setting them up for failure?"

As the days rolled forward, I was increasingly aware that this was exactly what we were doing.

I could see that the pull was so great on our kids and I thought a lot about how this Herculean pull was only to get stronger. Smartphones making screen time possible everywhere were just emerging and meanwhile, one-to-one programs were springing up all over and homework was increasingly shifting to computer screens.

Many schools began to give each student their own mobile device, such as an iPad or Chromebook, for school work. This allowed kids to defend unending screen time in the name of needing to do homework. When I first heard my son say the now-infamous line, "I need it for homework," I shuddered.

Questions started to nag at me, both as a mother and as a primary care physician. I worked many years as a researcher and wanted scientifically-backed answers to all the questions I was asking myself, such as, what is the impact of social media on kids, what is the impact of video games, and how much time on screens is healthy?

I was desperate to understand what types of limits were necessary around screen time and how to enforce such rules without ruining my relationship with my kids or my husband. My days were filled with a thousand questions and my nights with a thousand worries. Talking with parents, teachers and others about these issues, I knew I was not alone.

What surprised me most was how little discussion there was in schools and the press about all the topics that consumed me. Where were the public forums about screen time and youth?

I wondered how I could help get discussions going in order to answer the questions that were on my mind and share the findings with others. I knew what I needed to do, and that was to make a documentary. I had been making documentaries on key social issues that impacted me personally for over a decade.

The decision to make a documentary

My interest in documentaries began while I was growing up in Berkeley, California. I lived with my mom, who would rent out space in our small home to help supplement the rent. I didn't have siblings, so I often talked with the renters. One was an editor for documentary films and when I saw her films, I was immediately enthralled by the power of watching people tell their real-life stories.

When I was in medical school, affordable consumer video cameras hit the market and I was so excited when I bought my first one. I filmed strangers when I was out and about, asking them all types of questions, such as what they liked about their job. Other times the interviews I conducted were a bit more playful, like the day I asked people for their opinion on the tacky shirt my friend was wearing (my friend had worn the wackiest shirt we could find just for this very purpose).

During my Primary Care Residency at UC San Francisco, I started taking filmmaking classes when I was not working in the hospital. During this time, I made a short educational film involving a family who didn't want their elderly mother to know she had cancer, which is a common practice in certain cultures. I felt ethically torn about what to do and how to best handle the situation. Withholding information from patients was not something my peers and I had ever learned about in our medical education and I hoped to provide insight into all of the cultural and ethical issues that a circumstance like this one raised. With the family's permission, I filmed my journey to understand how to approach the situation. That is how my first short film, "If She Knew" was born.

What really got me hooked on pursuing documentary filmmaking alongside my devotion to being a doctor was that I began to see how documentaries could be used as the centerpiece for social movements. I saw how these films could be used in community screenings across the country to bring together citizens, policymakers and others to spark conversations and reveal solutions.

I found that the issues that often surrounded families dealing with mental health problems were not being addressed in our society nearly enough. I knew this all too well, both as a physician and as a daughter of someone with schizophrenia. My dad's illness began before my birth and as I was growing up, things were really hard.

As an adult, I had a lot of questions about my own relationship with my father, as well as the way in which our society failed to provide enough support for those who were in similar situations to mine. I wanted to find ways to help my father and grow closer to him. I also wanted to understand how society could better help all families dealing with serious mental illness. With my dad's permission, I decided to make a very personal documentary about my family's journey in order to find answers. The goal was to use the film as a vehicle to inspire conversations and motivate people to take action.

What resulted is a deeply personal documentary: "UNLISTED: A Story of Schizophrenia." In partnership with the United States' largest mental health advocacy organizations, "UNLISTED" was screened in communities across the country to bring people together to discuss the issues that are often regarded as taboo and rarely discussed.

What made the film such a success to me was hearing from so many people about how the film not only made them feel less alone, but also helped them feel more comfortable talking with others about their own mental health challenges and inspired them to discuss ideas to increase access to help for their loved ones. I was working day and night on advocacy but it never felt like work because it was so gratifying.

Inspired by "UNLISTED," I wanted to understand how people experienced mental health problems around the world. I was amazed that while global health was getting lots of attention via organizations such as the Bill and Melinda Gates Foundation, global mental health was almost completely ignored.

I was able to spend time in many countries to create the film "HIDDEN PICTURES: A Personal Journey Into Global Mental Health." Again, my goal was to bring people together through community screenings to encourage discussion about how to ensure that individuals and families all over the world get the support they deserve. The reach of this film extended even further through the organizing of various events, such as a global screening with 141 organizations on World Mental Health Day, and later by partnering with the World Health Organization in advocacy work. There had not yet been a film on global mental health and I was delighted to receive so many messages from people around the world thanking me for bringing attention to stories like their own.

The experience I gained from my earlier films gave me the confidence to make a documentary about screen time that I hoped would be an important tool for social change.

I thought about how such a film would need to be geared toward kids, parents, teachers and anyone who is interested in children's well-being because our tech revolution is massive and ever-growing. It was and is clear to me that we need everyone to come together to find solutions to ensure balance. I knew that community screenings would be the perfect way to foster conversations and build a movement.

The birth of the film "Screenagers: Growing Up in the Digital Age"

In my search for families who were willing to share their concerns about screen time, I was shocked to find that this was much more difficult than I had anticipated. I knew that I was not the only parent struggling to understand how best to raise children in our tech revolution, so I had expected that finding families who would want to talk in the film would be fairly straightforward. After all, we were not talking about mental illness. Finding stories for "Hidden Pictures" in places like South Africa and China was extremely difficult since mental health stigma is so prevalent. I had really believed that finding people to interview about screen time issues would be so much easier, but I was wrong.

Once I thought more about it, I realized that parents' hesitations made a lot of sense. Parenting is the most important thing we do. Sharing things we have tried to do, either attempts that have seemed to work or ones that have outright failed, makes us worry that we will be judged. I know that I too had this feeling at times while appearing in *Screenagers* with my family. Was I too lenient? Too controlling? Were the rules we came up with in the film "fair?"

Another reason parents were so hesitant to be filmed is that growing up, many didn't have the same exposure to screens as their children do today. This was brand new territory and feeling really unsure of any and all policies made perfect sense once I thought about it more.

Originally, I had not planned on filming myself and my own family for this new film, but I wanted to show, in real time, the challenges that families are experiencing. I also felt that it was important to show that the struggles that feel so personal are actually happening in almost every home in America. Given how hard it was initially to find families willing to share, I realized that mine had to go first.

So with their permission, I started to film my family. These clips mainly focus on my continued failed attempts to get things right with my kids concerning their screen time. As the film progresses, you see the lessons I learned and several solutions that started to work in our home. Fortunately, over the 3 1/2 years of making the film, I was finally able to find many families and youth who wanted to be in the film, even though it wasn't easy.

The finished film, *Screenagers*, explores the impact of things like social media, video gaming and tech in schools and considers all types of solutions that have the ability to create healthy screen time balance. Interwoven into stories of families are insights from psychologists, brain scientists and other experts attempting to shed light upon some of the impacts that tech can have on youth, as well as ways to ensure healthier screen time in our homes and schools.

Before Covid-19, more than 4 million people in 80 countries gathered to watch the film in person and discuss solutions afterward. Once Covid-19 hit, we started to hold community screenings online. The goal has always been to promote community participation that continues beyond the film screening. This type of work is hard and important and we all need to be working together for the long haul.

The birth of the film "Screenagers NEXT CHAPTER: Uncovering Skills for Stress Resilience"

A couple of years into the film's screenings, I was reading news reports and hearing from many parents about their teens' concerning levels of stress, anxiety and depression. Questions about the social and emotional impact of screen time were beginning to circulate.

Then, my daughter started having symptoms of depression and even as a doctor, I didn't know what to do. Often, when I stepped in and tried to help I would make her more upset! That was the last thing I wanted to do. Meanwhile, I wanted to understand how her time on social media, YouTube and other platforms was impacting her emotional state. What could I do and how was screen time playing into this?

I wanted to find solutions. What do we need to know about screen time in order to minimize any negative impacts on mental health? What skills can all teens learn, at home and at school, that can help them handle challenging emotions including stress, anxiety and depression? What specific things can all parents do to raise emotionally intelligent teens in our screen-saturated society? Finally, what could I do to support my daughter?

All of this led to the creation of "Screenagers NEXT CHAPTER." The film interweaves my personal stories with those of my own teenagers — particularly my daughter Tessa, who was struggling with depression. Featured alongside personal stories are experiments and brain science that I found fascinating, as well as insight from researchers, psychologists and parenting experts. The film reveals all sorts of steps that can be taken in order to provide teens with skills to navigate complex emotional and social challenges that have always been a part of growing up but have been heightened by our tech revolution.

All about improving our conversations about tech with youth

My goal for the *Screenagers* films was to improve conversations about screen time occurring between adults and youth. To this end, I geared the films for both kids and parents. I hoped that families would watch them together so they could see the story and science in the movie and then would have a not-so-personal way of discussing the often charged topics.

But this goal went beyond just sparking short post-screening discussions. I hoped to find ways to help foster productive ongoing conversations in homes. I knew this was really important to encourage because research shows that approximately 30% of parents and youth in the U.S. reported that they fight daily about screen time. That is, millions of families. For many other families, this fighting is not daily but it is still very frequent.

Some argue that it is inevitable and even developmentally appropriate. Nevertheless, ongoing battles can erode relationships in profound ways.

Why calm conversations can be so hard

There are many reasons why productive conversations between teens and parents are so difficult. From my own experience, I can relate to these three common points.

First, the elevated emotions of parents

My emotions ran high when I thought about the many factors that related to my kids' screen time. I worried about them feeling excluded, feeling inferior or watching shows that modeled values I disagreed with. I admit that I'm a bit of a control freak, but I hated to see them wasting so much of their time online. Why were they not outside hiking or doing some creative writing?

I would often, without thinking, start talking about all of my concerns not *with* them but *at* them — pouring my fears onto them in hopes that I could worry them into not doing or seeing the things on the internet that worried me.

It took me a while to realize that my emotions were making them not want to talk with me about screen time issues. Even when I was speaking very calmly, they could still sense my negative feelings.

Second, the defensiveness of youth

Youth feel lots of strong emotions when it comes to talking with their parents about screen time. Struggles over control and rules often come to a head when the screen is involved. Parents use it as a tool: "You can't have your phone if you don't..." to weaponize the conversation. Kids receive messages from the news, and other adults, that generally report very negative headlines about youth and tech use. Things like, "It's destroying a generation," and "It's causing depression." There is much less talk about how screen time can bring positivity to their lives. Over and over, youth have told me that all of this negativity makes them feel very irritated, defensive and even angry.

This scare approach also often happens in schools. Screen time discussions may only occur when a police officer is brought in to talk to the kids about cyberbullying or sexting. When an officer came to my daughter's middle school to speak about cyberbullying, I was surprised by the accusatory nature of her presentation. She literally said that she believed that all of them had cyberbullied in some way. I was speechless when I left the classroom.

Third, these are sensitive conversation topics

A third reason why screen time conversations can be challenging is that they involve complicated topics. The intensity of things that kids may see and read starting at a young age due to the internet is like nothing a parent would have thought possible just 10 years ago. For instance, they regularly witness intense pornography, self-harm, shark attacks, suicide and drug use in shows like "13 Reasons Why" and platforms like YouTube and PornHub. This kind of content can also come off as "how-to" instructions, which is particularly upsetting.

Even if one has installed blockers such as Net Nanny, the truth is that kids will be around screens in many settings. And many teens are wily enough to get around blockers anyway.

Knowing that it is important to talk about a sensitive topic, and knowing what to say are two completely different things. For example, many elementary-age children can now be exposed to pornographic images and videos. How can we handle this challenging topic? How does that conversation change as they get older?

How conversations became calmer in our home

Years back, our conversations about tech were not calm at all — we were undergoing everything I mentioned above. At some point while making *Screenagers*, I realized it would be helpful to have an agreed-upon time in the family to talk about tech — our rules, our solutions and so forth. My girlfriend told me about weekly family meetings she had in her house when she raised her teens years prior and that planted a seed in my mind.

So I talked with my family and we came up with this idea: Tech Talk

Tuesdays, a time carved out in the week where we would discuss issues around screen time. These issues would include screen limits for our family and broader issues of screen time in our lives and society at large.

Having this weekly practice started to help our family dynamic. We felt much more like a team than like opponents in a battle of wills. We started debating the issues of freedom of the press and how far that freedom should go, given all we saw happening online. Of course, we also talked about our own screen balance goals, how our home rules were working or not working, and what rules needed to be modified.

Things were calmer in our home. The stress level was lower and we were all relating better.

All of this led me to begin writing a weekly blog called "Tech Talk Tuesdays" about the topics I was discussing with my family so that it might help other adults have productive conversations with the youth in their lives — their own kids, those they interact with at school, in after-school programs, in faith-based settings and so on.

I started by sharing these writings via the *Screenager*'s website and then they quickly spread via all sorts of channels, like schools who were posting them in their newsletters. I have been writing and sharing these posts every week for over four years now. I am fortunate that my Co-Producer and Community Engagement Partner, Lisa Tabb, has been an incredible thought partner in creating these.

Having spent more than four years researching and writing the "Tech Talk Tuesday" (TTT) blog and seeing how much they were helping families, Lisa and I realized that adapting the most popular blogs and adding additional writings into a book could be helpful.

The writings in this book draw from iterations of my favorites of more than 200 TTTs. The vast majority are either brand new or significantly revised. Each topic section has questions at the end that are meant to facilitate discussions between you and your kids.

What this book aims to do

My goal with this book is to help parents raise kids in the face of our new screen world and to give a roadmap of important conversations to have with kids and teens.

This book covers all of the topics that I believe are essential for everyone to be discussing in their homes and schools. Such topics include video gaming, social media, sleep, mental health and communication skills, just to name a few. The book also covers the critical topic of ways in which parents can work with their kids to create healthy screen time limits and to ensure that those limits are followed.

This book, with the many conversation starters it aims to spark between adults and youth, provides a means by which youth can better develop insight into the many complex issues associated with our tech revolution. For example, what are their views on the societal trend to buy so many goods through Amazon rather than in person at stores? How do they feel about our new "attention economy," whereby companies employ all sorts of strategies to keep eyeballs on their tech products? Having conversations like these will help you raise compassionate thinkers who will be the leaders in their homes and beyond regarding tech issues.

Through my years of filming and speaking at schools, I have been disappointed with how few opportunities youth have to discuss the hundreds of topics that our digital age raises, as many of these directly impact them. The thing is, youth LOVE to talk about these issues. Granted, your child may not be open to talking about tech with you at this time — as was the case initially in my home — but don't worry, this book has lots of solutions for such scenarios (you get to learn from my mistakes).

Another intention of this book is to improve our children's science literacy by providing many research findings that can be shared with them. I have consistently found that youth are very interested in learning about research related to screen time. Unlike science that can seem incredibly abstract — such as chemistry (no offense chemistry) — experiments related to screen time and human psychology are much more relatable.

Being science-savvy is so important, especially now, as news headlines fly at our kids and media outlets try to distill research into catchy headlines. What is the actual science behind the words and are the media messages accurate? When Covid-19 hit, it only reinforced the need for us to raise science-literate youth.

How to have effective conversations?
Answer: communication science

Throughout the book, I share many evidence-based techniques that lead to productive, fruitful discussions that can help decrease friction and repair fractured relationships. It is all through using communication science.

Communication science is something I became interested in when I was a medical student, even though I wasn't familiar with the term at the time. I was intrigued by the fact that some physicians use words and mannerisms in a way that make patients and patients' families feel at ease and cared for. I could visibly see this on patients' faces. Then there were other physicians whose communication techniques would inevitably leave patients feeling worse.

My interest in interpersonal communication inspired me to do research in the science of it at UC San Francisco.

An ineffective communication approach:
the "scare tactic"

When I started making *Screenagers*, I saw that the main way kids were learning about tech was via scare tactics. Think, for example, of the schools that teach kids about cyberbullying and sexting, and how some of them have police officers deliver the message so it is clear that they should be really scared of the consequences.

Unfortunately, scare tactics have not proven to be very effective for long-term behavior change. Let me give you one example: Massive public health campaigns designed to combat smoking showed images of damaged lungs and provided testimonials from people diagnosed with lung cancer with the intention of scaring us out of using cigarettes.

It turns out that those campaigns had a surprisingly small impact on behavior decisions. What eventually turned the tide and cut smoking rates were two tactics: substantially raising the cost of cigarettes and placing firm limits on the places where people could smoke. Of course, continuing to educate people about the ill effects of tobacco is important, but if we had just focused on using scare tactics, we would not have made the significant progress we see today.

Scare tactics can work well for short term behavior change but it's important to examine a better way to shape behavior, which I call "share tactics."

But first, let's explore the science behind why scare tactics are not very effective when it comes to youth and screen time. The amygdala is the part of the brain that responds to fear and provides us with warnings that something scary is about to take place. Do you remember when you first watched a scary movie that played creepy music as the camera led you down an eerie hotel hallway? Even when you don't, the amygdala does. That's why you may get creeped out in empty hallways later on in life.

This is crucial. Learning from fear-inducing stimuli helps us avoid and escape danger. But what happens when your amygdala is shooting fear straight to your nerves and nothing bad actually occurs? You stop responding. This is exactly what is happening with our kids when we keep telling them, "Too much YouTube is bad for your brain" or "Playing violent video games will make you violent." If we constantly yell, "DANGER, DANGER!" and the warning is not in sync with our child's experience, they will tune out our words.

I understand that it is very hard to exercise restraint when things seem scary, since we feel like it is our job as parents to protect our youth. We worry about the risk of video games, social media, binge-watching, social cruelty, anxiety, grades and the list goes on and on. So what do we do?

Ditching a "scare tactic" for a "share tactic"

When it comes to getting our kids to engage with us on tech issues, I have found it more effective to engage in what I call a "share tactic" instead of a "scare tactic." A share tactic stresses the importance of sharing science and stories in a non-black-and-white way. It is about considering many perspectives when looking at topics. Scare tactics take the opposite approach. They are very black-and-white and one-sided.

People, especially tweens and teens, are not big fans of being told what to do and what to think. Instead of talking at them in a doom and gloom way, could you include them in the conversation? Listen to their experiences and opinions about the dangers of social media, video games and too much YouTube. Calm conversations involving statistics, real-life stories and areas of relatability are what get people — including tweens and teens — to think and act preventatively.

Of course, these share tactics help us work together to define and follow the rules so that we can also have sacred, screen-free times in our lives.

Ideas for how to use this book

Please know that you will still get a lot out of reading this book on your own without engaging in the conversation topics and suggested questions that I provide.

If you can have these conversations with your child, that is great. One thing that really helps me stay consistent with them is to pick a certain time to talk each week — or maybe twice a week. My family picked Tuesday nights during dinner. If something prevented all of us from being at the table together, I found other times — such as when we were all in the car — to hold "pop-up" Tech Talks.

It's also important to decide whether these conversations should be a time devoted exclusively to topics in the book or if they should involve issues taking place in your own home. For us, Tech Talk Tuesdays were a time to bring up any and all issues. For example, if Chase or Tessa would only turn in their phones after I had reminded them several times each night, then we would strategize about how to make the nighttime routine go smoother at our next Tuesday meeting.

I highly recommend starting most of your conversations by asking everyone to begin with something positive about the tech in their life. Examples of the positives of tech may be a good conversation a child had over Zoom with a grandparent, a new app they found or a new trending game or meme they like. When we started our tech talks, I quickly found that beginning with the positive significantly improved our discussions — my kids were less defensive and in a better mood. It was the perfect way to set the stage for talking about harder topics.

Before venturing forward I share these final thoughts

I know that many of us believe that managing screen time in our homes is extra hard because we didn't grow up with all of this tech in our homes. We didn't have parents dealing with these issues. Yes, this is true. Yet, I'm often reminded that just because one grows up with something doesn't mean they will know how to parent around it. For instance, think about drugs and alcohol.

I hope that when today's kids become adults and the topic of parenting and tech comes up, they will say something like, "I grew up in the tech revolution and at home, we talked about it all and things were managed pretty well. I feel pretty prepared." But they also might say, "I grew up in the tech revolution, and all I remember is a lot of fighting."

I want to emphasize one final point, which is that there is NO ONE WAY to parent! Each of us is different and that is the beauty of our humanness. The last thing I want this book to do is make anyone feel negatively judged about their parenting. There are so many factors at play in our selves and in our homes that make parenting such a wild journey. To me, the key is being open and humble with our kids about how we are on this journey to do the best we can, because we love them so darn much.

Chapter One:

Social Media

Youth today are inundated with adults telling them that social media is evil. They hear this via the press and from the adults in their homes and schools. In the meantime, they see lots of good things about social media. All of this works to make kids feel like we adults "don't get it."

Meanwhile, there are plenty of news articles and book titles that put kids down, with the idea that social media and cellphones are "ruining a generation." This, not surprisingly, makes youth feel insulted and leads them to become defensive.

I am to blame for this too. I was originally so focused on making sure my kids understood all the risks of social media that I forgot the key step — first validating that there are also many positive things about tech. I have come to realize that this validation cannot occur just once or twice through saying something like, "Yeah, hun, I know it is great that you can talk with friends on social media," and then returning to my fears of inappropriate picture sharing and on and on.

Talking with psychologists, I realized why it is important that we often let our teens know that we appreciate their feelings about social media. This is because we are asking our youth to hold two opposing views in their brains at the same time. On the one hand, social media has many positive aspects to it. And on the other hand, it also has negative aspects. Holding two seemingly opposite views side by side at the same time is hard for all humans, but it turns out it is particularly hard for younger brains. This is called dialectical thinking — holding two seemingly opposing views at the same time.

Young people's brains rely on more black-and-white thinking than those of adults. I have seen my kids experience plenty of the upsides of social media along with the downsides. For example, my son Chase's ongoing group chat with boys from his high school has been both a source of great fun and hard emotions for him. I remember during his senior year of high school, after he had sustained a concussion, some guys in his main chat group were inferring he was faking it. They suggested he was trying to get out of doing things. It was incredibly hard for my son to be dealing with the pain of the concussion while getting accused of being a liar for it. As a mom, how could I best engage with him about his online social life in a way that felt supportive and not too intrusive?

My daughter loved the conveniences of social media to help coordinate with her dance team or to stay connected with friends she had to move away from. At the same time, I have also seen her in emotional pain from agonizing over posting just the right photo on Instagram or being made fully aware that she was not being invited to social gatherings.

The social lives of kids have always been a confusing ground for parents to navigate. It has always been hard to be both engaged and also to give space — what is the right balance? Now, with social media, this challenge is more complicated than ever.

A Common Sense Media study found that fewer than half of parents in the United States regularly discuss social media content with their preteens or teens.[1]

Now is the time to change that statistic and to empower parents with the tools to feel more confident in talking with their youth about social media.

● ● ●

Appreciating Positives Aspects of Social Media

There are pluses and minuses to social media — it would be ludicrous to claim it was all one way or the other. Yet, I am the first to admit that my comments were heavily biased for a long time when I would have conversations about technology with my kids . Surprise, surprise, eventually, they were very resistant to talk with me about the topic. I needed to change.

I consciously spent several days in a row exclusively talking about the positives about social media. Soon, they weren't just more open to talking about it with me, but they also started to bring up things that bothered them about social media.

Having a conversation (ideally, more than once) about the upsides of social media and other communication tools in our tech times can be a very effective way to inspire calm conversations that can lead to deeper ones over time.

Let me start with a story I heard on Susan Cain's podcast series called "Quiet." Cain is the author of the book, "Quiet: The Power of Introverts in a World That Can't Stop Talking." In an episode entitled, "How Young Introverts Can Thrive on Social Media," we meet a young professional, Davis Nguyen, who has been an introvert for all his life.[2] The core of the story is how social media helped him achieve many goals despite being an introvert.

Davis grew up in poverty and was attending one of the lowest-ranked high schools in the country, but he aspired to go to a top-tier university. He decided to use the internet and social media to reach out to other teens across the country to ask for tips on taking the SAT and for help with his college essay. He says that he was happy that several people he did not know offered to help.

> Davis said:
> *"One girl from Harvard told me that one of my essays I'd spent 40 hours on was really bad. ... I'm so glad she gave me that feedback, because I was able to throw it away, and the next essay I wrote turned out to be the one that I turned in to Yale and Harvard. The fact that I was able to ask for help, I was able to get really good feedback."* (Davis was accepted at both universities.)

But the part of the story that is most remarkable is that he realized that he could use social media to connect to people he admired, such as Rolf Potts, the author of one of Davis' favorite books, "Vagabonding." Davis not only reached him, but he was able to help when the author said he would like to speak at Davis' school. This experience was so positive for Davis that he decided to use social media to reach out to other people he looked up to, which led to many new connections, including with author Susan Cain.

Davis said:

"Every week, I would do my research on one person who I look up to, and I would find a way to be helpful for them. ... It's not jumping completely out of my comfort zone, but just extending it just a few inches every week."

So, being able to venture out socially and make small steps can be a helpful aspect of social media. And by no means is Cain advocating that youth hide behind social media. Cain says in the podcast: "And that's the key. To help quiet kids to use social media as a tool for development but not as a crutch to avoid face to face encounters."

Let me give some other examples of the positives of social media that teens often describe.

CAN HELP SHY AND INTROVERTED YOUTH TO COMMUNICATE

It is common for adults to talk about how they worry that kids can only say things online and cannot talk face-to-face. Yet, many youth tell me that they are saying things online that they want to express but are just not quite ready to be having such conversations in person. They still have in-person conversations with some people of course, such as family and good friends. They just find that with the aid of social media, they can have more time to compose themselves and have conversations with people beyond their closest friends. In this way, things like Snapchat, email and texting can take away some of the anxiety that in-person interactions can create.

Of course, the problem is that if they do not, over time, get more comfortable talking in person with people, then social anxiety needs to be considered. The good news is that the vast majority of older teens I have met, who told me how they were shy as tweens and appreciated that they could communicate with peers through tech, developed increasing confidence in face-to-face conversations over time.

DEEP DISCUSSIONS WITH FRIENDS

My own teens and so many others I have spoken to talk about all the deep conversations they have over text and social media. And when I ask if these conversations are as meaningful as they are in person, many times, they say yes. On a few occasions, both my kids have shared deep conversations they had with someone on social media and I am always impressed with the level of honesty that goes back and forth.

STAYING IN CONTACT WITH FRIENDS FAR AWAY OR FROM PAST SCHOOLS

One great advantage of social media is the ease with which we can all stay in contact with people we care about. Kids can reach out to friends from their old schools or their old neighborhoods, making them feel connected even when they are far apart.

CONNECTING WITH COMMUNITIES TO FEEL UNDERSTOOD

Social media can provide kids with online communities that offer support. Kids who are feeling alone as they navigate life can often find fellowship in online groups of people who share an identity. Young people who are bisexual, gay, trans, etc., can find connections online.

MANY WAYS TO DO SMALL ACTS OF KINDNESS FOR FRIENDS

Social media has made it much easier to support businesses and social causes with reviews on Yelp and sharing recommendations. My family and I love the little bakery down our street. It is a bit worn down, but the owner is an incredible baker. I wanted to help spread the word, so I was happy to be able to give her a great review on Yelp. I did not expect it, but one day when I stopped in for some outstanding carrot cake, the owner thanked me for posting a review.

Being able to spread the word about friends' work, such as a talk they are giving, a book or a show or their pop up bread stand (which our neighbors have sporadically done around Seattle) feels so great. We parents don't take this for granted because it was so hard to spread the word before the tech revolution.

HOW I CHANGED AS A MOM

I know if you are like me, your mind was probably piping in with all the worries you had while you were reading the positives of social media above. It is the same for me. One example from my experience related to Tessa and her interest in watching "influencers" — also called "creators" and "YouTubers" — who she finds on social media and YouTube. Usually, the influencers she gravitates to are girls her age or slightly older.

At times, Tessa has looked up advice from these girls. For instance, Tessa may type in, "What to do when having a bad day" and start listening to whichever YouTuber catches her eye.

I worried about all sorts of things, like what might happen if the YouTuber gave her bad advice and only made her feel worse. When I would try to talk with Tessa about my fears, she would tune me out.

I needed to change my tune. I started saying more validating things to Tessa, such as, "What you are saying makes a lot of sense." I would also mention that it made sense that she would go to get inspiration from people online and that I did this too by listening to certain podcasts where people talked about psychology and life skills.

Eventually, by letting Tessa know that I understood that these videos did help her at times, she started sharing them with me. From this new place of understanding, we have been able to have interesting conversations about issues like when she should choose to reach out to a friend for input vs. turn to the internet, or if a sponsor behind a YouTuber could taint her genuineness.

IDEAS FOR CONVERSATION STARTERS:

1. How does tech help you make connections?
2. What connections over social media feel really good?
3. Do you think liking a photo is a small act of kindness?

What is the Right Age to Give a Phone With Social Media?

I get asked all the time what age is right to give a child a phone. What people are really asking is when they should hand over a small computer (i.e., a smartphone) with access to the world. Most parents are not concerned about giving their kids or teens a phone, per se. If it was just a phone, that would be easy. If it was just a phone with texting, that would be slightly more complicated, but it would still feel manageable.

Parents, like myself, often feel caught between a rock and a hard place. On the one hand, we hear from our youth that everyone is on such and such app, like Instagram, and they are the only ones without it. It also can be really hard if a sports team or another group is using social media to make plans together. We also know there are perks to a smartphone, like seeing when the bus is coming or having a camera or a calculator available at all times.

And then, on the other hand, we have legitimate concerns about social media — such as exposure to strangers, internal and external pressures to post and respond, desire for attention, access to porn and more. We also worry about social conflicts such as being excluded, inappropriate group chats, sexy posing and posting, making inappropriate TikTok videos and on and on.

There is no science-driven data that tells us that there is a specific age that is the right one to allow a phone and access to social media. Granted, when I hear of elementary-age kids with a phone and access to social media, I worry. I hope their parents are helping guide their experience and putting firm limits on phone use, because the risks of these devices are much greater for kids in elementary school. We must be aware of the risk of elementary-age kids who have devices.

GET TO CALM FIRST

Before embarking on conversations about these topics with your kids, first stop and recognize if you are having feelings of fear or worry. Make sure you have thought about how you don't want to transfer those emotions to your kids. You don't want to seem one-sided or overly concerned to them.

I remember a few times in those early days when I would go to my room and take many deep breaths before talking about the topic of smartphones. It was hard for me to put on a calm veneer when on the inside, I was a bundle of nerves.

DECISION TO WAIT UNTIL AT LEAST 13

I have spoken with several parents who wanted to wait until their kids were 13 years old to give them access to social media. After all, the official "appropriate" age provided by tech companies like Instagram and Facebook is often 13. But it can be hard since many kids may feel left out if they are 11 or 12 and most of their friends have access to social media except for them.

When kids have friends who also do not have a phone or access to social media, it helps parents hold out until their child turns 13. There is an organization called Wait 'Til Eighth, whose focus is on this issue. It's a place where you can find support.

TALK WITH OTHER PARENTS

When your relationship with your tween or teen has spiraled down into negativity around this issue, it can help to get outside perspectives. For instance, it helps to talk with friends who have kids the same age about what they do. Consider talking with parents from your kid's social circle.

If you learn that your tween really is the only one in their friend group without a device and that they are feeling incredibly left out and sad because of this, it might be time to let them have a device. Whether you make that decision or decide to wait longer, the following are key steps that can be useful.

TALK ABOUT THE ANTICIPATED FUN AND THE CHALLENGES

Talk to your child about what excites them about getting a phone and some challenges each of you anticipates. Challenges might be things like what might happen when they feel like friends need a response and their allotted social media time is up. Or how they can limit who to "friend" to decrease all of the Snaps they might get. And how should people treat each other online as well as in person? How does it make a person feel when the person they are with is glued to a phone and ignoring them?

SETTING UP EXPECTATIONS

Establish right off the bat that there will be defined times regarding use and nonuse. Make sure it is not said in a belittling manner like, "We have to do this because we all know you don't have good self-control." Rather, this should be understanding — point out how there are dozens of reasons why phones and apps pull for their attention, like friendships and the fact that tech companies create ways to keep them on the apps.

Even before coming up with specific rules, have conversations about times and places where it makes sense to have phones away. I wish I had done this more. It is such a powerful way to let them know that you respect their brain power in all of this and that their input is important. They may not get (in fact, they most likely won't) all of their preferences, but you are there to understand their hopes and wishes. Life is all about not getting everything we want. Life comes with all sorts of rules, but what is great in a family is that we listen to each other and care about each other's perspectives.

This is also a good time to discuss how you plan to be engaged with their use. The more this is about working with them, the better. You want to be able to check what is going on and talk about it rather than conveying the idea, "I will be monitoring you." From the start, it is about the idea that yes, things will be fun, but they will also be tricky at times and you are there to help them navigate this complex new social terrain they will be entering. It is not about your trying to catch them or their friends messing up. I can't stress enough how youth have told me how frustrating it is when parents have that mentality instead of a supportive one. When youth feel the latter, they tell me that it helps them stay out of a "sneaking mode." The more you keep an open line of conversation between them, the less they'll feel the need to transgress.

CHOOSING WHICH SOCIAL MEDIA

When starting social media, parents often feel better allowing just particular apps to start. If your child is really pushing for a particular platform because it is the main way their friends are communicating and they have felt incredibly left out by not being on it, then that is the app you will want to start with.

Some parents are more concerned about Snapchat than Instagram. This is in part because messages disappear once they have been opened and read. Other parents have expressed more concern over Instagram, with its flood of posing models and friends.

I decided to ask some teens what they would say to a parent who was wondering which social media app they should allow before the others. I share this to show that there is no clear cut answer and the key is having discussions with your youth to talk about pluses and minuses of each app and make decisions from there.

> Tye, 15-year-old boy:
> *"Personally, I believe Snapchat before Instagram. Firstly, because that's what I did and it felt so much more comfortable. Secondly, I feel like Snapchat is less chaotic because all you do is talk to your friends and see what they're doing. While on Instagram, it's very chaotic at first because you get all these ads, friend requests, and I always — and still do — felt like I had to post something. Also, there is a lot of responsibility that comes with Instagram because you have to be careful with what you post because if you forget that you posted something inappropriate and you lose a job because your boss found that old picture or video of you, it's your fault."*

> Isabel, 13-year-old girl:
> *"If deciding between getting Instagram or Snapchat first, I would have to choose Snapchat. For me, Instagram can cause more stress and feel toxic. While Snapchat, on the other hand, helps me*

connect with friends and make plans. There are some dangers with Snapchat because teens feel more invincible, I think, when sharing photos and texts, but it really depends on how you use it. If the teen is well-informed and knows how to handle their digital footprint, then I would suggest getting Snapchat first. These are mainly my preferences, though, and it varies from person to person."

Ellie, 18-year-old girl:
"I got my first phone when I was in 5th grade and Instagram had already been downloaded onto my phone off of my dad's iCloud account. I had no clue what it was or how public or private it was. I would post anything and everything. After one year of having the account with 0 followers, I had 2000 posts. My parents had no clue I had Instagram, and honestly, I didn't think much of it because it wasn't popular yet and no one really had it at that point. But from seventh to eighth grade, Instagram grew into the huge social media platform it is now. That's when I had to have a conversation with my parents about posting with purpose and that nothing is really private. I deleted the 2,000 posts I had up and made my account private to completely start over. Getting Snapchat was a lot more of a process because they had heard so many horror stories of girls having private pictures leaked. I had to put together a whole presentation to get Snapchat and then had a contract of what I could and couldn't do on the app."

Justin, 18-year-old boy:
"In my experience, Snapchat is just like texting while Instagram is used to document people's lives. I don't think you need to get one at a time though. I do not see any harm in getting both at once."

YOU CAN REVERSE YOUR DECISION

Parents do at times reverse decisions about allowing a main social media app. It is of course not the goal to permit, and then not, and to keep going back and forth. But it is important to know that it is always an option to change a decision.

Here is an example from one mom, Jill, who has a 12-year-old boy. She allowed him to have access to Snapchat for a while but then decided to reverse it. Nothing bad happened on the app but she explained to me:

> *"The more I looked at Snapchat, the more concerned I got. The app, as you know, deletes pictures and messages once they are read, so kids can basically send anything, which is scary. I noticed my son had over 600 friends, which is not really possible. Some were girls who looked like they were in their twenties and so many of the pictures were of young girls in sultry poses."*

Jill went on to say that she was worried about the pictures of girls being spread at the school and she did not want her son to be at risk of getting such a photo. She wrote that she and her husband decided to have him delete the app.

I spoke with her son, and he told me that he was not that upset about no longer having Snapchat. He has Google Hangouts, so he can still communicate with his friends online, and he also talks with them while playing video games.

MAKING IT SAFE TO COME TO YOU

We want our kids to come to us when they feel they have made a mistake, or when people are treating them poorly. Yet, they are in a time of life where the pull for peer acceptance and connection is heightened, and there are reasons they might not follow your rules or values. For instance, they download an app you did not approve of; they exceed the time limits you have set for them; or, they send an inappropriate picture of themself to someone.

I always tell my kids that I hope they will come to me with these issues and we will work them out together. The first step is talking it out and seeing what they are thinking and what their ideas might be for reparation. The actual situation would define how long, or if at all, there would be a consequence. And if a consequence is appropriate, the goal is not to over-punish them — when that happens, their anger toward parents can really become the focus rather than actual learning from their mistakes.

IDEAS FOR CONVERSATION STARTERS:

1. What age do you think is ideal for a person to get a cellphone? A smartphone?
2. What are some of the fun things you want to be able to do on a cellphone? Smartphone?
3. What are some of the tools that smartphones have built into them?
4. How much time do you think you should have per day on your phone?

• • •

Why Teens Choose Different Apps for Communicating

My team and I have surveyed teenagers — both boys and girls — about how, when and why they choose to communicate via their many apps. It can be a fun exercise to have your teens explain how and why they choose to use certain tech platforms for specific kinds of communication. Or if they don't have social media yet, what they expect to do in the future. It is important to be curious without judgment if you want your adolescents to be as open as possible. So, be sure to frame the conversation in a positive light.

INSIGHTS FROM NINA, 16-YEAR-OLD GIRL

INSTAGRAM: "I rarely use Instagram to communicate with one person directly. I usually use it to communicate something to all of my followers at once and no one in particular. Many teenagers have 'public' — being followed by everyone — and 'private' Instagram accounts [also called Finstagrams] — being followed by people you are actually friends with. Instagram has a simple button in their privacy settings if you only want people who you approve of to see your photos and videos. Otherwise, your account is open to everyone. Good quality photos that reflect well on me go on my public account. And posts that are more about the caption [private thoughts, song recommendations, daily woes] and have pictures as an afterthought are relegated to the private."

SNAPCHAT: "I use Snapchat for casual conversations like checking in with a friend after school. If I just want to say hi, Snapchat is the best place to do it. Since I am sending a picture along with the message, I don't have to think very hard about what the message is going to be. Additionally, since it is possible to send Snaps [which are just photos with no text at all], a conversation is not a necessary part of a Snapchat interaction."

TEXTING: "I use texting for actual conversation and communication. Many of the texts are in group chats and almost all of my plans are made in group chats. Texting is direct and concise, so I will usually text someone if I have a specific question or something that I need to coordinate. However, if I already have Snapchat open, I will just use Snapchat to relay logistics."

CALLING: "My phone calls are usually with my parents, who are not as adept as my generation when it comes to texts. Sometimes I will call my friends, but only if I have to talk to them about something that is timely or if my hands are busy so I can't text. If I'm on my way somewhere and need directions or want to know right then whether a friend wants to run an errand with me, I will call them because I am sure to get an immediate answer. Most of my phone calls are short and to the point and if I want a longer, more leisurely conversation I will use FaceTime."

FACETIME: "FaceTime is usually best for longer conversations and conversations that I would prefer to have in person but cannot. Sometimes it is simply because I am bored or lonely and want the presence of one of my friends, and sometimes because I have something serious or long-winded to talk about that would be too much to type out or too sensitive to talk about over social media. Oftentimes this will be drama or family issues.

I don't like FaceTiming very often because calls tend to drag on with neither person wanting to be rude and say they have to go when it is evident from the video that they are not doing anything. My friends that are boys don't FaceTime much. They do use an app called House Party that is sort of like FaceTime, but you can have up to 8 people on a call and they use this for playing video games together."

INSIGHTS FROM TYE, 15-YEAR-OLD BOY

INSTAGRAM: "I typically just use Instagram to see what my friends are up to so that I don't feel totally disconnected from my friends."

SNAPCHAT: "Same as Instagram. I do, though, use Snapchat a lot just to talk and communicate with my friends and family, and again to see what people are doing."

TEXTING: "I rarely text use texting. I typically just use it to stay in touch with my family."

CALLING: "I only really call my family, and usually, it's to catch up with relatives or to talk with my immediate family."

FACETIME: "I have used this a lot more recently since we're not at school, but typically I use FaceTime to talk with my friends and to see how they're doing."

EMAIL: "One of my most used ones, I use email to talk to family, coaches, teachers, etc. I use email almost every day."

INSIGHTS FROM ALI, 16-YEAR-OLD GIRL

INSTAGRAM: "Personally, I didn't enjoy Instagram because it often made me feel bad about myself. Therefore, I deleted my Instagram and started a new one for pictures of my dog. I just follow my favorite baseball players, actors and cute dogs, so now scrolling through my Instagram is a more enjoyable experience. I often post pictures of my dog (never of myself) and write to other nice people with dog Instagrams."

SNAPCHAT: "I used to do streaks on Snapchat, but I realized that it wasn't enjoyable. Now, I only use Snapchat to have a quick conversation with a friend or to send funny pictures of myself to my sister."

TEXTING: "Texting is my main method of communication. Whether I want a short or long conversation, I think that texting is the easiest and least stressful way to chat."

CALLING: "I rarely call people since it stresses me out a bit; I only call my mom if I have a quick question or if I need to be picked up from somewhere."

FACETIME: "I FaceTime people when I would have wanted to see them in person, but can't. When I was in public school — I'm homeschooled now — I used to FaceTime friends regularly to study together. Now I like to FaceTime a friend when I need to rant about something or if we have something specific to talk about. I like to use text when I'm bored and want to chat with a friend since it's awkward when you are FaceTiming someone and you run out of things to talk about."

IDEAS FOR CONVERSATION STARTERS:

1. When do you choose to use Snapchat?
2. When do you choose to use Instagram?
3. When do you choose to use texting?
4. When do you choose to use FaceTime?

• • • •

Feeling Lonely in a Hyperconnected World?

Step back 15 years and imagine someone described social media to you and then asked you the following: "Given what I just told you about social media, don't you think loneliness rates will go way down?" How would you have responded? I am pretty sure I would have answered yes.

Then smartphones, loaded with social media apps, were in the hands of youth all the time. As I saw more groups of teens looking down at their phones and barely talking with each other, I started to have second thoughts.

On top of this new "alone together" phenomenon, the research showed that teens were now spending about seven hours less with peers per week than before smartphones hit the scene.

Research validates that adolescents' feelings of loneliness have increased sharply since 2011, which is when screen time started becoming more ubiquitous. In her paper, "Less in-person social interaction with peers among U.S. adolescents in the 21st century and links to loneliness," San Diego State University Professor of Psychology, Jean Twenge, analyzed surveys of teens in eighth, 10th and 12th grade performed year after year.[3]

In 2011, when asked if they agreed with the statement, "A lot of times I feel lonely," 25% (the average of all grades combined) reported that they "mostly agreed" or "agreed." Then, in 2015, that number went up to 31%. The 25% figure was fairly constant for the preceding 10 years, and 31% is the highest level since the survey began in 1991.

It turns out that 31% more eighth graders reported feeling lonely in 2015 than in 2011, and 22% more seniors felt lonely in 2015 than in 2011.

In fact, a higher percentage of adolescents report feeling lonely now than at any time since the survey began in 1991. Twenge reported that "adolescents low in in-person social interaction and high in social media use reported the most loneliness."

Loneliness is an emotion, and our emotions exist to teach us things. They give us information about our experience in the present moment. In the best-case scenario, they are a buzzer that activates us to make a change. So if we have a sense that we are missing the company of others, i.e., a sense of loneliness, it is a signal to try to do something to lessen that unpleasant feeling. Maybe it's to make plans or attend a public gathering. It is important that we talk to our kids about these feelings and discuss ways they can gain skills to manage them when they inevitably arise — and to also assure them that the feeling will pass.

There are variations of loneliness. Here are some examples:

- **"No close friends" loneliness.** Maybe you have many acquaintances on social media or in your community, but you don't have close friends — no one to tell secrets to.

- **"I'm different" loneliness.** Perhaps you feel lonely because you are unhappy with how you look, your sexual orientation, or you just have a deep-seated feeling of not belonging.

- **"Left out" loneliness.** This can be brought on by seeing others doing things on social media or hearing about things at school that you were not a part of. You are experiencing loneliness from feeling like you are left out.

What does this mean for our teens and tweens? Are our teens lonely? Does social media provide an allusion of feeling social when in reality, some more profound need is not getting met?

We know that kids who report more time interacting in person with each other and adults are more likely to report greater emotional well-being and less loneliness. This means that we need to help them have times throughout their day when they are off devices. At home, this can look like screen-free dinners or family game nights. It can be collecting phones when friends come over or encouraging participation in sports or other social activities.

IDEAS FOR CONVERSATION STARTERS:

1. Do you ever feel lonely?
2. Do you feel like you are making a lot of connections throughout the day in person and online, but still feel like you don't have anyone to share your deepest thoughts with?
3. What can you do to deepen relationships in person and not online?

. . .

Distress Signals on Social Media

Several weeks ago, my daughter, now a senior in high school, was on her phone in the hammock she had set up outside. I got into the hammock beside her — very carefully, I must add — because hammocks make me motion sick. As we were lying there, I was doing my usual work of trying my best not to ask her questions about her phone — avoiding comments like, "Hey hun, who ya talking with?" Eventually, I could not hold back and I said gently, "Seems like you are in a deep conversation with someone." She said yes in a very agreeable tone, indicating that I had not frustrated her. She went on to say: "Yeah, my friend is feeling depressed, and we are talking."

Me: "Oh, that's great she told you."
Tessa: "Yeah, it's been going on for a long time."
Me: "How did you find out?"
Tessa: "She posted on her Snapchat story."
Me: "Oh, got it. I'm just curious, did a lot of people see it?"
Tessa: "No, it was just her story available to her close friends."
Me: "How many people is that?"
Tessa: "Like, 15."
Me: "What did she write on the post?"
Tessa: "Just that she was feeling depressed and, like, not getting out of bed."

Then Tessa shared a long paragraph she wrote to her friend, all about how it's so hard to motivate yourself to do things when you're feeling bad but how starting small can make such a difference. She went on to share her "victory technique," originally taught to Tessa by a different friend. In this strategy, you label every accomplishment as a "victory," even things as small as going to the bathroom. As these victories are acknowledged, momentum builds to do even more throughout the day.

In addition to all the advice Tessa had written, I was moved by all the supportive things she said to her friend. Tessa then told me she had to get out of the hammock — she was going on a walk with this friend. "Wait!" I exclaimed, "Let me get out first so I can do it slowly and get less seasick."

My conversation with Tessa reminded me that while not an everyday event, kids often get messages or see posts of friends who are going through hard times. Some teens say that it is helpful for them to be able to reach out to many people at once via social media, but this, of course, raises concerns. Will only the people it was intended for see it? How do peers on the receiving end know how to respond? And what happens when a person makes a post that worries their peers, but when asked, the person says nothing is wrong?

AN EXAMPLE OF WHEN TEENS ARE WORRIED ABOUT A FRIEND WHO IS SHOWING SIGNS OF HAVING A PROBLEM BUT NOT TALKING ABOUT IT OPENLY

Some months ago, while at a dance competition where our daughters were competing, a mom I knew told me how her teen daughter was worried about a friend. Her daughter (I will call her Jill) knew her friend (I will call her Mandy) made comments that she didn't like her body. Now, her posts were seeming pretty dark; she seemed sad and angry in her posts.

Jill's two other friends were also worried about Mandy, but they did not know what to do. The friends felt stuck because when they tried to talk with Mandy about their concerns, both in person and through written communication like texts, Mandy would skirt the issue. Jill and her friends wondered, were they overreacting? Was there something really bad brewing? They hated not knowing.

The good news was that the three friends worked together to sort out a plan quickly. They decided to talk with a mom who they felt could skillfully speak with Mandy's mother.

I asked my friend where things stood now. She said Jill was happy that they had the other mom as an ally and that she would be able to talk with Mandy's mom. She also said she hoped the other mom would not be too alarmist.

There are other times when there are serious crisis signals, and emergency intervention needs to happen.

I will never forget when Tessa was in seventh grade. She had an iPod at the time. One night, she came into my room and showed me a close-up photo of a girl's mouth open with many pills on her tongue. Tessa told me this was someone she was friendly with at school, and that this girl had just posted this for a small group of people to see.

I was so glad, of course, that Tessa knew to come to me. She tried calling the girl, but she didn't answer. Tessa and I immediately put our heads together and contacted the school to reach her parents. The situation ultimately was well-managed, and the girl got the help she needed.

Sharing these stories with youth in your life can be an excellent way to discuss these important issues. During Covid-19, many youth have told me about struggles they have shared with peers on social media. The key is that we let youth in our life know that our main goal is to ensure that everyone gets the help they need in hard situations.

HERE ARE SOME POINTS TO CONSIDER SHARING WITH YOUR KIDS AND TEENS:

- Let them know that you understand that sometimes people will put concerning things on their social media — more likely on their private accounts — things that give their friends concern.

- Let them know that you are not looking for an excuse to take them off social media, and that when things like this happen, you want them to feel safe to come talk with you. It is so important to say this, since tweens and teens worry that if parents know that issues occur, parents will rush to end or restrict social media. (That can be appropriate at times but that is not what I am discussing here.)

- Let them know that you understand that how their social world perceives them is really important to them and that you don't want to embarrass them. Saying this when no issues are happening can help build their trust so that they come to you when they need to.

- Let them know that if they come to you, your goal is to work with them and not to take over. You are there to help them drive, rather than to take the steering wheel yourself. Of course, there can be times when we as parents do have to fully drive, but these times are not as common.

- Let them know you want them to have someone to go to. Even though we want them to come to us, some teens might decide not to at specific times for certain reasons. Is there a person in your family, like an older cousin or an uncle they feel close to, that they also know they can go to?

- Let them know they should remind their friends that they really want to help and that it is not a burden. When a person confides in someone, that someone is usually honored that they did so — they get to feel trusted, appreciated and much more. Often, when a person is under the weight of hard emotions, they incorrectly believe that if they go to someone for support, they will be burdening them.

- Often teens will know at least one person who "overshares" and makes the whole friend group uncomfortable. Talk about ways your teen can gently bring this up with the "oversharer."

IDEAS FOR CONVERSATION STARTERS:

1. What things do you say to friends to check in with the hopes of getting a more honest answer?
2. Have you ever had a friend post things that made you concerned, like memes that refer to drug use, to being misunderstood, references to anorexia or other posts that read as cries for help?
3. Are you talking with anyone now who is going through a hard time?

· · ·

"Cyberbullying," Reworking Conversations so Kids Engage

Years ago, I would ask youth about cyberbullying and I could tell they got annoyed at the question. I soon learned why. They had been sitting through school assemblies about bullying every year since they could remember. Some of them told me they felt like they were learning the same things over and over, making them feel talked down to because much of what gets taught is obvious to them, like the need to go and tell an adult. They also told me that issues of bullying are often taught as if they are simple and clear-cut and that real issues that come up are much less black and white, and often do not look like what we think of as classic bullying. By the time they're in high school, kids will often say: "Please don't let one more adult tell me that digital posts are permanent or that cyberbullying is bad. Trust me, we know.``

In the late 1990s after the Columbine shooting, states started requiring schools to teach their students about bullying. It made sense because bullying is often associated with mental health issues and Columbine taught us that bullying often plays a part in horrific events such as school shootings. Since then, kids have been inundated with messages about the dangers of bullying. The curricula of these teaching programs are likely to be pretty strong, but somehow we have turned kids off of even the term "cyberbullying." I suspect we haven't hit the mark, and the lessons that they get every year in school feel out of sync with their everyday online experiences.

I have serious and long-held issues with the classic teaching around bullying because it mainly focuses on "bullies" and "victims" and depicts clear cut scenarios. However, the biggest reason that such teachings fail to engage our youth is that they miss the crucial truth that social cruelty and conflict online is very common and exists in many different forms.

So the question is, how do we engage our youth on these issues in discussions and at schools? We as parents need to get involved — this is important stuff.

From my work in schools talking with kids in assemblies, I eventually changed my approach and asked them, "Who here is tired of talking about cyberbullying?" Almost all hands would enthusiastically go up. I could tell they were relieved that the adult understood them and from there, I could engage them on the most important elements of these topics.

Let's go over some basic definitions and ways to talk with our kids about the topic that will hopefully engage them.

WHAT IS "CYBERBULLYING"?

First coined in 1999, there is no consensus on a single definition, although different versions usually include the use of digital technology to inflict harm repeatedly.

When do kids feel "bullied"? The reality is some youth use the term for any negative action they feel someone enacted against them, such as a snide comment on a couple of posts. Others feel bullied when they are the recipient of significant cruel behavior, like if a rumor is spread about them or if someone is making it very obvious that they are not invited to an event.

It turns out that kids use the term all the time to mean many different things. For example, a quote from Dr. Englender's new book, "25 Myths about Bullying and Cyberbullying":[4]

> *"It does seem as though the word bullying is applied to almost any situation where someone's feelings are hurt. In a 2018 study of more than 600 teens, I found that 62% of teens who believed they were bullied were actually using the word to describe different problems such as fights with friends."*

CONSIDER DISCARDING THE WORD "CYBERBULLYING"

Long ago, I stopped using the term "cyberbullying" when I talked with kids, including my own. I use terms like "social cruelty," "relationship strife" and "online conflict." I use anything but cyberbullying because they tune out immediately at that term.

If we can get away from using the terms "bully" and "victim," I think it will make a world of difference. We have so many media stereotypes of a "bully" and as our kids have let us know, it's often a lot harder to determine who is to blame and why in real-life scenarios.

Instead, we can use words like "aggressor" and "target" when that dynamic is clearly at play.

The important thing is to enable conversations about what is actually happening. Is it a fight between friends? Is someone jealous and trying to break up friendships? This is referred to as an act of "relational aggression," in which a person takes action to sabotage a friendship.

Often teens will see on social media that peers are out together and they were not invited, and they feel excluded and hurt. Was this purposeful aggression towards that individual? Maybe it was an accident. Maybe there is a conflict with one of their peers who did not want that person to join. None of this would be bullying, per se, but rather a social conflict.

Getting away from the broad term "cyberbullying" to more specific terms like "cyber-conflict" or "cyber-aggression" can help engage youth.

LOOK AT STATISTICS TOGETHER

True cyberbullying is not common, and teens express a lot of frustration that adults think cyberbullying is happening far more than it actually is. I remember so clearly that in the early days, when Chase and Tessa posted photos and commented on other people's photos, I would look at the comments with them, and scroll and scroll, looking for mean comments. I was impressed by how rarely I found any.

But yes, online meanness does happen.

Studies of middle schoolers report a higher incidence of youth saying they have experienced any cyberbullying.

WHAT SHOULD WE ENSURE OUR KIDS KNOW ABOUT ONLINE SOCIAL CONFLICT?

- Very often the person who is being the aggressor is doing it both online and offline.

- In the past, the main teaching was around telling the "victim" that they should tell an adult. The messaging is still to tell someone — possibly an adult, but it could also be a friend.

- In the past, the teaching was that "victims" should try to talk with the bully and stand up to them. Research has shown that while it can work, it can also backfire and make things worse. So this needs to be done on a case-by-case basis.

- "Bullying" can mean so many things and the key is to get support.

- Research shows that the main way youth should respond if they see a friend undergoing bullying-type behavior is not to confront the "bully," since this can increase their unkind actions, but rather focus attention on the person being "bullied."

- Save or copy the aggressive texts or conversations you or your friend receives to share them with an adult if need be.

- Don't reply: Block or report the abuse but try not to respond to digital aggression. Sometimes responding can aggravate the situation, and other times, you may find yourself behaving aggressively in return.

We know that it's always important to notify an adult, but research also reveals that not all kids or teens will tell adults, so talking with kids about steps they can take themselves to help a friend is key. When online meanness happens to them, they need to know they can turn to their friends (and ideally adults) to get support and to problem-solve together on ways to address the situation.

IDEAS FOR CONVERSATION STARTERS:

1. Do you think teachers and parents overestimate the amount of online cruelty (i.e., cyberbullying) that happens?
2. If yes, on a scale from 1 to 10 — 0 being adults only slightly overestimate, to 10 being adults way over estimate — what number would you say?
3. Which message have you gotten the most at school?
4. Have you ever supported a friend when online social meanness happened to them?
5. What have you done when social conflicts have arisen in your daily online life?

. . .

The Risk of Superficial Social Lives

Do your kids think social media has made our society more social or less? Plain and simple, we all will benefit from looking deeply and honestly at this question. In one week alone, I heard two stories about social media and disconnection, as well as one story of a teen who decided to limit her social media use to promote deeper connection.

The first story came via an email from a high school counselor. They wrote: "I had a conversation with my students yesterday about friendship. Most of them said they did not have any true friends. I asked why, and they said they couldn't trust anyone because of social media. One minute they think they have a friend, and the next minute, they are talking behind their back."

The second story came from a father who was telling me about his ninth-grade son. He described his son as introverted and said he spends very little time socializing face-to-face with friends, and yet he is often on Instagram and tells his parents that he is social. The dad is concerned about this disconnect between his son spending so little time with friends and his sense that these small online interactions are what he considers as his social life.

I remember talking with Simon Sinek, author of "Start With Why," about relationships and tech several years ago. He told me that when he was talking with a group of college guys and phones came up, the guys laughed when they talked about one of their friends who didn't own a smartphone. Simon noticed how they seemed to be dissing this guy for not having a phone. Simon decided to ask them if there was anything at all about the guy without a smartphone that they envied in any way. They stopped and started considering the question, and then one piped up said, "Well yeah, the quality of his relationships with others." All the other students nodded in agreement.

There are, of course, plenty of youth and teens who are very social in person as well as online. The real concern is for those who are not having in-person time. The other concern is that if in-person time is 100%

distracted time, i.e., if the friend is always on their phone, it can make for very unsatisfying social time.

What concerns many psychologists is when they hear about youth who talk about how they feel happy with their social lives, and yet they are doing very little in-person socializing. The concern is that these youth may actually feel satisfied, but these interactions might not be meeting fundamental human-relationship needs. What does it mean to be missing the in-person time to be goofy together? Or to be affectionate. Or to have face-to-face conversations about things that are hard in their lives.

HERE ARE SOME SOLUTIONS:

Be understanding that it is hard

We all want our kids, and ourselves, to have healthy, meaningful in-person friendships. While we can encourage our kids to join in-person groups where tech is put away, once our kids reach a certain age, they might not listen to that advice. Often, they want close friends and are frustrated that they don't have any in their life. So if we make remarks like, "just call so-and-so," that kind of response can feel invalidating to them, because if it were that easy, they would have done it.

There are many reasons they don't just call "so-and-so," and many reasons why they don't have any good friends at this particular point in their life. Sometimes the most comforting thing we can do is say, "This is OK, there are times in life when people can feel really lonely."

Talk about your friendships and connections

Another key approach is for parents to be more vocal about the things we appreciate about meaningful friendships. For instance: "I have been thinking about my friend David from high school and how whenever things were tough at home, he would come over and we would play records. He didn't mind that there was tension in my home and that I couldn't go out. He came to be with me nonetheless."

Or perhaps: "When I go for a walk with Mara, I just love how she asks me so many questions when I start to open up about something. Many other people I have known over the years immediately start talking about themselves, and well, I just know Mara doesn't do that."

Not just talking about our connections, but modeling how we create deeper connections is so vital. For example, I recently went for a short walk and knocked on a neighbor's door with the intention of connecting with someone I like. When I left my house, I didn't know which neighbor's door I would knock on, but I knew I had to act quickly before my time-pressured, stay-at-home self took over. I ended up having an excellent 10-minute discussion with an old acquaintance in her doorway, and then finished the interaction by saying how great it was to see her and inviting her to knock on my door anytime. It was short and sweet and perfect. At dinner, I shared the story with my teens, including the fact that right before I knocked on the door, I felt a twinge of self-consciousness.

Gentle questioning to get them thinking

We want to help our kids gain insights into their friendships — past and present — so that they can get a clear perspective on how satisfying their social situation is. Gently asking questions can be important for those youth who are more private about their social lives. Maybe it is just one question a day if you are like me and tend to ask about three in a row.

Some questions I have found useful are: "I'm curious. When you think of (name a good friend from when they were younger), what made that friendship so fun?", "Have you ever gotten to meet someone you knew predominantly online in person? How did that all go?", "When you think of your friends now, do you have any that you could tell personal things to and would they share them with others?" and, "When you think about good friends, what is it that you value most about them?"

Talk about social media breaks

Over the years, I have been impressed by the sheer number of teens who have told me that they get frustrated by all the "superficial" social interactions they have on social media. Many decide they need a break from it and get off it for a while. On a few occasions, Tessa has done this. Usually, it is just for a few days, but she says it often makes her happier. Chase has also gone through periods where he has majorly cut back on social media for similar reasons.

A national survey of adolescents found that 61% of smartphone owners reported taking breaks from their devices to get away from "digital drama."[5] 12% said they'd done so "many times." Of the remaining break-takers, 22% reported they did so "a few times," and 27% said they did so "once or twice."

One teen told me how she decided to delete Snapchat for a month for Lent because she often felt left out of things and seeing what everyone else was doing made her feel lonely. In preparation, she contacted her close friends, told them what she was doing and that they could contact her via text. Two days after she deleted Snapchat, she told me how much happier she was not to be reminded of what others were doing without her. "Ignorance is bliss," she said with a big smile.

IDEAS FOR CONVERSATION STARTERS:

1. There are many ways the internet can be used to have fun with friends. What is something you enjoy doing with friends while using tech?
2. Do you think social media has made our society more social or less social?
3. What are some of your favorite things to do with friends face-to-face?
4. Who would you like to spend more time seeing in person?
5. How might we connect more with our neighbors?

• • •

The Need To Be Seen and the Allure of Fame

Recently, a teen I was with was jumping up and down, exclaiming that she now had 10,000 followers and about 400,000 views on a video she had posted on TikTok. What does this increased chance of quickly gaining a massive number of followers and views mean for our youth? Could it be that soon, the number 10,000 will lose its power — just like the once exciting 100 views did in the past? What do our kids predict?

TikTok started to rise in popularity before Covid-19, but it exploded once screen time increased with shelter-in-place. I have become a bit obsessed with how often I hear parents or kids talk about how they know someone who quickly garnered a very large following. Then, there is the whole ripple effect of the fun of knowing "famous creatives," which is how popular people on social media are referred to.

A 12-year-old boy said to me, "I have a cousin who is TikTok famous, and then there is a kid in my town who has 3 million subscribers and works at our Chick-fil-A. So it is kind of cool to be able to get on there and watch someone I know."

WHAT'S IT LIKE KNOWING THAT YOUR FAME COULD BE JUST ONE POPULAR POST AWAY?

Often, I think about this new world where the possibility to become famous feels just an arm's length away. What does it feel like to be wondering as a 14-year-old, "Should I try to put up TikTok videos to become famous?" Or, as a teen girl considering, "Should I start YouTubing my morning routines or giving advice about clothes?" Maybe these teens decide not to do anything, but then a few months later, someone they know at school has suddenly become "TikTok famous." Do the thoughts start rumbling around in their brains again? Might they start thinking, "All it takes is just that one video that goes viral and bam, I could make so much money, have a ton of fans, and feel so wanted"?

Growing up, I envied the character Marcia Brady, not the actress Maureen McCormick. I really wanted siblings and two happy parents — the whole Brady Bunch package — and Marcia had it. I never even considered the possibility of being an actress, so I never had to have any existential angst of, "Should I try? Should I not?"

I have talked to teens who have struggled with questions like, "Should I go ahead and try to get a following?" and "Should I start a YouTube channel?" One 16-year-old girl told me, "I have really thought about doing this, but my negative bias has kept me from doing it." I appreciated her wisdom on the human brain's negative biases. At the same time, part of me wanted to say, "Wait, don't let the negative bias win! I am sure you could do it if you really wanted to." It was not her goal, so I didn't say anything, but later on, I mentioned a strength of hers that I saw, in hopes of providing a bit of ammunition for her to fight off negative thoughts.

But that said, some people are creative and gutsy and really like putting things online. Some do it with the goal of becoming famous, and others just really enjoy it.

Being seen does feel good. Teens tell me that being seen (getting views and likes) makes them feel appreciated. They say that if so many people see what they post, it implies that what they are doing is worth another person's time — and that can feel great. What are the upsides and downsides of striving for online attention? Why do some kids and teens spend so much time posting for online attention while others do not?

I'm sharing two stories of teens that I think will make for good conversations with young people in your lives. Both of these teens talk about the pros and cons of getting attention online.

A HIGH SCHOOL GIRL'S VIEWS ON THE PROS AND CONS OF ONLINE ATTENTION

Taylor Fang, a senior girl at Logan High School in Utah, recently won a writing contest. MIT Technology Review asked people 18 and under to respond to this question: "*What do adults not know about my generation and technology?*"[6]

> Fang wrote:
> "*Social-media platforms are among our only chances to create and shape our sense of self. Social media makes us feel seen. In our 'Instagram biographies,' we curate a line of emojis that feature our passions: skiing, art, debate, racing. We post our greatest achievements and celebrations. We create fake 'Finsta' accounts to share our daily moments and vulnerabilities with close friends.*"

> She continued with:
> "*When I got my first social-media account in middle school, about a year later than many of my classmates, I was primarily looking*

to fit in. Yet, I soon discovered the sugar rush of likes and comments on my pictures. My life mattered! ... I was looking not only for validation, but also for a way to represent myself ... Our selfies aren't just pictures; they represent our ideas of self. Only through 'reimagining' the selfie as a meaningful mode of self-representation can adults understand how and why teenagers use social media."

Fang then wrote about the cons of her online life:
"Yet by high school, this cycle of presenting polished versions of myself grew tiring ... I was tired of adhering to hyper-visible social codes and tokens."

So Fang started to do more things to foster her self-identity, like creative writing.

A HIGH SCHOOL BOY'S EXPERIENCE OF THE PROS AND CONS OF ONLINE ATTENTION

From a New York Times article, I read about another teen's story regarding getting attention online.[7] Rowan Winch, a 15-year-old boy from Pennsylvania, had been an avid social media user since middle school. He had big followings on several accounts, including his Instagram account @Zucccccccccc with 1.2 million followers. It took many hours a day to cultivate these accounts. He started at 6 a.m. and continued on the school bus, between classes, at lunch and during study hall. He kept his social media empire running with new memes, images and videos, trying to get to 100 posts per day.

Rowan's primary motivation for building these popular accounts was to develop his "clout." He explained to the reporter that this social currency is useful in many ways, like opening doors for jobs, getting internships, meeting a potential girlfriend and more. Another benefit Rowan discussed was the money generated from posting shoutouts on his accounts that other teens looking to garner more followers paid for. Some months, he made as much as $10K. A third reason he gave for loving the attention was, "with @Zucccccccccc, it felt like I had a purpose and was doing something that benefited a lot of people."

We parents worry about the many downsides of a story like this — i.e., Rowan's life being ruled by his obsession with clout causing him to lose in-person interaction time. The news story highlighted another big downside of Rowan's story, which was that he was completely dependent on one company, and when that company suddenly decided to stop his accounts, there was nothing he could do. One night, he was trying to refresh his @Zucccccccccccc account when he got a message that it had been disabled. Instagram gave no reason other than the vague notice that he was "violating a policy."

Rowan was devastated when his account shut down. "A lot of my friends think I've become depressed, and I think that's right," Rowan said. "I've been feeling insecure about a lot of things, like how I look and act and talk. I talk a lot less than I used to. I'm a lot less confident. Losing my account is the main reason I feel like this."

The stories above bring up rich discussion points. So much of why teens are driven to post things stems from the very basic human need to be seen. This reality warrants discussions about personal values. For instance, which ways of being seen align with one's core beliefs and which ones do not?

As a society, what does it mean that we direct so much attention to people in entertainment instead of to those who do amazing things to help people and the planet, for example? Here are a few questions to get a conversation going.

IDEAS FOR CONVERSATION STARTERS:

1. Do you know anyone who has made a viral video or who is famous on platforms like Instagram, TikTok or YouTube?
2. What are the upsides to internet fame?
3. What do you think would be the upsides for you? How about the downsides?

• • •

College and Other Transitions, Does Social Media Help or Hurt?

Transitions are challenging — from entering a new summer program to starting a new school to going off to college. Youth are facing these transitions with new forms of communication and self-presentation — yep, you got it, social media platforms. These platforms can both help and hinder transitions.

When it comes to getting roommates, youth often use social media to do some pre-meeting investigation and connection. I know of teens who said they were already "friends" with their roommate before they even met in person because of the cyber-snooping and Snapchatting they did over the summer. They felt having this friendship made the transition more comfortable.

Others have told me that this preconceived idea of who the new person was made them anxious about the upcoming transition because they didn't like or they felt intimidated by what they saw on their roommate's social feeds. When my son Chase headed to college, the university had a policy of not revealing roommate assignments until everyone got to campus. The policy stated, "We have found that roommate relationships are more positive and successful when they start out with face-to-face interaction, rather than on preconceived notions based on fragments of information or online communications."

Another issue college freshmen face is the constant contact they often maintain with their high school friends. This social tether is comforting, but can also at times engender FOMO ("Fear Of Missing Out"). We all know that people often present their best experiences on social media. My co-producer's son started college last year and during his first semester, he told her that from looking at his high school friends' social feeds, he surmised that they were having more fun at their respective colleges than he was. This made him question his college choice and made him feel envious and lonely at times.

A young man who is about to enter his sophomore year in college told me how unexpectedly lonely he was for the first half of his freshman year. It was challenging to meet people that he could relate to. Before entering college, he only heard how it was "so great" and "so fun," but no one ever mentioned how lonely it might be. For human connection, he frequently retreated to his phone to text his long-distance girlfriend. He realized that the crutch of ongoing communication with his girlfriend kept him from putting himself out there to meet people. Fortunately, during his second semester, he met a couple of people that he bonded with and he is now looking forward to returning to college.

All of this makes me think of a 14-year-old patient I saw two weeks ago in my medical clinic. At the end of our visit, this was our conversation:

Me: "Are you taking any risks this summer?"
Teenager: "Oh no, no, I don't do any risks." (Clearly assuming I was referring to risks such as drugs.)
Me: "No, no, what I was going to ask is whether you are taking risks such as asking someone you might be shy about asking to hang out? That would be a risk to ask them to do something, right?"
Teenager: "Oh gosh, yeah, that's true."
Me: "It can be so valuable to practice doing that — it can be hard but hey, you might get a new friend, so it could really be worth it. And, if you don't, well, you've gotten better at risk-taking... in the positive sense of the word."

He smiled a genuine smile, and I could tell he was happy we had this little exchange.

How our teens decide to present themselves online as they enter new social worlds and how often they take risks to meet potential friends is definitely worth discussing.

This made me think of a powerful episode of the podcast "Hidden Brain" called "Online Behavior, Real-Life Consequences: The Unfolding of a Social Media Scandal."[8] It goes into what happened to a high school student whose inappropriate online posts led to Harvard rescinding his admission. The story is told beautifully, and it is a great episode to listen to with older teens.

IDEAS FOR CONVERSATION STARTERS:

1. How has technology helped you stay in contact with people you care about?
2. What are the upsides and downsides of the ability to stay in touch with people?
3. How often are you surprised to see how different someone is in real life compared to their online presence?
4. When was the last time (including for you, adults) that you took a risk and asked someone to hang out? How did it go?

When They are Feeling Rejected, How To Help

Recently, I was speaking to a few hundred high schoolers in their school theater, and I started out by asking what things they enjoy doing related to screen time. They had fun throwing out all types of examples. I shared some things I love to do, such as Googling to find answers to almost any question — like recently, when I Googled what to do with leftover coffee and learned I could use it to make oatmeal, who knew? As we all talked about the upsides of our tech revolution, we joked about how long a documentary would be if it included all of the upsides. Some students offered four hours and others said 24 hours.

I always start conversations with groups of students by asking them about positive things they experience with their screen time, because I want them to know that I understand there are so many wonderful things to do with tech. Teens expect that any adult talking with them about screen time is going to focus solely on the negative. Once students see that I appreciate the many upsides of our tech world, they are more open to discussing ways to minimize the downsides.

When I asked the students about the things that happen on screens that negatively affect them, a student quickly raised her hand and answered, "Being blocked." She looked a bit self-conscious, so I quickly said, "Yes, teen after teen tells me about this. It's just so common." I was relieved to see her perk right up.

I went on to say: "It is so stressful when someone is blocked or unfriended. Often, they have no idea why they were blocked. I know how hard the not-knowing is. It is hard to feel rejected and then on top of that, to not understand why it happened makes it that much more upsetting."

Then, another student raised her hand. "Yeah, I hate it when I can see that someone has opened my Snap to them but they have not responded to me," she said.

I said: "These types of things can leave us feeling a lot of uncertainty and self-doubt. This can lead to going over and over things in one's mind and trying to find a reason." And so many heads nodded as I said these things.

There are many ways a person in life can experience rejection, and of course, many of these ways are now online. Here are some examples:

- When someone sends out invites to play an online video game and you don't get an invite.

- You get blocked. Someone can block you from Instagram or Snapchat. When you look at that person's feed, it displays a message like, "there is no content."

- You get "ghosted" when someone suddenly stops responding to your messages without explanation, often in texts or on other platforms.

- Someone breaks up with you over Snapchat, text, or Instagram. Sometimes, people even do this with a few words like, "I think we should just be friends."

- You get unfollowed on Instagram or Snapchat. You would only know if you went through your followers. You wouldn't get a notification.

- You are left unopened on Snapchat, which is when you send a Snap to someone and they don't open it. You can tell on your end that they have not opened it. This action is also called "leaving it unread."

- You see that someone posted pictures from a gathering that you were not invited to. Often this is on Instagram or a Snapchat story.

- You are left off a group text with people who would typically include you.

HERE ARE SOME WAYS I HAVE FOUND HELPFUL IN TALKING WITH MY TEENS ABOUT DEALING WITH FEELINGS OF REJECTION:

Let them know you are happy that they told you about the experience of rejection
I know that sounds obvious, but youth can have all sorts of things going on in their brains when it comes to telling a parent about these types of things. That little extra affirmation can go a long way.

Quickly recognize the feelings that come up for you
As their parent, you might feel angry or sad when your child shares the fact they got rejected. Try not to let your feelings flow out. This is a skill that I have worked to get better at myself. Instead, try to get to a place of calm and refocus your energy on really hearing what they are saying.

My daughter has such a sensor that even little signs of what she might perceive as my being upset could cause her to not want to reach out to me.

I remember a moment when Tessa was being a bit reserved and then she had this look of insight in her eyes, and she said to me, "Mom, I realize I often get worried telling you things because when you feel sad or upset, I feel bad that I made you feel bad." Another time she told me that she was worried I would overreact.

Don't demonize the internet
If your child tells you that they were not invited to join a group video game or that they were left out on social media, try not to say negative statements about the platform on which it occurred. Many youth fear telling adults about what is happening online because they worry that their game or device will be taken away.

Validate that it makes sense that they are upset
Tell your child that feeling rejected is one of the hardest emotions we experience. Then stop. Try not to attempt to fix it right away with things like, "Oh, I am sure it was a mistake," or "Well, you never liked that person anyway." Instead, right when they tell you, try to stay in validation mode for a while. It is incredibly comforting for youth to feel understood at that moment. In *Screenagers NEXT CHAPTER*, psychologist Laura Kastner says, "If there is one skill I would teach parents, it's validation."

Talk about times when you were rejected
Share the things you feel that you did well and not so well and what you learned. What is great about such sharing is that teens may open up to you in ways they would otherwise not have.

In *Screenagers NEXT CHAPTER*, I talk to a dad (who happens to be a school counselor) about whether he ever shares how his day went emotionally with his kids. He replied:

> *"I don't think so. You mean, like, just kind of saying how I'm feeling about something other than being angry with them for not doing something? I can't think of a lot of examples of checking in emotionally and letting them know what's going on."*

Suggest trying a "perspective plunge"
Have them imagine ways the other person could be seeing things that might explain their act of rejection. Consider doing a role-play where they act ast the other person and talk about why they did what they did. In doing so, they may realize that the person who made them feel bad could be overwhelmed with stuff happening in their own life. They may get insight into how different people experience hurt and why their coping skill may be to block or unfollow.

Talk about the pain of not knowing why and the courage to ask
One of the hardest things about being rejected is that often, a person does not know why they were rejected. The not-knowing can be agonizing. So what is there to do? Asking someone what happened takes an incredible amount of courage and we need to let our kids

know this. Because it is so hard, it is often the norm for many kids and teens (and adults, of course) to not ask at all. Strategize with your child ways to talk to the person who blocked or ignored them. Even if they decide not to, having a conversation about what they could do is a great teaching moment.

Ideas you suggest can include starting from a place of questioning, not accusing. You never know, maybe there was a mistake and the person didn't realize they didn't include you in the group chat.

Discuss any regrets

Is there anything your child regrets doing or saying to the person who rejected them? I love the phrase "Wise Remorse" (from mindfulness teacher Joseph Goldstein) to describe the idea of becoming mindful of something you did that you now regret. What did you learn from that experience? Might you want to tell the person involved that you are now feeling remorse?

IDEAS TO GET THE CONVERSATION STARTED:

1. When do you feel good about being included in things online?
2. In what ways have you experienced rejection through technology?
3. How often do you not know why you got rejected?
4. When have you approached someone to try to understand what is going on? Did you do so in person or online and how did those times go?

. . .

Should Social Media Not Have Likes?

On Thanksgiving in 2019, I was sitting around with family in Berkeley as we cooked and talked. Phil, my cousin-in-law, said, "Hey, I just got this message," and he showed his phone to us. It said that when he posted things on Instagram, people could still like them, but the amount of likes would no longer be specified. The amazing thing is that all posts appearing in his feed — his posts and everyone else's — no longer displayed the number of likes. When he opened his post, Instagram still showed at the top how many likes it had, but only he could see that.

My eyes immediately lit up. I knew and had written about how Instagram was hiding likes in other countries, but had not heard about it in the U.S. yet. It made me think of my son, who has talked about how cool it would be to make a social media platform about fostering positive connections by getting rid of likes and promoting a more positive social media experience.

Maybe Instagram is really going to do this. The company is hiding likes in several countries, including Canada, Brazil, Australia, Ireland, Italy, Japan and New Zealand. In late 2019, Instagram brought the disappearing likes to a small number of U.S. users, including Phil. By the time you read this, it may have changed, of course.

"Our interest in hiding likes really is just to depressurize Instagram for young people," CEO Adam Mosseri said in a Business Insider interview.[9]

Mark Zuckerberg, CEO of Facebook — Instagram's parent company — said at F8 in 2020, "We want people to be less interested in how many likes a post gets, and focus more on connecting with other people."[10]

You will still be able to see likes on your own posts, just not everyone else's, eliminating the comparisons that often happen.

This was being tested with select groups with plans to roll out to more people in the future. That is why my cousin-in-law Phil had his Instagram changed. He was not asked for permission beforehand and he had no option to ask for it. Instagram seemed to be testing accounts at random. (Or not random, who knows?)

With all this news, I decided to try something new at a workshop I was holding at an all-girls middle school. I asked the students to pretend they were the head of Instagram and to make an argument either for keeping likes or doing away with them. I was not surprised that so many of them raised their hands to volunteer to talk. I find that young people are eager to talk about all sorts of issues related to their digital lives, even when at home this type of interest may not be apparent for all kinds of reasons — including that a teen may feel defensive about their screen time.

The teens gave many pros and cons to having likes displayed. One girl eloquently spoke about how many YouTubers make a living from getting likes and that this new format of Instagram would be unfair to them. She also added that other platforms do not use likes and if a person preferred that, they should go to the other sites.

Several students also articulated some downsides of having likes, such as how it takes a toll on someone's self-esteem if their friends see that their posts aren't getting a lot of likes. One girl said she favored not having likes because they encourage people not to be "real," but instead to be like an "avatar." Another student added that even with the new system, it would still negatively affect the account holder's feelings since they'd still see the number of likes their own post received.

Many celebrity influencers responded positively to the change.[11] Cardi B said removing likes is a step in the right direction, but she emphasized that the comments section is often more damaging than the number of likes in an Instagram post. She said, "This is just my opinion ... I mean what makes you feel more insecure, getting no likes or people constantly giving opinions about you, your life, your topics?"

Kim Kardashian West agrees that taking away Instagram likes could be beneficial for our mental health. Attending The New York Times' DealBook Conference, Kim said, "As far as mental health, I think taking the likes away and taking that aspect away from [Instagram] would be really beneficial for people. I find myself to be extremely mentally strong and I have people who are obsessed with the comments, and I find that to be really unhealthy."

"While the feedback from early testing has been positive, this is a fundamental change to Instagram," Instagram's PR department said to me in an email. "We're continuing our test to learn more from our global community." They told me that Facebook is also testing, on a smaller scale, the impact of hiding likes.

A senior in highschool who will attend Colorado University of Boulder said to me,

"The majority of my whole Instagram feed right now is food, friends and fun CU Boulder accounts. I love that whole side of the app, but I hate how fake Instagram has become. The pictures that are posted are the one good shot out of the 200 pictures taken. That one photo is usually touched up using Facetune and

then layered with filters that make the posts look more bright and perfect. I am totally at fault for this and do the same thing, but it definitely gets hard at times scrolling through an Instagram of 'perfect people.'"

IDEAS FOR CONVERSATION STARTERS:

1. How important are likes on Instagram?
2. What about Instagram makes you, or anyone you know, feel good or bad?
3. What do you think about Instagram's experiment to hide likes? Do you predict they will, in the end, adopt this new format or not?
4. Do you think Instagram and other apps could do more to help combat negative emotions that are evoked on social media?

Chapter Two:

Video Games

Most likely, your child or teen is not addicted to video games. But they still could be spending more time playing video games than you would like, and you may have questions about how to ensure healthy video game use in general.

They may be passionate about games like Minecraft, which has had a resurgence of popularity after a relative dip. Perhaps it's Fortnite, Call of Duty, Overwatch, League of Legends or others. On average, at the end of any given day, 70% of boys will say they played video games.[1] Of those that played, the average length of time per day is two hours and 19 minutes. Overall, boys play five times longer on console games than teen girls and three times longer on computer games. Interestingly, girls almost match boys in the amount of time on average they spend playing games on phones. Teen girls average 26 minutes a day and teen boys average 35 minutes.

As parents, we have many concerns — are they wasting away their time when they could be doing more important things? Are they meeting strangers online who have bad intentions? Why are they so moody after playing for a long time? Are they playing video games during class time?

Then there is the issue of violent video games. How do these games involving war and fighting impact aggressive thoughts and behaviors? When he was in middle school, my son loved going to his friend's home and playing Call of Duty, a first-person shooter game, for hours. Knowing that they were playing a game all about killing others really affected me emotionally. Playing a game about killing people was antithetical to my whole being. "Breathe deeply," I would remind myself, "It is just a game." But I needed to know more, which was part of the reason I picked up my camera and started making *Screenagers*.

On top of everything is the sheer number of hours many youth want to spend on games. Why is this? For one thing, psychologists, behavioral psychologists, mathematicians and others work to keep video games changing in real time so that the player experiences the most satisfying "challenge zone." We all know that if we play, say, tennis with someone far worse than us, it is annoying and boring and makes us want to stop. And in the same vain, if we try to play with someone much better than we are, we become annoyed or embarrassed and want to stop. When we find that perfect partner, perhaps one who is just a tad better than us (that is what I always preferred), we get in the flow and want to keep playing. It turns out that video games are designed to shift in real time to keep the player in a specific zone known as the "challenge zone."

As parents, we can be at a loss when it comes to limits and how to enforce them. How can we deal with the fits when it is time to get off a game? What about the kids who play games to such an extent that they experience significant negative consequences in their lives, like damaged relationships, sleep, grades, etc.?

Andrew, whose story was featured in *Screenagers*, experienced this. He was a high school senior, an A student preparing for college who didn't think much about the six or so hours he spent each day playing video games.

Andrew told me how proud he was to receive an honors-based scholarship to a private college in Washington State. And yet, when he got to campus, Andrew floundered.

He told me, *"Around three weeks in, I had a paper for an English class, and I forgot to write it because I was up so late gaming."*

It became a vicious cycle. The more he worried, the more he gamed — sometimes all day and all night.

It went on like this for three weeks until Andrew realized he likely would fail his classes. One night, he took off from college and drove to his hometown to stay at a friend's house until his mother drove by his car one day, looked inside and saw all his belongings in the back.

Andrew's mother got him to come home, and that is when Andrew's parents fully realized the depth of his problem. They found an internet addiction treatment program called reSTART — a residential program in Washington State. They were finally able to get Andrew to attend.

I wanted to know how the hours of Andrew's video gaming as a highschooler impacted his relationships at home and I spoke with his younger sister, as well as Andrew. This is what they said in a scene from *Screenagers*.

Andrew's sister spoke about what the family did to convince Andrew to get treatment finally:

> *"We each wrote a letter to Andrew that said how much this behavior, this addiction, had impacted the whole family. My letter talked about how I missed, you know, hanging out with him as a kid and how I really hoped he'd be around longer."*

Andrew:
> *"I didn't realize how much my sister cared about me. I don't know how to phrase this. I've always felt, like, kind of disappointed that I wasn't a better big brother to my sister and I always felt, like, that distance between us and I always kind of was like, oh, I wish we were closer."*

Andrew's sister:
> *"It felt like he was a million miles away even when he was probably a few feet away from me. Most of the time, he'd be on the computer. It felt like he was in a different world."*

Andrew:
> *"She said it was... she said it's like I don't have a brother, that he might as well be dead."*

The impact of video gaming on family relationships can be a serious thing — the missed opportunities for becoming closer and the frequent arguments over gaming can create a house full of tension.

Of course, it is not just the gaming habits of youth that can lead to this disconnect, but also those of a parent. Seeing how gaming can negatively impact family bonds in so many homes makes me passionate about writing about solutions in this chapter.

This chapter will help guide discussions on how to increase the positives of video games while also decreasing the negatives, and how to work together to find balance.

Recognizing the Positives of Video Games

In my journey to learn how to be a better parent in our digital age, I realized how often I was speaking negatively about video games. The truth is, there are positive elements of video games. Spending time talking about these things is validating for our kids who like games and thus makes them feel understood, but it also reinforces the idea that how they make their decisions around gaming is important. For example, what games does a child decide to play and why? Are they having positive interactions with others while playing? Are they learning and growing in any way through gaming? How do the games they choose fit with their core beliefs?

So, let's talk about the possible upsides of video games. And for now, let's put aside concerns about types of games, amount of time and so forth.

FOSTERING CONNECTIONS WITH PEOPLE IN OUR LIVES

At the clinic where I'm a physician, one of our wonderful medical assistants told me she was looking forward to getting home that night for her weekly dinner with extended family where they played video games — primarily Mario Kart. Most weeks, about 10 adults and kids converge, and given that only six people can play at a time, the person who loses the round has to give up the controller. She said they all spend a lot of time laughing. At dinner, they have lively conversations.

Parent-child connectedness via games can be a source of good feelings in families. The way to connect with family through games can extend further — like in the case of a young person I know who loves to play chess with their grandparent remotely.

When it comes to peer social time, I am always struck by the amount of laughter that video games like Mario Kart and Just Dance generate for my kids. Being together in person can be particularly positive for strengthening peer friendships. Of course, lots of positive friend time happens over headsets and game-playing as well.

LEARNING TO COLLABORATE VIA TECH

Since tech is involved in all sorts of schooling and jobs, being able to communicate well with others through using tech interfaces is a good skill. It has been suggested that playing cooperative games is one way to foster online communication and teamwork that might strengthen skills in other tech-related group projects.

On this topic, Jane McGonigal, a game developer, said in an NPR interview:[2]

> "You know, gamers are used to working in teams, and they're used to using resources like wikis and forums to sort of share what they're failing at, give tips for other people so that they can get to the goal faster."

STRATEGIC AND CREATIVE THINKING

Games like Minecraft can definitely engage youth in stimulating creative thinking. As they create, they also get the benefit of feeling accomplished and proud. Another creative game that focuses on making things is Guitar Hero, which was pretty popular in our home several years ago.

Some games require strategic thinking, like Civilization. Portal is another game that incorporates puzzle-solving skills and taps into eighth-grade physics — so much so that the sequel, Portal 2, is a teaching tool that some K-12 physics teachers use.

Recently, Chase decided to learn how to play League of Legends. His friend was an avid player and he started to teach Chase. It is an incredibly complex game, and Chase has been impressed by how much strategic thinking the game employs.

OTHER UPSIDES OF GAMES

Teens tell me how they turn to phone games in the same way that one would turn to a fidget toy — to distract the mind away from mildly anxious feelings like boredom.

Another upside of games is that they can improve spatial skills and eye-hand coordination. There are also ways to be physically active via video games, such as with Dance Central, Just Dance and Wii Fit.

IDEAS FOR CONVERSATION STARTERS:

1. Besides the upsides of video games here, what are some other upsides?
2. What do you think about video games in terms of fostering connections?
3. What games have you played that you found to be really creatively crafted? For example, the animation, the story or the way the game works.

· · ·

What Video Game Developers Learn From Casinos

I presented *Screenagers* at schools, churches and associations on a trip to Hong Kong a few years back. One of the most interesting screenings was at a conference for health professionals who treat addiction. Did you know that, according to the National Center for Responsible Gaming, about 1% of the U.S. population has a gambling disorder?[3] In Hong Kong, it is almost double that rate.

Near misses, short-term rewards and promises of a bigger win to come are some of the tricks that video game developers have adopted from slot machines designed to keep players playing. In an article in The Economist, "The Scientists Who Make Apps Addictive," writer Ian Leslie explains:[4]

> *"The machines are programmed to create near misses: winning symbols appear just above or below the 'payline' far more often than chance alone would dictate. The player's losses are thus reframed as potential wins, motivating her to try again. Mathematicians design payout schedules to ensure that people keep playing while they steadily lose money."*

Leslie goes on to talk about another trick slot machine designers use.

> *"A player who is feeling frustrated and considering quitting for the day might receive a tap on the shoulder from a 'luck ambassador,' dispensing tickets to shows or gambling coupons. What the player doesn't know is that data from his game-playing has been fed into an algorithm that calculates how much that player can lose and still feel satisfied, and how close he is to the 'pain point.' The offer of a free meal at the steakhouse converts his pain into pleasure, refreshing his motivation to carry on."*

Video game designers also use the "pain point." But instead of free dinners, players are offered incentives like discount coins or other in-game rewards to keep playing. It appears random, but game developers have analyzed data, so they know when players are about to reach their pain point and quit — which is when they step in with a pick-me-up.

MIT professor and cultural anthropologist Natasha Schüll explains these manipulations in her book, "Addiction by Design: Machine Gambling in Las Vegas."[5] In it, she explores how the casino industry went from a social activity around a craps table or roulette wheel to a solitary experience of individuals zoned out in front of machines. Soon after her book was released in 2013, Schüll began receiving invitations to speak at tech companies and conferences attended by marketers, developers, and entrepreneurs. They wanted to learn from her how to hook more people!

I suggest we talk with our kids about some of the casino tricks and how they relate to the games and social media we all use on our devices.

IDEAS FOR CONVERSATION STARTERS:

1. There are many fun games. What are some that you think are particularly engaging?
2. Are you aware of how games and apps hook you in with rewards, like Streaks on Snapchat?
3. Do you think companies have a responsibility to monitor and limit their habit-forming games and apps or do you think it is OK to hook us in?

• • •

Beware of "Loot Boxes"

In 2019, England's Prince Harry publicly shared his major concern with video gaming in general, and Fortnite in particular.[6] At an event at the YMCA in London, he said game companies are working "to keep you in front of a computer for as long as possible." He spoke about having friends who are struggling with their children over the game. He had just returned from a "babymoon," so clearly, parenting was on his mind. (By the way, I had to look up babymoon, and it is a vacation you take with your partner before you have your baby — usually in the second trimester.)

As of 2019, video gaming worldwide is a $152 billion market, according to the Global Games and Esports analytics company, Newzoo.[7] That is larger than the global film and music industries combined. Some estimates put the value of "virtual goods" within gaming at more than $50 billion. No wonder everyone is looking for a piece of this market.

And with many of the games come "loot boxes," which are packages filled with prizes, weapons, gear and other tools that advance gameplay. Gamers earn access to loot boxes by reaching certain levels or paying real money with in-game microtransactions. When a kid sees and accepts a pop-up offer for a 99-cent loot box and accepts it, the credit card attached to the game will get charged. (Do you even remember authorizing it for in-app purchases?)

Shooting games are not the only ones with loot boxes. You will also find them in games like Candy Crush and Roblox, as well as games geared toward younger kids like Smurfs' Village.

Loot boxes are said to resemble gambling. Being able to spend real money for another chance to advance in a game is not that different from putting one more quarter in the slot machine in hopes of winning more.

A 17-year-old boy in Canada spent $7,600 on loot boxes in Fifa 16.[8] The 10-year-old son of one of our team members paid more than $200 in a week on Fortnite loot.

There are countless other instances of microtransactions gone wrong. In response, seven countries — China, Japan, South Korea, Singapore, Australia, the Netherlands and Belgium — have restricted, or are considering limits on video game loot boxes. Last year, the Belgian Gaming Commission found loot boxes to violate the country's gaming laws, and declared them illegal. This means game developers need to completely remove loot boxes of any kind from games shipped to that country. Failure to do so will result in high fines and prison time.

Belgium's Minister of Justice, Koen Geens, told the BBC that giving children access to loot boxes is a mix of gaming and gambling and is "dangerous for mental health."[9]

In the United States, at the urging of Senator Maggie Hassan of New Hampshire, members of the Federal Trade Commission said they would look into the use of loot boxes and their likeness to gambling.[10] In an effort to give parents a heads up, games that are rated by the Entertainment Software Rating Board now have labels indicating whether a game has loot boxes.

The video game industry's trade group, the Entertainment Software Association, claims that loot boxes enhance a player's experience. They said in a statement to The Washington Post last year:[11]

> *"Contrary to assertions, loot boxes are not gambling. They have no real-world value, players always receive something that enhances their experience, and they are entirely optional to purchase. They can enhance the experience for those who choose to use them, but have no impact on those who do not."*

IDEAS FOR CONVERSATION STARTERS:

1. What do you know about loot boxes and why are they so appealing?
2. Billions of dollars get made off of virtual things in loot boxes — what do you think about that?
3. What are the downsides of loot boxes?
4. Do you think that loot boxes and other in-game incentives are like gambling?

. . .

Different Parent Approaches
Concerning Violent Video Games

When my son was over at his friend's playing a lot of Call Of Duty in middle school, it made me sad and worried. I was concerned about the possibility of the game subconsciously teaching him to devalue people due to the way the characters get treated within the game. When I talked to him about my feelings, he would talk all about how he knew it was just a game and he was sure it wasn't negatively affecting him.

Scientists have done many experiments demonstrating that right after kids play a violent video game, they are more likely to exhibit more aggressive thoughts and behaviors than kids who played nonviolent games.[12] The effect size, when averaged out over many youth, is small. Yet, it is unknown whether certain youth are more susceptible to becoming aggressive after playing violent games than others. Such information could help direct attention to more susceptible youth to ensure they have alternatives to violent games. What is particularly concerning to me is that in experimental studies, playing violent video games is shown to decrease prosocial behaviors.[13]

While tragic school shootings have been perpetrated by boys known to have played many violent games, it wouldn't be correct to fully blame such a tragedy on games. Millions of boys play violent video games and do not commit any violent actions, let alone shootings.

Yet, real-life experiences show us that playing high-adrenaline games can make certain youth feel charged up and perhaps more aggressive afterward. For example, families may report that there is more yelling in the home than usual.

Games like Grand Theft Auto depict men sprinting after people with broken beer bottles in hand and characters using knives and hammers to attack people — including males who attack females. This brutality is what is so hard for many of us parents to see our kids interacting with.

Beyond the issue of aggression is that of the impact on a person's nervous system. I vividly remember when my son was 18 and had not played Call of Duty for a couple of years. He started to play it again, and I noticed a change in his demeanor after playing the game. At one point he said:

> *"Wow, I have been so surprised, but I am so revved up after playing Call of Duty that I have a hard time falling asleep afterward. It's this internal anxious feeling that is hard to describe and disconcerting."*

1. Some parents prohibit violent games in their home

Care providers can decide to have a policy of no violent video games in the home. I've instilled this policy in our home. I just had to have it that way. I could not emotionally bear having the games played in our home. I am not saying that every family needs this rule, and in fact, there is a potential price for it, as kids may favor spending more time at a home where violent games are permitted.

When Chase was in middle school, Fortnite was not yet out, and I do not know how I would have responded to it. Yes, it is violent, but much less brutal than Call Of Duty. Perhaps I would have allowed exceptions to my rule at the time.

2. Some have rules that time spent on violent games must not exceed time on nonviolent games

For example, if kids are playing games, they would spend perhaps 30 minutes on Mario Kart and then 30 minutes on Fortnite. This can be tricky to enforce fully, and perfect adherence should not be the goal. If it is close, then I consider that a big win. What is useful about this rule is that it provides consciousness of the messages of violent games versus the messages of games that are not violent.

3. Some make sure to have engaging nonviolent games

Games that focus on strategy or creativity, like Civilization or Minecraft, are examples of very engaging nonviolent games that require creativity and strategic thinking. Minecraft has an option embedded that allows the game to be played as a shooter game, so be aware of this option if you don't allow violent games in your home.

4. Some make playing violent games contingent on having talks about realities of violence

If your family decides to allow violent games in your home but you want to ensure a real understanding of how unacceptable violence in the real world is, you can set up times to talk about these things. It should not be seen as a punishment for their playing and enjoying these games, and instead as a time to reflect on the realities of war and violence. For example, you might have your children consider ways people work to prevent war and help people in war zones, or how those who have been in war — such as the U.S. veterans who have returned from Iraq and Afghanistan — have been affected by things like PTSD.

5. Some share opinions of older teens with their youth

The views of older teens can have a significant influence on kids' thinking. Many older teens and college students do have opinions about when violent video games should be allowed, and it is often later than one might have guessed. If you find a young person in your family or social circle and have them talk with your youth, this can help your child consider things in a new light.

I recently had a conversation with my son's friend, Thomas, who is a freshman in college. We were talking about Fortnite. I asked him what he thought the appropriate age should be for the game. He had to stop and think awhile, but ultimately said he thought 10 was definitely too young, but 13 years old would make sense. He added that violent video games were not allowed in his home while he was growing up and now looking back on it, he is happy about that.

In addition to the above, I want to add that some families make sure games are played in the least violent mode possible For example, there is a setting in Call of Duty where blood does not get shown.

IDEAS FOR CONVERSATION STARTERS:

1. What are your thoughts about violent video games?
2. Some people think playing action-packed games makes playing something like Minecraft less appealing because it feels so slow in comparison. Have you heard any friends say that? Do you feel that way?

3. If you were an older teen talking with a kid about these types of games, what might you say?

· · ·

The Upsides of Having Intermittent Breaks From Gaming

What happens when you have an active, involved kid with good grades who wants to play video games for three straight hours, seven days a week? A father came to me with this dilemma and explained: "My son is in seventh grade, plays on two sports teams and is an overall good kid. But I still think three hours is too much time."

His question made me want to look more into the potential costs of long stretches of uninterrupted screen-time activities like video gaming.

Clifford Sussman, MD, is a child and adolescent psychiatrist who specializes in helping youth regain balance after tech overuse. He and I have presented together at the American Academy of Child and Adolescent Psychiatry Conference on the topic of excessive video gaming.

Dr. Sussman co-wrote a review of the neurobiology of the brain while video gaming — including theories about what many successive hours of video game playing does to the reward system of the brain, which involves the chemical dopamine.[14] I spoke with him about this science and will share our conversation here.

Researchers have found that excessive use of anything that produces a heavy and continuous release of dopamine causes changes in the brain, such as reducing dopamine receptors. This happens with instant gratification activities like video games and entertainment media.

Dopamine causes a pleasurable feeling by being secreted by one neuron and then taken up by receptors on a nearby neuron in the reward center of the brain. But if too much dopamine is released, the receiving neuron will make less receptors, so as not to be flooded. This is because the body is always working to stay in homeostasis, or balance.

Sussman said: "If you have fewer dopamine receptors, it's like you have fewer receptors for pleasure, and it's almost like being desensitized for pleasure. You are more bored by everything, you feel worse at rest because you are not getting rewarded."

He sees it all the time in his clinical practice. His patients' parents will tell him all the time that when their son or daughter binges for hours on a game, they are like a different person afterwards — irritable, often angry and talking about how bored they feel and how they want to get back on the game. Sussman called it "reward withdrawal."

When the person stops playing the video game after many hours, other things can indeed feel more boring, for the theory is that their dopamine receptors have been reduced. So now when they do something that does not produce the same level of dopamine, it will be even less stimulating since there are less receptors for it.

Less response to rewards leads to less pleasure from everyday things. We don't want that for our kids.

Dr. Sussman shared with me how he identifies that someone is engaging in an excessive amount of gaming by inquiring whether "... there's a balance between what I call high-dopamine and low-dopamine activities."

I had never heard anyone talk about activities in terms of high and low dopamine.

Sussman wants to make sure that youth have time to engage in activities that are not only on screens that serve up consistently high levels of dopamine. The idea is that by doing so the neurons can replenish the dopamine receptors.

Sussman said that doing homework, playing a sport, exercising or playing a board game are all types of low-dopamine activities. All these activities require more delayed gratification than most online video games. Delayed-gratification activities on a screen would be things like using a word processor or photo editor. When gratification is delayed, lower levels of dopamine allow dopamine receptors to start to be replenished.

I asked Sussman if a low dopamine activity implies that the person experiences less enjoyment from it and he said:

> "It's not the level of fun, it's more how long you're waiting to get a reward. Even doing an activity like playing a board game. That's, let's say, entirely based on a video game and entirely based on

some of the types of rewards you get in a video game. Because a lot of board games now are wonderful because they're inspired by video game creators. The point is that you've got to set up the board, you've got to read the instructions, you have to wait for your turn. It's not all just coming at you continually. Baking is the perfect example."

SOLUTIONS DR. SUSSMAN SUGGESTS

Change the conversation

Rather than talking about activities as "work versus play," consider talking about activities as high-dopamine and low-dopamine activities. High-dopamine activities are ones where there is a constant and high flow of dopamine from things like video games, web surfing and watching shows. Low-dopamine activities produce delayed gratification. They can be enjoyable and can lead to a sense of well-being that comes from finally achieving things like completing a homework assignment. Some examples include exercising or playing board games, which are still fun but have a slower pace. Another good example is baking, which is enjoyable and followed by a short high from the reward of eating the baked good.

Alternate high and low-dopamine activities

Dr. Sussman says that the issue is not so much the total number of hours of high-dopamine activities on screens, but rather how often breaks get taken. Having time off high-dopamine activities is essential so that dopamine receptors can return to more normal levels.

For teens, he suggests only about one hour of a high-dopamine screen activity before taking a break. And for younger kids, it should be more like 30 minutes. And then whatever amount of time was spent on a high-dopamine activity should be followed by that same amount of time for a low-dopamine activity (on or off screens — but ideally off screens).

So if a teen girl played an hour of Fortnite, she would then engage in a low-dopamine activity for an hour before going back to high-dopamine screen activities. If a teen spends two hours on social media, they should then be off of high-dopamine screen activities for two hours.

Sussman thinks cooking is a great low-dopamine activity because of all the steps you have to take before getting to the pleasure (dopamine rush) of eating.

The whole idea is to help kids avoid the habit of really long binges.

Plan out scenarios in advance

Work with kids to plan in advance how they will get off their screens when the allotted time is up. For example, if a kid with one hour of allotted screen time enjoys playing Fortnite and they know one game takes at least 40 minutes, then they should be self-aware enough to not start a second game. Instead, they should do something else during the remaining 20 minutes of their high-dopamine screen time.

Consider a certain type of timer

Dr. Sussman said to me: "Kids, and even older kids, lose track of real-world time when they're on a screen. We call it time distortion. In other words, you don't really realize how much time is passing in the real world. Visual timers are great. They make one called the Time Timer where you just turn a dial and you see a visual representation of how much time is remaining. It's kind of like a more modern version of an hourglass."

Have consistent time blocks for gaming

Dr. Sussman said: "If you have a consistent amount of time that you give your kid for their screen time, then usually they're expecting it when it's time to get off. And there's not as much of a power struggle when it's time to get off."

I know it is very challenging to maintain consistency, but it does make such a difference. When my kids were younger — say 10 and 11 — they knew they had an hour a day on the weekends for video games and we did not have many power struggles over that time limit. Chase often played a game called Contraption. We did not have any console games until he was about 13, when we got a Wii game. Every six months or so, we would renegotiate how much video game time he would have.

IDEAS FOR CONVERSATION STARTERS:

1. Consider creating a list of ideas for high and low-dopamine activities both off and on screens.
2. Do you think taking more breaks between screen time activities could improve your mood?
3. Do you recall a time you binged on screen time and felt particularly low afterward? Maybe sad or angry, or perhaps you had a headache?
4. You can visit Dr. Sussman's website as a family and watch some videos he created that show animations of the science.
5. I think it can be interesting to talk about how one feels during the day doing certain screen time activities versus at night. Personally, at some point in my early 20s, I realized that I could not watch TV or movies during the day unless I was home sick, because afterward I would just unexplainably feel blue. It was not from binging and I still have that response to this day. I don't see how Sussman's ideas would explain this, but it has me wondering.

• • •

Video Games and Making the World a Better Place

One week, I started thinking about these three things. First, I believe that all parents would answer yes to the following question: "Do you hope your child helps others now and in the future?" Second, on any given day, research tells us that 56% of eight to 12-year-olds and 64% of 12 to 18-year-olds spend some time gaming on a mobile device, console or computer.[1] Now, here is the third and crucial truth — few of the games that young people play today are about themes related to helping others or making the world a better place.

In the same week, I was blessed to meet for coffee with a dear mentor of mine, Dr. Bill Feoge, who was instrumental in eradicating smallpox. He told me that the day before we met, he was speaking at his alma mater and a student asked him his advice on what career path to consider. Feoge told me that he answered this way: "First, I would think about topics that, if not addressed, can destroy humanity and will make us a blip on the evolutionary timeline."

All this has inspired me to share some experiences and stories that can get us talking about the pro-humanity games that exist and how we can inspire young people to think creatively about what they can create.

Let me start by talking about one of the first games I had my kids playing when they were young — about 10. Do you recall the quiz-based game called "Free Rice"? It is a free online game in which a player picks a category and skill level to be quizzed on and with each correct answer, grains of rice (and other supplies) are donated to the World Food Programme. Quiz categories were few in the early days, with topics like English and Geography, but now there are over 20 subjects.

The game was created by a father, John Breen, to help his child improve his vocabulary. Which makes sense because it is a parent's dream game, since we all get a bit of a buzz when our kids learn things. I realize this is not much of a game and that explains why my kids never wanted to play it for long; it was great for short spurts of time and changing the topics kept it more engaging. However, the real upside of the game was the sense that they were doing something to help others.

The story of the computer game, Foldit inspired me. As a child, Adrien Treuille thought up games in his head all day long. Growing up in New York City, he would look outside and see the flows of people. His brain started blending his love of games and his fascination with large groups of people, and he wondered how they might fit together. BAM — he thought about how he could get masses of people working together online to solve complex, important problems.

But what problem? He thought about the proteins in our bodies or in pathogens and how if the proteins get misshapen, they can cause diseases. On the flip side, manipulating how proteins fold can cure diseases. Could ordinary, unscientific people armed with knowledge about basic principles of proteins solve puzzles around protein folding? He created a puzzle game. When he launched it in 2008, the servers crashed within 24 hours because so many people wanted to play.

There is a great short video featuring Adrien talking about the origins and story of his game, and it profiles a 15-year-old boy who loves working on these Foldit puzzles. This video can be found by searching, "The Making of EteRNA".[15] Share it with your kids.

While there are some games about exploring and appreciating the world, such as Abzu — a game that takes the player deep into the ocean as a diver tasked with restoring life — there are not many.

An obvious objective a game could have is wiping out pathogens. Two games come to mind in this genre: Pandemic 2 and Plague Inc.. Plague Inc. was created by 33-year-old James Vaughn. In the original game, the player acts as the plague and the object is to destroy humanity. I was happy to learn that he and his nine-person team are working fast to make a new variation of the game where the player's objective is to destroy the pathogen.

I wish more games were based on themes of helping others. For instance, how to strategically overcome fires and other natural disasters, stop epidemics, improve city traffic, save bee populations, prevent wild-animal extinction, decrease global pollution, provide housing to those in need — to name a few.

IDEAS FOR CONVERSATION STARTERS:

1. Why do you think that there are relatively few games about helping humanity?
2. Can you think of ideas for "pro-social" games?
3. If you were to create a game about solving a scientific problem, what would it be?

. . .

Strategies for Effective Video Game Limits

The entire topic of setting limits around video games is extremely challenging for so many families. In *Screenagers*, we meet Chris, a quiet 12-year-old, and his grandmother and care provider, Amaryllis. She was really struggling with Chris playing video games for long periods of time. He would yell and kick the wall when his time was up.

In the movie, Amaryllis said: "He can get violent. He would kick the walls and hold his face and start crying and holding his eyes and he doesn't … it's like he loses it. I don't like to see him like that."

I have spoken with many parents of kids and toddlers who have complete emotional meltdowns when interactive games get taken away. As kids get older, it manifests in different ways, like giving the silent treatment when they are angry about rules. Just like kids, teens can also get volatile when screen limits are imposed.

For the past nine years, I've been talking with psychologists, behaviorists, gaming experts and countless parents and young people about how to rein in video game time. Here are some of my top takeaways.

LET THEM EXPRESS THEIR CONCERNS

It can be helpful to give teens as much control as possible when discussing the issue. You might say something like, "I know it's really frustrating to stop in the middle of a game, particularly when you are playing with friends, since you would be letting them down, so can we plan for that?"

FROM CONSUMER TO PRODUCER

I often ask kids to calculate how much time they think they spend in a week on video games. From there, I say:

> *"Let's say that is 10 hours. That means for 10 hours, you are consuming what those video makers have made — their ideas, their creativity. But what about your ideas? They have a hold of your brainpower. Sure, you enjoy the game, but do you want to hand over that much time of your brainpower?*
>
> *"Perhaps exchanging some of your consuming time for producing time will make you feel better about yourself as you work on your creativity and brain muscles. What if you spend some of your gaming time writing ideas you have for a game you might create? What if you start learning a bit about coding a game?"*

See if your child will commit to designing video games for some percentage of the time they spend playing — even if it's just for a weekend.

LET TECH DO THE WORK

With Apple's Screen Time app, you can set all phone games to go off at a specific time. Make sure your phone is linked to your child's, otherwise they can just push the button that allows them to extend the time.

Xbox and other console systems have parental controls that allow parents to set a time limit for game playing. On Xbox, you can set which games can be played, who can play them and how much time each person can spend on a game in a day or a week. One of the key things is to make sure the child can see when the time will be up. So if they see time will be up in 10 minutes, that might mean they will stop, since they know another game takes 20 minutes. One rule that can help is allowing that unused time to carry over into the weekend, within some limits — perhaps a max of an hour or so.

TRY USING TIMERS

Setting up a system where a timer goes off some minutes before game playing must end lets the child start mentally preparing for the big shut down. Ideally, the timer will go off say, five minutes later, and the child will get off at that time.

PRAISE THEIR ABILITY TO FOLLOW THE RULES

This was something I had to work on, but it has proven to be successful and I am a major convert. I learned to praise my kids by "holding up a mirror with specifics" when they follow through on tech rules, such as turning off a video game. Even if there was pushback and grumpy words, I learned to focus on what went right instead of focusing on any disappointment. So let's say I had to ask my son more than once to get off his video game, but he finally did and sat down for dinner. Rather than start talking about how frustrated I was that I had to ask more than once, I learned to say: "Hey, I know that was hard for you to stop playing, but you did it anyway. You came to dinner and sticking with your word shows a lot of respect for yourself and our family."

I learned a lot about the power of specific praise from school counselor and author Tammy Hudson Small, Ph.D. Tammy explained that even if a child or teen gets really angry and slams a door when they finally come to dinner, you can do something called "creative recognition" at the dinner table. The following is an example:

> *"You were really angry and I get it, having to stop playing is hard. You got angry, but you could have been even angrier and refused to come to dinner. I appreciate how you were able to cool down in your room and then come to dinner. It shows a lot of tenacity to work through those angry feelings and still show your commitment to making our dinners work, even when you're frustrated."*

KNOW THAT THE STORM BEFORE THE CALM IS NORMAL

Many kids become intensely angry, frustrated and just downright flooded with emotions when video games have to get turned off. This is known as "surge extinction" — or in behavioral psychology, it is referred to as "extinction burst."[16]

Take, as an example, a pigeon that has learned that she receives a small amount of birdseed when she pecks at a lever. She will, of course, then peck at that lever frequently. If the lever stops producing the pellets, the pigeon will first try pecking it just as she had in the past. When no food comes out, the bird will try again and again with increasing frequency and pressure. It can look frantic. This is called the extinction burst.

The evolutionary advantage of this extinction burst is clear. In a natural environment, an animal that persists in a learned behavior, despite not resulting in immediate reinforcement, might still have a chance of producing reinforcing consequences if it tries again. This animal would be at an advantage over another animal that gives up too easily.

After a period of frantic activity in which their pecking behavior yields no result, eventually, the pigeon's pecking will decrease in frequency. It would be a really useless trait to keep pecking at something without ever getting a response — just as it would be useless for a child to keep begging for more video games once they have learned that the parent will not say yes after certain times on certain days.

CREATE ALTERNATIVES

Alternatives to video games are crucial. Taking on a building project like making a birdhouse, making an airplane model or beading a necklace are all examples. The fact is that some youth may resist, saying they are not interested in doing anything. There are many ways to expose them to new activities that might, hopefully, catch their interest.

I sometimes give my kids a "two-minute introduction," where I quickly show them something they might like to do. They know I will be very quick and that there will be no pressure. I have shown them videos of kids doing martial arts and beading projects. One I particularly loved was an entertaining Indian chef, who I showed to my son. Chase follows his videos and has made Chicken Tikka for the family a few times now.

Sometimes, parents take a bit more of a forceful approach. I remember when Michelle Obama's daughters were preteens, she once talked about how they got to pick two extracurricular activities they wanted to do and she would get to pick the third. Michelle told the interviewer, "Maybe that doesn't sound fair, but life is not always fair."

Of course, we parents can provide good alternatives. I know playing board games sounds like a cliché, but I am amazed at how much laughter I have with my two teens when we play a game like Boggle.

If your child already participates in a lot of outdoor activities, that is great. Author and psychologist, Laura Kastner, Ph.D., told me in an interview for *Screenagers*:

> *"The whole myth of the overscheduled child, it's really, really over-hyped and what we should worry about is kids that are not having enough activities after school. 40% of teenagers have no after school activities at all."*

ASK FRIENDS FOR ALTERNATIVES

I am amazed at how rarely we think to borrow things from friends. I love exchanging board games with friends — this lets us learn about games they love and decreases the need to buy new things. Another thing I have done is brought some of the books that my kids enjoyed to friends' homes who have similar-aged or younger kids. We have also benefited from people loaning us their books. There is a much higher chance that our kids will like the books when we know they were a hit with other kids we know. I was delighted the other day when Tessa told me about a book swap she was doing with some of her friends.

GET OTHER PARENTS INVOLVED

Finding another couple of parents to do a once-a-month activity with your child or teen can be an excellent way to start new pastimes and strengthen relationships. This could be a group of fathers and sons getting together once a month to cook a meal and learn new cooking techniques. Simple recipes that I love to do in group settings are spring rolls using rice paper or sushi that only requires seaweed, rice and fillings like avocado and carrots. Sometimes my teens roll their eyes at the thought of such a night, but once everyone is in the kitchen, laughter and good vibes start to flow.

"MY HOUSE, MY RULES"

My wonderful neighbor told me how she operates with her kids (ages nine, 12 and 15).

> *"We just have a Wii at our house and have tried to stick with active video games. No guns, etc. Wii Sports, Just Dance, Mario Kart. No video games on phones for us. I tend to do 'my house, my rules' with other kids and allow for the same at friends' houses."*

FIND SUPPORT

Letting your friends know you are struggling over video gaming rules is a smart move on many fronts. First of all, you will quickly realize you are not alone, and second, you can learn all sorts of rules and strategies you hadn't considered before by sharing. Also, it's a nice way of finding like-minded parents among your kid's friend group and can lead to play-dates where all parents agree that some of the time will be screen-free. You might even find parents who want to ensure that only nonviolent games are played when the kids are together.

In *Screenagers*, we see Amaryllis, the care provider of 12-year-old Christopher, go to a wonderful counselor who works in a community center.

Amaryllis: "I don't like confrontation; I don't know how to set limits. I don't know how to set boundaries. Once you get on, as long as you're not bothering me, everything is OK."
Counselor: "And I know that that has to stop."
Amaryllis: "Yeah."
Counselor: "We have to create this balance where he has activities with people, where he's moving, and also he can get his reward by using the technology. The consequences for Chris are, 'when you're disobedient when you fight me on the homework, when you come with bad grades during the second marking period now, that is not acceptable. I'm not going to take the two away, but I'm going to bring them down to 30 minutes.'"
Amaryllis: "OK, he's gonna sit there and argue and cry, you know."
Counselor: "That is a reaction to your limit setting that in time will stop because he's going to know that 'grandma is firm and no matter how I act up, grandma is going to say no.' If you stay firm and consistent, they will follow your lead because they love you. They still want you to be proud of them, right? All kids want that. And, they realize that you're the only caregiver that they really have."

Eventually, Amaryllis does indeed get better at setting limits. We also see that she has encouraged Chris to find new hobbies, including getting more involved with taking care of his pet.

IDEAS FOR CONVERSATION STARTERS:

1. On a scale of one to 10, with one being super easy and 10 being super hard, how difficult is it for you to stop playing a video game?
2. How many hours do you think is the right amount of time per day to spend on video games?
3. If you were to come up with a game, what would you call it and what would be the strategy?

Clues to Uncover
True Addiction to Video Gaming

Many people use the word "addiction" to casually describe something they do often or compulsively. We hear people say things like, "I'm addicted to chocolate," or, "I'm addicted to my cellphone." Clinical addiction is a different matter. A clinical diagnosis is defined by:

- Negative consequences: problems with relationships, work and school

- Tolerance: wanting to engage in the object of addiction more and more to get the same effect

- Withdrawal: feelings of anxiousness and physical symptoms when away from the object of addiction

- Unable to stop: serious difficulties with trying to cut down or stop

The World Health Organization (WHO) added "gaming disorder" to its International Classification of Diseases in 2018.[17] The disorder is characterized by "impaired control over gaming, increasing priority given to gaming over other activities to the extent that gaming takes precedence over other interests and daily activities, and continuation or escalation of gaming despite the occurrence of negative consequences."

As a health care professional, I have welcomed this move by the WHO. A formal classification of the disorder should eventually increase the availability of treatment services and insurance coverage for such treatments.

The American Psychiatric Association (APA) is considering adding Internet Gaming Disorder as an official diagnosis. This is based on studies that show psychological and physiological patterns similar to those with a drug addiction.

How do researchers do this? One of the many advances in radiology over the past few years allows for a higher resolution of brain anatomy and an ability to understand the brain in action by performing a functional MRI imaging (fMRI). This radiologic test measures blood flow in the brain, and we know that when an area of the brain is in use, blood flow to that region also increases.

Functional MRI images of brains of people with video game addictions show many similarities to the brain images of people with drug addictions. The fMRI images of the brains of those with video game addictions at rest reveal, on average, alterations in the volume of an area called the ventral striatum, which is associated with the feeling of reward. People with drug addictions also show this pattern.

Additionally, when people with video game addictions are put in an fMRI scanner and shown images of video games, their brains light up in a similar pattern to people with drug addictions who are shown pictures of drugs.

What is particularly important to note is that studies have shown that people who have received treatment for video game addiction report their urges to play decreasing, and their fMRI patterns become more like the brains of non-addicted people.[18] Hence, the brain changes observed during their addiction period are not permanent.

While these types of studies give clues as to what may be happening in the brain with problematic gaming, they are also preliminary and much more research is needed.

Internet use related to things besides video games — such as social media, binge-watching videos and constant phone use — can become a true addiction, leading to negative consequences in a person's life. These areas have gotten less attention, in part because less research gets done on them and so less is understood from a psychological and physiological perspective.

So what are some of the clues that indicate a person is experiencing real consequences from their gaming use? The way that health care professionals begin to assess the situation is to have a person fill out a questionnaire. There are several different questionnaires used to assess Internet Gaming Disorder.

Going through such a questionnaire with your child can be a good way to discuss issues around addiction. Let's look at the "Video Game Addiction Questionnaire", developed by Dr. Paul Gentile of Iowa State University.[19]

Video Game Addiction Questionnaire:
Answer "Yes," "Sometimes," or "No" to the following questions:

1. Over time, have you been spending much more time thinking about playing video games, learning about video game playing or planning the next opportunity to play?

2. Do you need to spend more time and/or money on video games to feel the same amount of excitement?

3. Have you tried to play video games less often or for shorter periods, but are unsuccessful?

4. Do you become restless or irritable when attempting to cut down or stop playing video games?

5. Have you played video games as a way of escaping from problems or bad feelings?

6. Have you ever lied to family or friends about how much time you play video games?

7. Have you ever stolen a video game from a store or a friend, or have you ever stolen money to buy a video game?

8. Do you sometimes skip household chores to spend more time playing video games?

9. Do you sometimes skip doing homework to spend more time playing video games?

10. Have you ever done poorly on a school assignment or test because you spent too much time playing video games?

11. Have you ever needed friends or family to give you extra money because you spent too much money on video game equipment, software, or game/Internet fees?

Total your "Yes," "Sometimes," and "No" answers. If you responded "Yes" or "Sometimes" to at least 6 of these 11 questions, then this would indicate a gaming problem.

Questionnaires like these do not provide a definitive diagnosis. Such a tool can miss people who have a problem (a "false negative"), or it can label someone as having a problem when they do not (a "false positive"). For this reason, combining taking the survey with talking to a health professional is always recommended if there is true concern over a gaming problem.

There are books on the market for parents who are concerned about the effect that video gaming and the internet is having on their children. Parents may want to try to pause screen use for several weeks. These books go over, step by step, ways to do a screen time or video game "detox," and include Dr. Victoria Dunckley's "Reset Your Child's Brain" and George Lynn's "Breaking The Trance."

IDEAS FOR CONVERSATION STARTERS:

1. Do you feel like your gaming creates negative consequences in any part of your life?
2. Do you ever feel anxious when you can't get access to your favorite video game?
3. Should the risk of gaming addiction be taught in schools?

. . .

Advice to Parents
From a Recovered Gaming Addict

Cam Adair is a former gaming addict. After nearly a decade of gaming for up to 16 hours a day, Adair quit and launched the website GameQuitters to help others break gaming's hold on their lives.[20] Members from 95 countries participate in GameQuitters' community forums and other resources.

When Fortnite hit the market and started grabbing youth's attention with a fierce grip, I thought it would be fruitful to ask Cam for some of his insights. I was particularly concerned that kids were struggling to control the amount of time they spent playing Fortnite. Teachers were dealing with kids falling asleep in class more than usual. A college freshman who was not much of a gamer found himself rushing back from class with the intention of playing for a half an hour before doing homework and then heading off to basketball practice. Then, he started noticing that once he would begin playing, it was suddenly time for practice and he had not yet done his homework. Luckily, this older teen had enough self-awareness and drive to change this habit quickly.

Fornite was incredibly ubiquitous, in part because it is the first popular game that was free and able to run on the simplest of computers. Fortnite is a survivor-style game where multiple players simultaneously compete to be the last one standing.

I asked Cam for some advice for parents in general, and on the global Fortnite phenomenon in particular.

Q: First, what helped you to quit?

"The biggest thing that helped with the cravings was becoming aware of them and disassociating with them. Meditation and exercise helped me a lot, but the biggest thing that helped with the cravings was becoming aware of them. I started to feel the sensation in my body and recognize that it was controlling me."

Q: Why do you think so many kids are obsessed with Fortnite?

"Anytime a game is this viral, it creates challenges — especially for teenagers because everyone is playing it. To not play Fortnite in high school right now is to be a social outcast. That's hard for a teenager."

The battle royal element in Fortnite can also be problematic because there is no way to pause in the middle of a game without losing. It's also very competitive, and we know competitive games tend to be more addictive.

Clinical psychologist Jordan Foster shared how Fortnite is a combination of many popular games like Pokémon Go, Minecraft, and Call of Duty. In Fortnite, you can find fighting aspects, economic aspects and social aspects, all of which appeal to many teenagers."

Q: How can parents help kids stop playing Fortnite when their time is up?

"One simple tip is to understand the natural pauses in the game. Most games of Fortnite last 20 to 30 minutes, so if you ask your son or daughter to come for dinner and they are in the middle of a game, you will meet resistance because if they stop now, they will lose.

"Instead, try to plan ahead. If you see they are halfway through the game and dinner will be ready in 20 minutes, tell them not to start another one after it's done so they will be ready for dinner — and if they do, you will unplug the modem, and they will lose their game.

"When your kids know you understand how their games work and you will maintain your boundaries while also being compassionate and working with them, they are likely to respond better than if it's abrasive and a fight. Most importantly, parents need to get educated on video game addiction and warning signs."

Q: What advice would you give parents?

"Parents have to be better educated and firm with their children's relationship with technology. It's challenging these days because, as a parent, you're up against a billion-dollar tech industry that has a greater interest in selling their technology than they do in your child's health. Games are different from when I was growing up, especially with the integration of gambling-like game design, loot boxes and in-app purchases. If you notice technology causing problems in your home, or your child has mood swings without them, you must take action immediately. You must set firm boundaries and stay strong in them.

"Lastly, it's easy to feel a lot of shame and guilt as a parent, especially if your child is having challenges, but you must let go of that and open yourself up to help. Parents need to come together more on this subject."

Q: What advice would you give kids?

"Learn more about why you do what you do. Why do you behave the way you do? What needs do gaming or technology fulfill for you? What draws you to it? Are there voids created in your life without gaming?

"The more you understand about your relationship with gaming and technology, the more power you will have to make informed decisions for your highest good. It's not about gaming being good or bad; it's about whether it's serving you. It's about whether gaming or technology aligns with your values, goals and the vision you have for your life. Yes, gaming and technology are fun and entertaining. But fulfillment comes from engagement, not entertainment. Living a life of purpose comes from being a creator of the life you want, not as a passive consumer of content."

The intense desire to play games for long stretches can happen with any game at any time. That is why it is vital for us as parents to set limits for appealing ones like Fortnite. If you are unsure whether your kid needs strong time constraint rules, try this three-step approach:

1. Ideally, with their input, decide the amount of time they have until the game needs to get turned off. Take into account the usual length of each game. For example, in Fortnite, a game usually takes 20 minutes.
2. When that time is up, do they shut off the game themselves?
3. If not, talk to them about what is happening and why they think they are having a difficult time.

IDEAS FOR CONVERSATION STARTERS:

1. What are your favorite video games, and what makes them so appealing?
2. Are there situations where you use games to escape?
3. When you have tried to turn off your video game and failed, what things did you learn at that moment? (The more we let kids know it is not a moral failing to not be in control, the better. The more we engage them in thinking scientifically about the process of willpower, the better they become at it.)

Chapter Three:

Mental Health

When I think of my life to date, the most intense pain I have felt have been caused by my teens enduring long spells of emotional pain. My son Chase sustained a serious concussion and battled the sometimes agonizing physical and mental repercussions for years. And then there is my daughter, and I have to admit that I waited until this book was almost complete to return to this section to write about her experiences of enduring depression.

Tessa was starting ninth grade. The year before, we moved across the country and she was doing very well and meeting lots of new friends. She was involved in school activities and her mood was good overall. Then sometime into ninth grade, she started to get quiet and at times cry, and she would say she did not understand it, but she didn't feel good.

At the onset of her depression, I was on a seesaw in my head. As her mom, I was hoping it was just high emotions that would pass, but the weeks turned to months and she stopped wanting to do the things she used to enjoy, like going to dance classes. She started overeating and would talk about how it helped numb her feelings.

Everything felt so fragile to me. I would say something to try and help, and she would burst into tears or leave the room. When this would happen, all I wanted to do was hug her and apologize. I wanted to apologize for making things worse at that moment, apologize for how my baby had to endure all these negative feelings, and more than anything, I wanted to apologize for not being able to make it better. Every day, I would dwell over what I could do to make this end. I cried a lot.

I was surprised to find that even though I am a primary care physician who has evaluated teens and cared for many adults with depression, I felt completely lost on how to best support my own daughter.

Tessa would talk about the negative thoughts circulating in her brain.

Often, she would start to look sad and then not be able to study or do things. I would gently ask if she could explain what her mind was saying. She would say she couldn't, and I could see the frustration and sadness in her eyes. She wanted to be able to express things, she wanted to be able to do things to make herself feel better, but she felt trapped.

I just kept telling her:

> *"Hun, this is your brain, this is not you, and this is not forever. We don't know why the brain does this at times — why depression happens — but it is common, and we have a team of people here to help you. You are doing the best you can, 100% percent. Never doubt that. You are doing the best you can with the tools you have and what is happening in your brain. I love you; we all love you; so many people love you. We are all going to work together to get you through this."*

Fortunately, we found Diane, a wonderful therapist for Tessa. Diane worked weekly with Tessa, and Tessa enjoyed the sessions and felt that they were helping her. I was glad that I, and sometimes even the whole family, was able to sit in on some sessions. In these sessions, Tessa would talk about what we were doing that helped and what we were doing that didn't, and Diane could help us unpack the reasons why. This helped us feel closer and better prepared about what to do when we were at home and Tessa was not feeling well.

Eventually, Tessa tried medication, and while there was a period of starting and stopping and changing the medicine, one medication finally did begin to help her some.

I needed to learn strategies to best help Tessa, and Tessa needed her own coping skills. As we were learning these new tools, I realized I wanted all kids and adults to learn what we were learning — not just for depression symptoms, but for all of the many challenging emotions that youth experience growing up and will at times experience as adults.

Most youth learn very little about how to understand emotions like anxiety, stress and depression, but they learn even less about the skills that can help them cope with these challenges. It is shocking to me that in 2020, only three states require their school districts to teach mental health.

Many young people turn to the internet for a host of health related information. In one survey of 14 to 22 year olds, researchers found that approximately nine out of 10 (87%) reported having gone online for health information — the top five topics searched being fitness (63%), nutrition (52%), stress (44%), anxiety (42%) and depression (39%).[1]

In that same study, they monitored survey answers suggesting moderate to severe depression. They found that 90% of respondents who met criteria for either one reported having looked up information about depression on the internet.

On the one hand, the internet can be a really wonderful resource for helpful information for people who are struggling emotionally. On the other hand, how often is the information inaccurate and worse yet, how often is it suggesting harmful coping approaches? Or connecting people to groups or a person that does not have their best interest in mind?

Tessa's depression was most active during ninth and 10th grade. Things were better for her for most of the 11th grade, and now she is in her senior year. Bouts of depression come and go for Tessa, but not nearly as acutely as in those earlier years. Tessa is much, much better. When she was struggling the most, I sometimes sought counseling for myself. I needed help with thinking through the ways I could best support her instead of racing in and trying to solve things on her behalf. I also have friends who are adolescent psychologists that were very helpful. I wanted the insights that they gave me to be offered to everyone, and that mindset also inspired the film.

What was so key for me during this time was finding other parents going through what we were going through. I have four friends who are moms trying to cope with their own teens' emotional challenges. Calling them was my lifeline at times, and knowing that I could also support them meant so much to me.

My own experience has proven to me that one of the strongest antidepressants available to any of us is the ability to help others. This really hit home with Tessa, who is in the film too.

When the film was in rough-cut form, I asked her to watch and make sure that she was OK with the footage and that she still wanted to be in the film. It was important to me that she was really sure. After viewing it, she said, "When I watch the other teens in the film tell their stories, it helps me so much that I absolutely want to help others by sharing my story." Many of the other teens in the film also told me that they wanted to be in it to help others.

Chase has had his own battles to fight. His injury has forced him to deal with chronic physical pain and it has been incredibly hard on him. Often, the pain could not be pinpointed to a particular cause, and as a physician, I had extra awareness about the psychological anguish that can come from this unknowing. As a mom, I have had many sleepless nights feeling emotional about Chase.

He has also found it therapeutic to talk about his experiences as a way to help others. In Chapter 10, you will learn how tech has helped improve his well-being despite the pain.

This chapter covers a large range of mental health topics. Having all of these talks with our kids not only helps them with their own emotional wellbeing, but it also provides more tools to help people get through challenging times.

· · ·

In a World of Happy Posts — Why Expressing True Emotions is so Important

Emotions are often challenging and confusing, and it truly baffles me why we don't spend more time in schools and homes discussing this reality with our youth as they grow up.

In filming *Screenagers NEXT CHAPTER*, which in part explores the science of emotions, I asked a 7-year-old girl to list all the feelings she could think of. She rattled off her list of words such as "angry", "sad", and then she said "bold." Suddenly she stopped, tilted her head and looked at me inquisitively and asked, "Is bold a feeling?" I did a double take. Was it? Right then and there, I was reminded of how confusing feelings are, no matter one's age.

Feelings can be pesky annoyances all the way to fiendish liars. For example, depression can often say lead people to believe lies such as, "You are the only person who has this", "You are a flawed individual and you better not tell anyone what you are feeling, for they will surely think less of you," and, "Look this is your fault, you are good for nothing and you deserve to feel awful." There are many more lies depression tells and anxiety tells quite a few as well.

Throughout my 25 years in medicine, I am constantly reminded of how people's fear of telling others about the hard emotions they are dealing with means they do not get support and treatment. Many individuals have told me that their emotional challenges began in their teen years, but they never felt OK to talk about it with others. When someone tells me that I am the first person they have confided in about their struggles, my heart always aches, thinking about how they have had to suffer not just from the feelings, but from the extra burden of feeling so alone.

Youth have long received all sorts of messages through television shows and movies about what feelings are OK to talk about and which are not. I think about all the shows in which characters are shown displaying anger, but almost never expressing feelings such as guilt, regret, sadness or fear, to name just a few.

Now, in addition to shows, there is the whole new landscape of social media. Ask any young person if they think there is a lot of filtering of emotions happening on social media apps, and they will give you an impassioned "yes" and tell you that it is not just other people who do this, but that they also partake.

One eighth-grader told me:

> *"I remember in a time of my life where I wanted people to know that I was happy. Let me just show this to the entire world how happy I am. I would post over and over and over again until I almost believed it myself. When I obviously wasn't very happy. But I wanted to be. I wanted to be happy so bad, but I just wasn't."*

If a teen is upset about something, what will they do with that upset feeling? One thing they may do is called "down-regulating" the emotion, which is when someone tries to lessen a negative feeling by doing things to avoid feeling it. A person may do this to try to feel less negatively affected by the emotion — to both feel and try to look better than they really are.

Researchers know that a downside is that suppressing feelings can hinder resolution, thereby extending the emotional pain. But they wondered how it could impact the person's thinking abilities and cognitive processing.

James Grossman at Stanford has been conducting studies on this very question for over two decades. He wanted to understand what happens when a person is told in a study to down-regulate their emotions — also called "suppressing" emotions. What happens to that person's cognitive abilities to process and recall the information.

In one of Grossman's studies, participants were asked to watch an upsetting film showing a man getting into a motorcycle accident.[2] Researchers told some of the participants before the film to suppress any emotional reaction they had to the film, and they told the other group not to suppress their emotional responses.

They found that the participants told to suppress their emotions recalled far fewer details about the movie than those who were not instructed to suppress their emotions. Clearly, their brain had to actively suppress the emotions, leaving less brainpower to take in what was happening on the screen.

From this study, another interesting cost of suppressing emotions was determined. It caused participants' blood pressure to rise higher than the control group, who had been free to express their emotions. Stress-related increase in blood pressure is taxing for the body and is associated with problems such as heart disease. A fascinating additional finding was that not only did their blood pressure go up, but when they had to explain the film to someone else, (while still suppressing any emotions the film may have caused them) the person they were talking to had an elevation in their own blood pressure, which was not the case for the control groups. The researchers do not know why these people experienced elevated blood pressure, but it might be that they were sensing the tension in the other person — whether consciously or subconsciously — and this led to the observed rise.

James Grossman told me in an interview:

"What we found in laboratory studies and in the field is that when people try to use suppression, they can look cool, but they don't feel cool. And furthermore, their thinking process is slowed down. So if you give people information while they're suppressing, they don't remember it as well. So if I'm a teenager and I'm really upset about something that a friend of mine said or something that happened at home, and if I'm trying to suppress that emotion, that may make me so busy cognitively that I can't really pay attention to what the teacher is saying or what the homework is all about. And if you add that up day after day it can mean very, very different trajectories academically."

There is no question that with the increased exposure to media on devices, our youth are growing up with far more ideals of beauty, handsomeness, and ways to act or express oneself than ever before.

Suppression can of course be very advantageous at times. Say a person is feeling a lot of anger and they start lashing out at someone. It most likely would be much more effective to step away and start breathing and thinking about calming down, to lessen the intensity of the emotions and not just act from that emotional place.

I wanted to know what schools were doing to effectively teach emotional intelligence, and I went to a school district that brought together young men of color for a leadership program many times over each school year. In these meetings, the boys were encouraged to share as much as they wanted to. It was a very kind environment.

In one of these meetings, I was fortunate to meet one young man who stole my heart, a 14-year-old named Julio. He told me how hard it was for him that his father was in jail. Yet, he did not like talking about his feelings and had never shared these emotions with his mom.

He was able to get into a program that brought middle and high school boys of color together in ongoing ways to teach them social, emotional and leadership skills. The boys meet at their schools in groups with mentors and at regular intervals. All the boys from the various schools would come together and talk in a circle, hearing speakers and working in smaller groups.

I felt energized when I was at one of these group meetings because I could see how engaged so many of the youth were. One of the exercises was to have everyone in the circle stand up and share whatever they wanted to share. Group leaders encouraged everyone to speak by telling them how they all mattered and that no matter how little they wanted to say, their words were important — they were important.

In the film, we witness a powerful scene during this circle time where a boy in 12th grade stands up and talks about his father recently dying and we see him begin to cry.

Next, Julio stands up and says to the circle while looking at Tray:

> *"I feel with Tray and what you said when you talked about your dad. That opened up the door for me. I can't talk about my dad like that. Most of my childhood, I didn't have him or talk about him. I can't talk to my mom about this. Until this point, I've never talked about the struggles that I've had. Not having my dad. In my seventh and eighth grade, I made the basketball team, but I never got to play because my grades were trash. And I felt lonely. So I want to thank you guys for giving me the opportunity to have my voice be heard."*

One of the leaders of the program, a wonderful school administrator who was at the circle when this scene transpired, said to me:

> *"To say I can't even talk to my mom about it. That, for me, let me know that that practice, that sharing, that experience for other young men to see that not just for him, but think about the effect it has on the other young men. That's the powerful piece that they don't get to see."*

Julio, later explained to me how impactful that moment in the circle was:

> *"That was the first time I've ever talked about how I felt about my dad. That day, I told my mom that I talked about how I felt about my dad. My dad has been gone for a lot of time and I really needed him. And she was very receptive to how I was feeling. She wasn't judgemental. After that, I think I got a lot closer with my mom."*

The following are ideas about what parents can do.

DISCUSS MEDIA AND VIDEO GAME LITERACY

Talking about the ways males and females are displayed in shows in regards to expectations about emotions is so important, more so now than ever. Start with the shows and videos they watch.

I recall how frustrated I was that my son was so glued to the series "Arrow", which is about a superhero — who of course never talks about feelings or shows any emotions. The whole idea of a male hero who is stoic beyond belief consumed him.

I worked to stay calm and to ask him questions about his take on the superhero and how he felt about the messages the show was sending. It was useful to ask what he thought a younger kid would learn from it. So, if Chase was 11, I might ask, "What do you think an 8-year-old might take away from the show about what it means to be a real man?"

Media literacy also must include video games that now contribute hours of messaging to our kids and teens about emotionless males. In games, many people are killed, and yet there are no emotions expressed and no negative consequences shown (other than perhaps losing a round).

DISCUSS SOCIAL MEDIA LITERACY

Ask your kids questions like how often they think a person's post is in line with their true emotional life. Teens tell me often that when they are not feeling good, they purposely post photos where they look good in the hopes of getting lots of likes, so as to boost their mood. This may help in some ways, and yet there can be downsides.

DISCUSS HELPFUL AND UNHELPFUL SUPPRESSION OF CHALLENGING EMOTIONS

Using a story from my life is something I often do with my kids when it comes to issues around feelings. For example, I might share with them how when I am on a call discussing a questionable bill, my frustration with the person on the other end can quickly mount (in part because I was waiting twenty minutes to finally speak with someone). I work very hard to suppress my frustration because it is not at all my goal to let my feelings out on this person. In that way, I am glad to be regulating my emotions.

Take a different scenario. I am working at my medical clinic and I'm feeling emotional about a conflict I am having with my husband. I work to suppress my emotions so I can provide the best medical care possible. I soon recognize that I am really having a hard time concentrating so at lunch, I call him. I get to express my feelings, we work things out, and when I get back to see another patient, I can focus much better.

IDEAS FOR CONVERSATION STARTERS:

1. What ways does our screen world promote hiding true emotions?
2. What do common messages in shows and video games convey about what and when it is appropriate for girls to express emotions? How about for boys?
3. Can you recall being upset at school, having to hold it together, and finding it was really hard to concentrate?
4. When was the last time you told someone about your emotions and felt it was helpful?

• • • •

How Tech Impacts Teen's Stress and How To Help

When people get asked to rank their level of perceived stress, teens on average report higher levels than adults. Teens also have higher levels of the stress hormone, cortisol in their blood streams at any given time than adults.

There are many reasons teens report stress, including academic-related stress and stress caused by relationships with peers and family. There is also the stress of trying to feel "good enough," or trying to belong to a peer group — just to name a few. Screen time and stress can be intertwined.

Youth tell me many positive ways technology helps them to cope with stress, such as contacting a good friend to get advice or using it to make a song. Both of these uses help them relax and feel more competent. Many teens turn to YouTubers for insights on how to cope on a bad day or how to approach a friend who is ignoring them. Others tell me that they achieve instant stress reduction from watching funny YouTube videos.

On the flip side, there are many ways screen time can promote feelings of stress. One of the big ones is managing social media — both the relationship issues that can emerge and the sheer volume of things that demand their attention.

I interviewed a 15-year-old girl who told me about the stress she feels from social media and all the "Snaps" (i.e., messages) she gets:

> *"I'll send streaks. At 8 o'clock, I'll put my phone down. I'll go eat breakfast. I'd come back, and I'll have like 17 different snaps from people. I have to make sure I'm not ignoring them. And they know I'm not ignoring them. It's just a lot."*

While adults often talk a lot about their fears of cyberbullying on social media platforms, far more often, tweens and teens tell me other ways that screen time leads them to feel stress.

Here are a few of the many other examples they give:

- Seeing others out without them on a Snapchat story
- Seeing the guy they like in photos with his new girlfriend
- Seeing one image after another of the popular girls looking their best
- Having someone open their Snapchat so they know their message has been seen, but then they don't respond
- Not being invited to be in a group video game or an ongoing group chat
- Having someone not respond to a text message
- Having someone comment something snarky on a post they made
- Having a guy repeatedly ask them for a photo or to meet him somewhere
- Feeling bad when they have to go to bed and cut off a friend who is texting a lot because they are going through a hard time
- Arguing with family about screen time

So often, youth tell me that immediately turning to a screen is their go-to when they are feeling stressed. One 12-year-old boy said, "When I'm feeling stressed, I go on my phone, Snapchat, YouTube."

Teens are fully aware of how using screen time to cope with stress can help in the short run, but often only makes things worse. For example, when they feel stressed about having to write a paper, it's easy to escape the feeling by watching YouTube videos, but they will only feel greater stress as the night goes on. They have not done work on the paper and then it just spirals, with less sleep and so forth.

THINGS PARENTS CAN DO TO HELP
YOUTH DEVELOP SKILLS FOR STRESS:

1. Help them stop and define "stress"

We all know that "stress" is always the word of the day. It gets thrown around all the time. It can be helpful to do the following when your child (or yourself) says they are feeling stressed.

Stop and think: "Hey, I just said 'stress' — or hey, you just said 'stress.' What emotion is it really?"

See what the person who used the word "stressed" comes up with. Maybe they really mean tired or overscheduled or angry about something or perhaps even sad.

Just doing this one step — identifying the core emotion, gives us the ability to address it with more skill and forethought.

2. Help them identify "challenge stress" vs. "overwhelming stress"

How can we help our kids see stress in new, more helpful ways? Some degree of stress is healthy and desirable — this is often called "challenge stress." But feeling overwhelmed by stress is not desirable.

Talking about "challenge stress" vs. "overwhelming stress" is key. You may start by asking, "What is happening in your life that is challenging?" And then help them define the stress by saying something like: "There is some good stress. For example, a cross country runner might be feeling stressed about a meet on Saturday, and that keeps her making sure to practice all week. And frankly, she is excited about Saturday's race. So the stress is a good thing — motivating her to work hard and to step into a risky situation."

Overwhelming stress might look like this example: A student is in three clubs, two meet on different days before school and one meets after. They have several challenging classes. Meanwhile, peer issues are happening. So now they find themselves having a hard time falling asleep. Once they have identified what type of stress they have — challenge or overwhelming — then problem-solving is warranted.

3. Let teens lead when it comes to problem-solving

When they are experiencing overwhelming stress, ask them if they have any ideas for how to solve the problem. Research shows that teens experience increased levels of stress when their parents jump in and try to solve problems. This is what I did so often with my teens and I needed to change. I was fascinated by the science that explained to me why I needed to let them lead.

Investigator Jessica Borrelli wanted to study what was happening when parents stepped in to problem-solve for youth. She studied a group of 8 to 12-year-olds and their parents.

I am going to let her explain in her own words here, but know that her team would attach devices that measured physiological responses for both the teens and their parents during their interactions as a way to measure physiological stress.

Dr. Borrelli said in an interview with me:

> *"We tried to develop a task where parents would be tempted to become controlling, and we thought that the type of situation that would evoke that behavior would be a situation where teenagers are failing. So we created a computer paradigm where teenagers are asked to do a complex puzzle. We tell the parents ahead of time not to help. And then we watch as mom, after mom, after mom ends up actually stepping in and helping. And then what we do during this experiment is we're actually monitoring moms' and teenagers' cardiovascular reactivity. What we found was when they stepped in and tried to help their children with the task, they showed decreases in stress and their children showed an increase in stress."*

It was helpful to learn about this science to really help explain that when I go into problem-solving, it lowers my stress but increases that of my kids. I have learned to say these two things that have made all the difference:

- "Do you have any ideas for facing this stressful situation?"
- "I am here to brainstorm solutions whenever you want me to — just let me know."

These phrases let my kids know I have faith in their problem-solving skills and also puts the sense of control in their hands — if they want my input, they have control to ask me for it.

Maybe a teen like the one above, who is feeling stressed by school, will come up with solutions such as getting help in how to address the peer conflict, taking a break from one of the morning clubs, or seeing if they can swap one of the classes for another that is more enjoyable.

SHOW THEM THE WAYS YOU HANDLE YOUR STRESS

Parents have told me how surprised they were when they stopped to think about it. They realized they rarely share their coping strategies for stress with their kids. My teens know that exercise is my number one stress reliever. I am not an Iron Woman athlete, but I rely on my daily dose of movement. It makes all the difference in the world for my stress levels.

They also know that other than texts, I have no notifications that pop up on my phone. They know that I don't bring screens into my bedroom when going to sleep because sleep is so important to me.

ENSURE THEY HAVE "STOPPING POINTS"

Gone are the days of "natural stopping points" because videos, online games and social media platforms are all specifically designed to be an endless chain of events. That means as parents, we need to create the stopping point.

If a 13-year-old knows that screens get put away at 9 p.m., they have to learn to not keep postponing work. Having times when they need to be off social media and video games ensures they have time to recharge

by doing things like playing with a younger sibling or helping chop vegetables at dinner time.

IDEAS FOR CONVERSATION STARTERS:

1. What screen time activities help you relieve feelings of stress?
2. In what ways does screen time contribute to your stress?
3. What are other ways you handle your feelings of stress?

• • •

Helping Youth Understand Clinical Depression

Ishmael is one of the sweetest teenagers I've ever met. He lives in Oakland, California with his mother and two little sisters. He has an older brother that no longer lives at home. Ismael was 15 when he shared his story of emotional hardship with us for the film *Screenagers NEXT CHAPTER*.

He told me the following:

> *"After school, I would come back home and I would just be in my room. I'd be like, I could sleep like for the whole day ... I wouldn't be social. I wouldn't talk to my mom. I wouldn't talk to my brother. I wouldn't talk to my sisters. I would just be in my room all day doing nothing. Just getting used to feeling depressed."*

His mother added:

> *"He isolated himself. So when that became, you know, OK he's spending a lot more time — the door closed. His windows. The room is black and he's just there. He would always say, 'It's because you don't understand. You don't get it.'"*

Ishmael explained, "My mom, I try not to be emotional in front of her because I try to be strong for her."

It was so moving to hear Ishmael talk and at this point, he was choking up with tears and so was I. He experienced feelings of worthlessness, sadness and felt almost no pleasure in doing things for months and months.

THE SIGNS AND SYMPTOMS OF CLINICAL DEPRESSION

Let's take this time to cover some basic but essential education about clinical depression. In this way, our kids will know about warning signs in themselves and in their friends and other people they will meet throughout their lives.

To screen for depression, health professionals use a screening tool called the PHQ-9. I'm writing about this PHQ-9 questionnaire because talking about it with your kids can help them better understand the symptoms of depression and gauge whether they or a friend are experiencing it now or in the future.

I have shortened some things, but the PHQ-9 essentially asks the following:

> *"For at least several days a week for two consecutive weeks: Do you have little interest or pleasure in doing things? And/or Are you feeling down, depressed, or hopeless?"*

The person needs to answer yes to at least one of those two questions. If they do, then they answer the following questions, which are on a scale from "not at all" to "nearly every day."

- Do you have trouble falling or staying asleep, or sleeping too much?
- Do you feel tired or have little energy?
- Do you have a poor appetite, or conversely, do you overeat?
- Do you feel bad about yourself, or feel like a failure, or do you feel like you've let yourself or your family down?
- Do you have trouble concentrating on things?
- Do you move slowly? Do you speak very slowly? Or the opposite, do you feel overly fidgety or restless?
- Thoughts that you would be better off dead, or thoughts of hurting yourself in some way?

- If you've checked off any of these problems, how difficult have these problems made it for you to do your work? How hard is it to take care of things at home? Get along with other people? (These questions get rated on a scale from "very much" to "not at all.")

Answers then get scored. The PHQ-9 questionnaire can be found online and talking through it with your child can be a good way to discuss the main symptoms associated with depression.

Also, we know that depression in boys can manifest as significant irritability or hostility and the questionnaire can unfortunately miss this. There is also the fact that some teens will start using or increase the use of substances such as marijuana or alcohol as a way of trying to cope with their emotions. Some will not be even aware that it is depression that they are experiencing, and some will not realize that their emotional state is a big factor in why they are using substances.

As a parent, trying to figure out if your child is experiencing clinical depression can be excruciatingly difficult. I know for me, I just had no clue how to interpret my daughter's words and behaviors in the early days — was this just teen girl moodiness or was this something else? Talking with other parents and getting insights from professional psychologists made all the difference.

STRATEGIES FOR TREATING DEPRESSION

There are many different ways to help youth who are dealing with depression. Here, I touch on some of the main strategies: therapy, behavioral activation and the importance of building a support team.

Some form of counseling is a crucial first step. It is key that the youth can relate to the therapist — that they feel heard, that they can trust the person, and that they do not feel as though the therapist is only listening, but that they are also engaged and suggesting new ways to problem solve and rethink things. With so many factors, it is no wonder that it can take a teen meeting with two to four people before they find someone they feel good about working with.

Counseling is all about helping youth to start seeing things in a new light. There are many types of therapy, and one of the most common ones used to treat depression is called cognitive behavioral therapy. The "cognitive" part of it helps patients rethink the things they are telling themselves. For example, if a tween constantly thinks that no one likes them, the therapist will make sure the child feels heard and validated. And then, once the child does not feel judged about these thoughts but instead feels like the therapist has empathy and concern for them, the therapist can help the child see how their feelings do not fit the facts. The therapist will enquire about family members and friends who have shown signs of liking them. The therapist might then ask, "How can it be that all these people like you and yet you think you are not likeable?" Through these explorations of thoughts and real life data, the goal is to help shift the youth's thinking away from their negative thoughts towards more helpful ones.

Part of Ishmael's road to rising out of depression was ongoing counseling. He liked his counselors, which, again, is key for healing.

Ishmael said: "I started seeing school counselors, and then they started to like trying to help me. I would tell them about my problems and my thoughts, and they would tell me that I'm a good person."

The other primary intervention is the "behavior" part of cognitive behavioral therapy. It has to do with helping the youth start to perform behaviors they used to find pleasurable so that, in time, the feelings of pleasure can come back. This is what depression does to a person — it saps away motivation and pleasure and it becomes a vicious cycle. With less motivation, people are engaged in fewer activities that can bring joy via fun — like time with others that can create a sense of self-confidence. They do less and are alone more and their depression just gets worse and worse.

Given that a teen with depression has very little motivation to do things, it is brutal to witness as a parent on the sideline. I have been there. I kept thinking and at times saying to Tessa things like, "Hun, if you go for a jog, you will feel so great afterward," or, "Why don't you call that girl you talked about last month, maybe she wants to hang out?" or, "Hun, why don't ... "

My suggestions often only made Tessa more upset. I learned it would make her feel worse about herself. Rationally, she knew there was merit in what I said, but she would think to herself, "I must be such a loser because I just can't do those things."

For behavioral activation to occur, a support team is so key. Developmentally, adolescents need distance from parents. Our suggestions need to be doled out sparingly and in conjunction with input from others.

Ishmael's mom felt awful that he spent hours in his room with the blinds down, doing so little. She would suggest things for him to do, but her words were not enough. When Ishmael started seeing a counselor, she continued to give him suggestions about things he could do — which is the behavioral activation I mentioned above. Ishmael also had a friend who gave him a ukulele and encouraged him to try playing. Slowly but surely, Ishmael started to watch videos on how to play, and he started to enjoy it. As he got better at playing the ukulele, he started to feel better about himself, creating a positive loop that helped to lift the depression. One of my favorite moments in *Screenagers NEXT CHAPTER* is when we see Ishmael playing the ukulele for his little sister, and her little legs are swinging back and forth as she looks at her older brother with a big smile and a gleam in her eyes.

I needed help finding ways to get Tessa to do things to help her feel better. I knew that being with little kids was a consistent mood booster for Tessa. Since I could remember, whenever she would see a child younger than herself she would want to stop and interact with them. The interaction would always leave her with a big smile on her face. Before her depression, she loved babysitting. But with the depression, she would lay in her bed feeling useless and she did not reach out to the families she babysat for prior.

One of the families she babysat for was in the neighborhood. Normally, I did not like getting involved in Tessa's jobs because I felt strongly that the whole process around getting work is part of personal growth and learning. But with her depression, I decided a bit of engagement could make a world of difference. One day, I asked the mom if we could chat outside for a minute. When we met, I told her how Tessa was struggling with depression and did not have her usual initiative to reach out to babysit. I asked if there was a way that she could reach out to Tessa to have her come and play with her kids or to babysit.

I felt so vulnerable asking her this — I didn't like coming across as if I was overly involved in Tessa's life, as I work hard not to be. Also, I wondered if the mom would be worried to have Tessa babysit, knowing she was dealing with depression.

I was not worried about telling the mom about Tessa's depression because Tessa had told me many times that she was fine with telling adults if it was related to her feeling better or my feeling better — i.e., for both of us to be getting support and solutions through it all. Also Tessa felt close to this particular mom.

When I asked my friend her whole face lit up. She said, "Oh, I am so glad you told me, and I love Tessa and would love her to come over and sit!"

That is what happened, and it was one of the many small steps that contributed to getting her back to her old self.

This same team approach happened with her teachers and counselor. As a family, self-advocacy was a top priority and we always encouraged our kids to talk with teachers and counselors when they had concerns or questions. We wanted them to know early on that school is like a job — that they are learning how to navigate relationships, be responsible and a host of other skills. We let them know that mess-ups, failures and forgetting things was how people learn. We would be there to help them but not to pave the roads for them.

As school became incredibly difficult for Tessa to maneuver, we knew that her abilities were being overcome by the weight of her depression. My husband and I spent many nights talking about when and how we would intervene. Tessa was in ninth grade and we were aware that developmentally, it made perfect sense that having parents get involved in school was a charged issue. So we saw her counselor and I spoke with psychologist friends to figure out a plan. Ultimately, we let Tessa know that just a little check-in with her teachers could help the staff know what was going on and how they could help support her. The teachers were grateful when I talked with them and Tessa was as well.

Medication can be helpful in the treatment of depression. By the time an adolescent and parents are considering medicine, it has a long and rocky road. It is not like teens go into a doctor's office reporting feeling blue and the doctor immediately says, "Oh, here take this." For a medicine to be offered, many symptoms and issues will have to have been occurring for a long time. Also, it would have to be determined that counseling on its own is not sufficient.

Then, there is the emotionality that comes with thinking of starting the medication. Teens and parents have heard many things that can concern them about medicine — some true, some not. Either way, there are issues with medication and it can be hard to know what to do. On top of that, there are no ways of knowing which medicine will work, so it is a guessing game — but an educated guessing game. This is the reality of medicine that works to impact emotions and behaviors positively. Frankly, this is true for many medicines we physicians use to try to help a person feel better physically. The whole point of antidepressants is to help a patient suffer less and get to the point where they can participate in things they love again.

IDEAS FOR CONVERSATION STARTERS:

1. Have you discussed depression in any class or assembly at school?
2. Does knowing about the PHQ-9 help you understand depression better?
3. How often do you see people post online about their sadness or depression?
4. Do you know anyone you think might be depressed?

. . .

Exploring Why Depression Rates are Increasing

Current data reveals that about 19% of girls and 6% of boys 12 to 17 will meet the criteria for a depression episode in a given year. Since 2011, there has been a 59% increase in teens who meet criteria for a depression episode (which includes mild, moderate or severe).

I want to make a few comments about this data. This percentage is higher than those who have actual clinical depression because the screening questions are designed to not falsely miss people who are suffering (i.e., there are some "false positives" in this 59%, but there are few "false negatives"). This number may also include false positives because some of the teens may have been sleep-deprived upon taking the survey. We know that many teens are sleep-deprived nowadays and that their answers on this questionnaire can mimic that of depression.

Also, researchers wonder if boys are truly this much less depressed than girls. Perhaps they are less in touch with feelings, less likely to admit to them and some symptoms get missed on the questionnaires.

Depression symptoms started going down for teen boys and girls through the '90s, and then leveled off. And then around 2011, they started going up again. I want to talk about all the reasons why we might be seeing this rise, and I hope you will discuss these ideas with the kids and students in your lives. They get all sorts of headlines with quick answers, but the reality is more complex. Depression symptoms stem from a complex intersection of environment, events and genetic wiring.

The fact that about 59% more teens meet the criteria for a depression episode now than nine years ago is very concerning. I want to point out that during this time period, there has been an increase in adults reporting depression symptoms as well.

We know access to social media and the internet has dramatically increased over the same period of time. How does this relate to more teens reporting depression symptoms? It is far too simplistic to say that this recent rise in reported symptoms is caused solely by screen time, but what part does screen time play in this dramatic increase?

We all know that for any teen, their online life can lead to some level of depression — such as experiencing intense cyber cruelty. We also know that when youth spend large amounts of time on screens, it can be a red flag that they may be experiencing depression.

Let's look at all the possible reasons for depression: I'll start by considering possible non-screen time reasons for this increase, and then I'll discuss screen time's impact. I will use the word "teens" to refer to both teens and tweens.

NON-SCREEN TIME POSSIBLE REASONS FOR DEPRESSION:

**Could it be that teens are more likely
to report their feelings on surveys?**
Before the late 1980s, teen depression was not widely talked about in the U.S., in part because the medical world paid relatively little attention to it. The talented comedian Gary Gulman, who had depression

in his youth, remarked that the treatments available in the '70s and '80s "pretty much were 'Snap out of it' and 'What have you got to be depressed about?'"

Over the past decade, many celebrities have opened up about their mental health struggles — such as Lady Gaga, Serena Williams and Prince Harry, to name just a few. Also, famous YouTubers, who are particularly relatable to teens, sometimes talk about their depression. Since teens are exposed to media more often than in the past, opportunities to hear about these experiences have multiplied.

By the way, I believe it is a real gift that in this country, more and more influencers are being open about their experiences with mental health problems. The reality is that in most of the world, this is not the case. For example, when I made the film "Hidden Pictures", about global mental health, I was amazed that in India, China, South Africa and even France, it was nearly impossible to find any celebrities who were publicly open about their mental health challenges.

Could it be that overall, things are harder now for teens than in the past?

Teens often talk about the stress of not being good enough. The level of competition teens feel at school and in sports is much higher than when we were growing up. Meanwhile, academic loads can be daunting. The number of academically successful teens who tell me all the cool things they love to do in and out of school, and yet say, "Oh, no, no, I am not going to apply to such-or-such college, I would NEVER get in" utterly astounds me.

Other societal stressors are important to factor in, such as the stress families experience with rising health and housing costs, decreasing relative wages, job losses, worsening anti-immigration sentiments, climate issues and funding shortages for social support programs, to name a few. There are many ways things feel worse now, but it is important to remember there were plenty of intense stressors in the past as well.

Possible reasons due to screen time

The rise of reported depression symptoms starting in 2011 correlates with the increase in screen time and smartphone ownership, so of course everyone wants to know if social media and overall screen time is causing the rise in depression.

Researchers have hypothesized that if social media is a risk factor for worse moods, then a teen who spends more time on screens should have a higher chance of reporting depression symptoms.

Indeed, when researchers have analyzed surveys that asked teens questions about depression symptoms and time they spent on social media, they have often found that more time on screens correlates with a higher chance of reporting depression symptoms (or other markers of low psychological well-being.) The correlation often starts after about two hours a day of social media. Some studies do not show a relationship but most do.

These correlation studies do not prove that social media, or lots of time on screens, cause depression. To establish causation, researchers would have to randomize thousands of teens into two distinct groups — one group that would be allowed to use social media and one group that would not — and then to follow them for many months. The researchers would record whether the "using" group was more likely to develop depression symptoms. But what about the group that is feeling sad about being left out of social media? You can immediately see all the complexities and impossibilities of trying to conduct such studies.

CAUSES FOR THE CORRELATION BETWEEN SOCIAL MEDIA AND THE INCREASED CHANCE OF DEPRESSION SYMPTOMS:

Could it be due to negative experiences on social media?
Negative feelings and experiences happen on social media at times. In *Screenagers NEXT CHAPTER*, we hear teens say:

> "If you post something, someone comments something mean or rude on it, it makes me upset."

> "Oh, I'm not as skinny as her. I can't afford to go on that trip."

> "You can see if they've opened your Snapchat or if they haven't opened it, and I know that they've opened someone else's, it just feels so bad."

"Guys asking for pictures. They don't want anything to do with me otherwise. It hurt me."

"I see people doing fun things, and then my anxiety just kind of takes over."

There are many other possible reasons of interest. Middle school counselors tell me how students often come to them feeling upset because they keep seeing on social media that they are being left out of things. Much less often, they report being cyberbullied (of course, being excluded can indeed be a form of bullying).

Could it be because time on social media can displace time needed for well-being?

Time on screens and social media can usurp activities that are known to foster well-being. One of the big ones is that many more teens report getting insufficient sleep than ever before, and some research has found that this lack in sleep can explain a lot of the rise in depression symptoms.

Other examples of crucial things being displaced include less in-person time, reduced chances for a person to challenge themself in ways that help them gain feelings of self-worth, fewer positive mentor opportunities due to less after-school jobs, and less physical activity.

Could it be that teens who are feeling depressed already (due to genetic wiring along with events at home, school, etc.) are more likely to spend longer amounts of time on social media?

Teens with depression generally experience a loss of energy and find it really hard to do things that they used to take pleasure in. Screen time is low energy. In addition, with all the YouTube videos online and other entertaining options, teens can easily distract themselves from hard feelings.

So what do I make of all of this?

I believe all the reasons above, both non-screen and screen-related, are contributing to the increases we are seeing in teens reporting depression symptoms. As a physician, educator, researcher, mom, and as someone who has been out in the world with the *Screenagers* films, I have heard all of these reasons from teens.

Time on screens and social media are important risk factors. So as parents, we want to work with youth to help them make smart choices on screens, ensure that they have plenty of time off screens, and help them obtain skills to work through hard emotions effectively.

IDEAS FOR CONVERSATION STARTERS:

1. What are your thoughts about the many reasons depression symptoms are going up?
2. What screen time activities can help improve your mood?
3. In what ways can social media-related issues lead to more depression symptoms?

. . .

Anxiety, What Every Family Should Know

I was on a plane reading the book "My Age of Anxiety" by journalist Scott Stossel when tears started pouring out.[3] I was reading this scene from Stossel's life:

> *"One night, when I was fourteen, I woke up at three in the morning with one of my bouts of screaming panic. Hearing my cry, my father lost control. He stormed into my room, trailed by my mother, and started hitting me repeatedly, telling me to shut up."*

Stossel's psychiatrist once said about Stossel's father: "He didn't have a lot of tolerance for anxious behavior. Your anxiety would make him blow up with anger."

My heart aches for Stossel and I want to do all I can to help people of all ages remember that as humans, we don't choose to have anxious feelings, we don't choose to have feelings of depression, and we don't choose to have the difficult emotions, thoughts and behaviors that are a part of our lives.

I also feel for Stossel's father. He needed help and was not getting it — in part because his mind hindered his ability to see outside of his mindset. But I believe that if he was asked: "Are you happy? Are you proud? Are you content with how you get angry and violent with your son when he is experiencing anxiety?" His answer would have been "no." Maybe not right away but with the right help, I think the chances are very good.

Knowing how to lovingly and effectively be with our kids and teens as they experience difficult emotions and display challenging behaviors is immensely complicated. But there are lots of solutions — knowing strategies and sharing them with our friends, colleagues and parent groups is crucial in stopping stories like Stossel's.

HELPING OUR KIDS UNDERSTAND THE DIFFERENCE BETWEEN ANXIOUS FEELINGS AND CLINICAL ANXIETY

Anxious feelings
We often use the word "stressed" in our society, which can mean many different things to the person saying it — such as feeling that something in their life is out of control, feeling overburdened, or irritated, or many other things.

In the same way, when a person says they are feeling "anxious," it also can mean many different things. This is where the skill of stopping to think about the core emotions behind these words is a great one to hone. Understanding leads to the most effective interventions.

It can be helpful when thinking about anxious feelings to know that often the anxious feelings are actually fear. Fear of an uncertain future, fear that you did the wrong thing (regret is a type of anxiousness), fear of what will happen if you ask someone if they want to video chat, and then the fear of how that person will perceive you.

Since 2002, Washington State has been surveying sixth, eighth, 10th and 12th graders every two years about health issues, including mental health. The survey is called the Healthy Youth Survey.[4]

Here are the 2018 results regarding anxious feelings for eighth-graders in King County, Washington. This is the county in which Seattle is located — where I live.

Eighth-graders reported the following:

- 58% reported that at least sometimes, they "felt nervous or anxious in the past two weeks."
- 46% reported that at least sometimes, they were "unable to stop or control worrying in the past two weeks."

12th-graders reported the following:

- 69% felt nervous at least sometimes
- 59% were unable to stop or control worrying at least sometimes

Unfortunately, they only started asking these questions in 2018, so I cannot provide any data from previous years.

There is an incredible shortage of data in this country that makes it hard to effectively compare data about anxious feelings of youth over the past years. Here is one of the few studies that exists. The American College Health Association surveys students from many colleges over many years.[5] They have been asking if students "ever felt overwhelming anxiety in the past 12 months." In 2011, roughly 50% reported yes, and in 2016 approximately 58% reported yes.

Clinical anxiety

The numbers here come from the main comprehensive study on youth mental health, called the National Comorbidity Study-Adolescent Supplement.[6] When any book or scientific paper references rates of adolescent clinical anxiety, this is the paper to which they are referring. (The numbers here were rounded to the nearest tenth.)

By age 18, 32% of youth will have met criteria for some type of clinical anxiety, ranging from very mild to very serious.

By age 18, 19% of youth will have met the criteria for severe clinical anxiety — meaning it has caused severe impairment and/or distress.

The study revealed the prevalence rates of specific types of clinical anxiety. It found that by age 18:

- 19% of youth will have met criteria for having had a specific anxiety phobia (These were ranked from mild to severe, and the majority met criteria for "mild")

- 9% will have met criteria for social anxiety (the majority met the criteria for "mild")
- 5% will have met criteria for PTSD
- 8% will have met criteria for separation anxiety
- 2% will have met criteria for generalized anxiety (the majority met criteria for "severe")
- 2% will have met criteria for a panic disorder (the majority met criteria for "severe")
- 2% will have met criteria for agoraphobia (the majority met criteria for "severe")

Unfortunately, the data collected for this study was done in the early 2000s and published in 2010, and there has not been a follow-up study. I know this is shocking. I have spoken with the researchers, and they told me that one of the reasons a follow-up study has not been conducted is due to a lack of funding from the government.

Diagnosing Clinical Anxiety

Some anxious feelings are to be expected and are even helpful. For example, anxiousness in anticipation of a test coming up can help a person to study. When anxious feelings are often out of proportion for the situation and the feeling does not fit the fact, this may indicate the possibility of clinical anxiety.

HERE ARE TWO SCENARIOS THAT WOULD
BE CAUSE FOR CONCERN:

- A teen worries all the time about tests. Long before they are even going to happen, the student is consumed by fear. The teen loses sleep and has lots of intrusive thoughts about failing.

- A teen experiences significant anxious feelings when they imagine talking to other people or raising their hand in class. This has resulted in them being extremely behind in school and not having any friends. While the student desperately wants to change, they can't move past their anxious feelings.

When I'm working with patients in my clinic, I assess anxiety in teens and adults. I ask everyone who comes into the clinic at some point in the visit, "Are you experiencing any anxiety or depression?" The incidence of anxiety and depression is significantly higher in a medical setting than in the general population, so it is important that I ask about these things. And so often, I see how relieved they are that I asked. When I see people in my clinic and have identified a concern about anxiety, the number one question I then ask is, "Are you avoiding things?" Their eyes light up and they often respond, "How did you guess that?"

The main questionnaire used in health settings to help diagnose clinical anxiety is called the GAD 7. I really recommend going over these questions with your kids.

It starts with these questions:

Over the last two weeks... How often have you been bothered
* by the following problems?*
Feeling nervous, anxious, or on-edge?
Not being able to stop or control worrying?

If the teen answers yes to either, they are then asked if they have these symptoms:

Worrying too much about different things?
Trouble relaxing?
So restless that it's hard to sit still?
Become easily annoyed or irritable?
Felt afraid as if something awful might happen?

The final part assesses how distressing and/or debilitating the symptoms are and asks:

If you checked off any problems...
How difficult have these made it for you to do your work, take care of things at
* home, or get along with other people? (Options are from "Not difficult at*
* all" to "Extremely difficult")*

When symptoms are ongoing, there can be real suffering and they can possibly lead to the avoidance of certain situations. So, while it is common for teens to feel a bit nervous about going up to talk with a peer, a more intense nervousness would indicate a more severe problem. This might present itself through an avoidance of most social interactions and a sense of isolation.

When anxious feelings lead to a lot of suffering via constant worrying and a lot of negative consequences, these are signs that a person's anxiety is a clinical problem that should be addressed with professional help, such as from counselors or therapists. In therapy, a person is provided with many skills and at times, medication.

STRATEGIES TO HANDLE ANXIOUS FEELINGS THAT YOU CAN TEACH YOUR CHILD

Because we know that anxious feelings are so common, it makes perfect sense that we take the time to talk about evidence-based ways our youth can handle such feelings in healthy ways, (vs. things like drinking alcohol and other unhealthy ways of coping).

A few of skills that I recommend discussing with youth in your life:

SKILLS TO HELP WITH ANXIETY

These skills can be helpful even for youth who do not have clinical anxiety but for whom anxious feelings are getting in the way of doing things they would like doing, such as having more friends, worrying less often and so on.

Skill One: The Three Xs

Child psychologist and author, Lynn Lyons, described a skill she calls the three Xs, which she teaches to many of her patients:

"The first X is you will expect worry to show up. You would say something to yourself like, 'Oh, there it is. So I'm about to take a test,' or, "Somebody else got into this school.' You have to recognize that. That's your worry.

"The second X is you are going to externalize it. You pull it out, you give it a name, and say something like 'Hi, Pete, nice to see you.'

"The third X is that you are going to experiment, so you do the opposite of what the worry is demanding. The worry demands attention. You decide not to get in a discussion with it and, instead, you are going to pivot. You pivot into getting started on your homework. Or if you're falling asleep, pivot into thinking about something that is sort of mundane enough that it doesn't really matter to you."

Skill Two: Does the feeling fit the facts?

When a person has anxious feelings, they can stop and ask themselves, "Does the feeling fit the facts?" If it does, then it is all about problem-solving. For example, a student has a test tomorrow and they are anxious because they cannot figure out what is going to be on it because they had problems with their Zoom. Well, this anxious feeling does fit the facts, so the goal would be for the student to problem solve. Maybe they decide to call some friends who are in the class to discuss the upcoming test.

Now, let's take another anxious feeling. Maybe a child is feeling worried about a friendship. They want to call that person to see what is going on, but they are too afraid. Does that feeling fit the facts? Is something awful going to happen if they call? Will they be shunned, mortified, rejected by that person, and all their friends? No! So if the feeling does not fit the facts, the goal would be to do the opposite and to call that person.

It is easier said than done to do the opposite of our fears. But that is the goal and when we can do it. It is great for building self-efficacy, even if one does not feel that way at the moment. I know this personally. This approach of, "Does the feeling fit the facts" is something one of my past therapists taught me, and it has been very useful over the years. My teens also use it at times.

Skill Three: Exposure therapy (also referred to as Exposure Response Prevention)

The goal of this type of therapy is to work toward no longer avoiding things that a person wishes they were not avoiding. It is about eventually doing the things the person is avoiding over and over, so they get used to the uncomfortable feelings and learn how to do actions despite anxious feelings. Meanwhile, the more the action is done over time, the more anxious feelings will lessen.

One of the most common reasons exposure therapy is done is to help someone get over social anxiety. In making *Screenagers NEXT CHAPTER*, I met Olivia, a 15-year-old who had clinical anxiety for several years and it included a strong fear of talking with unfamiliar people. So something like ordering food from a person at the cash register could be really hard for her.

Her parents were able to get her professional help and begin exposure therapy. One of the tasks was not only to have her practice ordering food, but also to make the task harder by purposely embarrassing herself. By practicing tolerating the feelings of embarrassment, the level of anxiety was lessened in all types of interactions with people. For example, she would practice by going to a mall food court and ask for sushi at a pizza place. She told me how hard it was at first, but how it got easier with time. It really helped her to do these exercises.

The important thing to know is that a teen does not need to have clinical anxiety to gain benefits from employing exposure techniques. Many youth and teens are so worried about talking in class. Let's review how we can help them lessen this with exposure activities.

1. Start by setting a time with a supportive teacher to practice outside of class to ask questions and to offer answers.

2. Make plans with a teacher before a class to have an answer ready, so that when the teacher asks the question, the student will raise their hand and propose the answer.

3. Do the same prep work together to think of a question the student could ask in class. Then, the student is reassured that the teacher thinks this is a "good" question that is valid and reasonable.

4. Create a goal of how many times in the class they will raise their hand to answer a question or ask a question. For instance, pick four times a week and have an accountability plan with a reward or treat when they accomplish the goal.

5. Finally, they will start to raise their hand and participate more in other classes where they have not been working with the teacher.

Skill Four: The "TIPP" skill (from Dialectical Behavioral Therapy)
"TIPP" stands for Temperature, Intense Exercise, Paced Breathing, and Paired Muscle Relaxation. The TIPP skill is all about helping a person overcome intense anxiety, depression or other strong emotions. It gives concrete action steps that, when completed, help to change a person's physiology, which helps in turn to change their personal emotional state quickly.

Here is the breakdown of the action steps:

T:
Temperature — the person applies a bag of ice to their face for a minute or two. Many teens also talk about how useful it is to put their faces into an ice bath of water for a few seconds. I have known many teens who find this action to be a physical shock to the system that often stops the flood of emotions, as their mind pivots to feeling cold. Tessa never had formal DBT counseling, but she learned some of the skills and she has used this temperature one in the past. It really helped her quickly lower intense uncomfortable feelings.

I:
Intense exercise — the person takes the energy of the emotions and does some quick jumping jacks or other quick exercises.

P:
Paced breathing — the person works to consciously slow their breathing. They might breathe in for five seconds and then breathe out for seven seconds. This activates the parasympathetic nervous system that results in calmer feelings.

P:
Paired muscle relaxation — the person breathes in and tenses a body part at the same time, such as the arms, while paying special attention to the feeling of the contractions. Then, when they breathe out, they release the contraction.

IDEAS FOR CONVERSATION STARTERS:

1. There is a need for more research on both anxious feelings and clinical anxiety of youth in this country. What type of research could you imagine doing?
2. If you were to study anxious feelings as they relate to screen time, what would be some interesting questions that you could see researching?
3. What strategies do you find helpful when you are feeling anxious?
4. What skills mentioned here could you ever consider using or telling a friend about?

. . .

Talking About Our Emotions Builds Their Resiliency Skills

I believe that talking skillfully with the youth in our life about our past and present emotions and the ways we navigate such feelings are some of the best resiliency teachings we can do as parents.

I have worked to become more skillful in talking about my anxious feelings and other challenging emotions with my kids over the years. I have learned how to share with them what is appropriate and to not communicate things that would be burdensome. One tool has been to run things by people whose insight I deeply trust before sharing things with my kids.

I had a very intense childhood, and I don't ever overshare or burden them with certain details of that time of my life. Burdening our kids with our past traumas or making them stand as our care providers is not good for them at all!

Naming the feelings we have and stating how we handle them is something kids and teens appreciate. I have spoken to many who say they wish their parents would talk more about their own emotional states.

I have interviewed many parents over the years and asked about whether they talk with their kids about their emotional challenges and ways they have addressed them. So often, parents have stopped, scratched their heads and said that they have never thought about it, but now that I had asked, they realized they had not.

I asked one father the following question, "Do you ever talk about your emotional experience of what your day is like?"

He responded: "I don't think so. You mean like just kind of saying how I'm feeling about something other than being angry with them for not doing something? I can't think of a lot of examples of checking in emotionally and letting them know what's going on."

It's a good idea to talk more openly about your present and past feelings and the things you have done or you are doing to manage the emotions.

In doing so, here are a few of the positive things you will be modeling:

- It is natural to be feeling all sorts of feelings — anxiety, worry, anger, sadness, and also happiness at times — and to not feel guilty about that.

- Trying to understand what we are feeling can be challenging. For example, when we say "stressed", what do we mean? Overwhelmed? Afraid? Getting to the core of an emotion can help address it more effectively.

- No one can fully control the thoughts and feelings that come into their head. So, that might mean that your anxious feelings don't fit the facts.

- We have choices of how we want to handle challenging emotions. You model this when you talk about the things you have tried to help handle your own emotions. For example, maybe you say: "I am feeling anxious and it just makes me want to avoid the feelings and watch movies, but actually that is making me feel worse. I realize I need help, so I am going to start talking with someone who can help me."

I find what psychologist and author, Laura Kastner, Ph.D., once told me about parents who want their teens to open up to them about what is going on emotionally, but who don't model this openness themselves to be very interesting. She said:

"Have these teenagers seen their fathers or even their mothers talk about mistakes, embarrassment, shame, disappointment, regret? It's an emotional language that they need to learn from our modeling it at the dinner table and other places. But it's also a sense of vulnerability that they need to sort of master."

I loved meeting and filming one family where the dad, mom and son talked about how the father changed from telling his sons to "man up" to valuing discussions about emotions.

The dad said:
"I come from India, and over there, you know, you don't show the sign of weakness. Crying is the sign of weakness. And I didn't want them to be weak. And I'd say, 'Why are you crying? So what's wrong with you?' And they will try to explain, and I say, 'Come on, be a man, man-up.'"

Then his son said:
"When I'm stressed out, it's helpful to just talk about it with someone. Cause it's like you don't wanna hold in all that emotion because it's just not healthy. I kind of feel like I try and make it so that he doesn't feel uncomfortable talking to me."

The dad:
"And he'll say, 'So you can talk to me, you know that, right.' And I say, 'Yeah, I know.'"

The son:
"I think mom is good at talking with people. I do think that she does tell me when she's going through something emotional."

The dad:
"Now I see how they approach it with their mother, and I see the positive impact it's having on the kids. If I had not recognized that or changed that, they would have been different kids today."

TAKE-HOME POINTS FOR SHARING OUR FEELINGS

Let me reiterate that this is not about overwhelming our kids with our hard emotions, but gently and skillfully naming what emotions we are experiencing at this moment in time.

Youth deserve to feel that they matter. When they were little, they might have brought us a warm cloth for our head and now, maybe they lean in to hug us. Letting them feel needed is a real gift. When we let our kids pamper us a bit, they often light up.

I have such strong memories of when I was sad about something and how my kids fully jumped in to help me feel better.

It is truly empowering when we get to help others. The beauty is that it reduces the anxious feelings of the person who receives the help and also reduces the stress of the person giving the help. Standing at the sidelines and seeing someone in emotional pain and not being able to do anything is very stressful.

IDEAS FOR CONVERSATION STARTERS:

1. Have you felt any new feelings of anxiety this week?
2. Do you notice anyone else in the family feeling anxious? How does that make you feel?
3. Is there anything that you do to bring down your own feelings of anxiety?
4. Are there any ways that you have helped others this week by bringing down their levels of anxiety?

A Dozen Ideas for Finding Support

I wholeheartedly believe that the ability to ask for help is one of the best resiliency skills we provide our children and teens. For some youth, asking a math teacher for help with a problem set can be challenging enough, let alone asking for help when they are going through an emotionally challenging time. The vulnerability lies in letting someone know what is really going on inside, as well as asking for help.

Meanwhile, for us parents, the digital age can add new complexities because when our teens aren't doing well emotionally, not knowing what is happening on their screens can feel really unsettling. Is there an intense issue happening with peers? Are they looking up information about what they are feeling that is making them feel worse? The reality of screen time makes having a calm conversation about support that much more important.

In my medical practice, teens come to me experiencing hard emotions such as depression, and tell me how they have not told anyone about what they are experiencing. This always feels like a punch in my stomach. To be suffering is hard enough — but to be suffering completely alone is just so awful. I gently respond, "I am so glad you came here today and that you told me." As I say those words, I can literally see the relief on their face.

I often think of the image of a teen in their room alone, curtains down, with thoughts of worthlessness — the teen and their parents feeling so isolated and confused about what to do. I have a dream that someday we will look back and say: "Do you remember when it was so common for teens in emotional pain to be alone in their rooms day after day? And that we accepted that? Shocking, isn't it?" Instead, teens would have wonderful support teams — friends and the family giving them care in all sorts of creative and effective ways.

Seeking support can be incredibly daunting. For example, a teen might not like their assigned school counselor, and the school won't let them change. Or it is hard to find a therapist with available appointments, even before knowing if they will be a good fit. Meanwhile, the cost of seeing such a therapist can be prohibitive.

As a nation and as a world, it is imperative that we continue to think creatively to expand ways people can be of help and how people can receive help. A few years ago, I lived with my family in India where I spent a year as a Fulbright Scholar making films about programs in which local residents were being educated on how to provide basic mental health support to people in need in their communities. These programs have been extremely effective. As parents talk more openly and regularly with our kids about mental wellness skills and resources, we are actively enriching our communities — just like I witnessed throughout India.

HERE ARE SOME IDEAS FOR SUPPORT RESOURCES

As you talk with youth about this topic, it will be great to hear from them about what support resources they know of and who they talk to.

School counselors

At times, my teens were fortunate to have a school counselor they liked going to when they were facing challenging times. I highly recommend that we encourage our kids to meet with their school counselor, even when all is going well, so as to establish a connection. That way, if they end up in a hard place, they are more likely to go to them for help.

School Nurse, Health Centers, Social Workers

Sometimes, the school nurse is skilled at supporting students when they are experiencing emotional pain — not just physical pain or a cold, or whatever it is that we think of when we think of the nurse. The nurse may have ideas for local resources as well. Many schools have access to social workers who offer helpful ideas and can be a wealth of support.

Finding a person to help with screen time issues, such as compulsive video gaming

Looking for a behavioral counselor can be helpful. Behavioral counselors help clients develop new, more helpful habits while breaking other ones. Restart, an internet-gaming addiction treatment center in Washington state, has some names of people as a place to begin. The good news is that doing sessions over Skype is possible with many of these types of providers.

Often when there has been a lot of tension and fighting in the home over screen time, family sessions with a school counselor or therapist can be immensely helpful. Their job is to ensure that everyone feels heard and to help set up small goals for everyone to achieve.

Finding a counselor or therapist outside of school

Psychology Today has an online tool that allows you to look up providers in any city. Sometimes looking at directories of professional groups, such as American Depression and Anxiety or Association for behavioral and cognitive therapies, can help.

Getting ideas from friends is incredibly helpful, especially if you have friends who are in the field or who have gone to people for support. Some people advise against going to the same therapist as a friend, but given how hard it is to find someone to see, I worry less about this issue. If it is a question of your teen going to someone who also sees his or her peers, then talking with your teen about this is important. The key is for the teen to understand that legally and ethically, the therapist will not share information with others, i.e., their peers.

It is perfectly reasonable to ask a therapist for a short call to assess if they seem like a good fit. It is hard to tell over the phone and in a short time, but at least you have a sense right away if it is a definite no.

It can be hard to know if the therapist is "a good fit." How do you know if the meetings are making much of a difference? If after a few sessions, the client has not gotten specific insights that have helped or have a few particular things to be working on, then talk with the provider and assess if it makes sense to return. Or speak with others, such as a good friend, to help you decide.

Churches, synagogues, and other places of worship

There are some incredibly gifted and supportive people in these communities. In many houses of worship, there are specific people trained to work with youth. The youth pastors, youth rabbis, or youth group leaders are all great places to start.

Mental health organizations

Here are a few examples — and of course, there are many other great organizations.

NAMI[7]

NAMI is a wonderful organization that I have partnered with to do advocacy work with some of my past films. Check out what they do. NAMI has local branches nationwide. They offer all sorts of support groups, and in fact, I used to attend one in Seattle when I was working on a film about my father who had Schizophrenia. I went because I needed support to help me process my complicated relationship with him.

NAMI has a great program called Family to Family. They also go into high schools to speak and much more. NAMI has a helpline at 800-950-6264.

Recently, I was thrilled to learn that a couple of the NAMI affiliates, such as one in New York, have started something called Parent Match.[8] The program trains parents who have had experience with a child or teen having mental health challenges to be able to provide free, one-on-one emotional support to other parents currently going through a similar situation.

The Jed Foundation[9]

They originally were focused on suicide prevention amoung collage-age students, but they have since branched out. For example, they now take on mental health more broadly and have many resources for younger teens and their families. I highly recommend watching a video the Jed Foundation produced called "Seize The Awkward" with your child.[10] Many teens I have spoken with think it is very well done.

Child Mind Institute[11]

For online information about children and teens, the Child Mind Institute has some unique resources. They did a month-long campaign called My Younger Self, where they conducted short interviews with actors, famous athletes and others who faced challenging emotions growing up. Watching a few of these shorts with your teen could help with a discussion about these topics.

Youth Mental Health First Aid[12]

These are free day-long courses designed to help parents learn how to understand the mental health issues of youth and learn things they can do to help. On the website, you can find if there are classes near you.

Mental Health America[13]

This organization has affiliates across the country, has many programs, and also works to increase mental health access locally and nationally. Their "Finding Help" page is helpful for the nuts and bolts of finding mental health support.

Crisis Text (CT)[14]

This organization is a resource that many youth and adults report using and finding helpful. People who volunteer for CT receive 30 hours of training before they start and they volunteer several hours a month. My good friend is a volunteer and we spent an afternoon together where she showed me how their training works and examples of the work she does with people. It was powerful. A person can text about anything they are struggling with, and the volunteers are there to provide supportive interactions. Even though it is called Crisis Text, the texter does not have to be in an imminent crisis; they get all sorts of people seeking support for things like eating issues, problems with peers and just people dealing with hard emotions.

IDEAS FOR CONVERSATION STARTERS:

1. If you are having an emotional time, is there a website or organization you go to? Have you ever heard of any of the ones listed above?
2. Who might you reach out to if you are having a difficult time? A school counselor? A school nurse? Your friends, a teacher, etc.?

Chapter Four:

Sleep

As adults, we all have sleep stories. Some of us are "great sleepers," some of us have naturally always stayed up late, some of us have battled with sleep issues — including myself. Since college, I have experienced long stretches of insomnia.

Because I dealt with insomnia, in medical school, I started focusing on ways to improve people's sleep. Now in my work, I talk with people about things they can do to improve their sleep.

As a parent, I did all I could to help my kids get a healthy amount of sleep when they were young and did my best to create structure and policies to help them as they became teens.

The data is irrefutable. When youth get adequate sleep, it helps prevent problems with mood, obesity, risk-taking behaviors, academics, substance abuse and mental health.

The worrisome thing is that more and more young people are failing to get enough sleep each night. We know this from the research as well as from teachers who report that teens are falling asleep in class at an increasing rate. Tweens and teens themselves tell me all the time that they see others sleeping in class and how they so often struggle to stay awake too. They tell me how much they hate the feeling of wanting to stay awake but being knocked out by intense drowsiness.

During my medicine residency, I had a few run-ins with my own sleep starvation that were really scary. While working in the ICU, every third day we had to spend the whole night in the hospital — which could mean working 30 hours straight without sleep. I recall one time in the ICU at 5 a.m., when a patient rolled in who was rapidly losing blood internally from his GI tract. I was the one giving the orders to initiate his stabilization. Even with my body pumping adrenaline, I was so tired that I felt drugged and nothing could snap me to full attention. I was splashing my face with ice water and hitting myself to try to stay awake — it was torture not to be able to get my mind fully working. Quickly, I realized I needed help and got the team to find backup. Thank goodness, another physician was able to get there quickly.

Thankfully, a few years after my training, new laws were enacted to limit the number of hours a resident could work each shift in the hospital, in part to prevent such situations.

There are many new challenges that keep youth from getting a healthy amount and quality of sleep — technology is playing a major part in this trend. Increased screen time is associated with less sleep for today's youth. It is now widely known that light at night suppresses the secretion of the sleep-inducing hormone melatonin from the brain's pineal gland. Blue light has a particularly strong impact. Thus, the American Academy of Pediatrics recommends that kids and teens be off screens an hour before going to bed. For younger kids, this is easier to enforce. For teens, it is a very hard recommendation to follow since, like many of us adults, they want to be able to check in with friends or homework before bed. The truth is, the effect on sleep from delayed melatonin release is tiny compared to the main reason screens can interfere with sleep, which is their constant pull for attention. Pings throughout the night, pinging others, binge-watching, scrolling and shopping are the activities that keep us awake far more than the light. Therefore, small changes, like getting a new screen color, are not the answer.

I believe that improving sleep for our youth is so important that I have dedicated an entire chapter to it here. Let's get started.

· · ·

Sleep Deprivation — A Major Public Health Issue

The American Medical Association, the Center for Disease Control, and the American Academy of Pediatrics all report that chronic sleep loss among American adolescents is a major epidemic and a public health crisis.

I was shocked when I read the latest research data we have concerning teens and sleep deprivation.[1] In 2015, when ninth through 12th-graders were asked if they got at least seven hours of sleep each night, 41% of them said they did not. That is a major sleep shortage. Compare this to the percentage found in 1991, when many of us parents were in high school. Only 26% reported less than seven hours of sleep most nights.

It turns out that during the 1990s, the rate of sleep deprivation increased until the 2000s, where it stayed stable at about 35% for nearly 12 years. In 2012, things started to worsen abruptly, such that in 2015, 22% more teens reported not getting seven hours of sleep compared to 2012.

While 41% of high schoolers report getting less than seven hours most nights, the latest sleep guidelines from the American Academy of Sleep Medicine (AASM) are as follows:[2]

- Children 6 to 12 years of age should sleep nine to 12 hours per 24 hour period regularly to promote optimal health.
- Teenagers 13 to 18 years of age should sleep eight to 10 hours per 24 hour period on a regular basis to promote optimal health.

WHY SLEEP MATTERS

Take every important aspect of life, and sleep loss can negatively impact it. With teens, insufficient sleep can lead to an increased risk of obesity and Type 2 diabetes, as well as mental health issues — including an increased chance of reporting depression and suicidal thoughts. It can also lead to worse academic performance and a higher chance of accidents.

Multiple health risks have also been linked to teens' sleep loss, including more drug use and problems with violence and delinquency.

For example, data has revealed that adolescents who get the least amount of sleep on school nights are most likely to report alcohol use and more likely to have alcohol-related problems such as binge drinking, drunk driving and doing regrettable things while intoxicated.

One key area experts are concerned with is the ongoing development of the brains of youth.[3] Brains of young people go through structural maturation up until age 24 for females and 26 for males (on average).

Structural maturation includes increased myelination of neurons, which is a wrapping around each neuronal axon that makes signals travel faster and prunes away certain neurons. They are also responsible for more developed connections between different regions of the brain.

Before this realization, researchers thought the brain was structurally crafted by elementary age and that changes occurred only due to learning from the environment and experiences. The brain starts to whittle away at certain neuronal connections while strengthening others, starting in the teen years. This is impacted by what happens in the child's life and what they do day-to-day. The environment and experiences in a child's life help the brain become more specialized.

It's concerning to me to learn that when researchers look at the brains of youth who are chronically sleep-deprived or who have large variations in the amount of sleep they get each night, they are more likely to show brain morphology that differs from their peers that get more total and regular sleep.

For example, researcher Adriana Gálvan and her team conducted brain imaging studies of adolescents and then had the teens keep sleep diaries.[4] They found that those teens who reported large variations in the amount of sleep they got per night were more likely to have neuronal organization that implies less brain maturity than those teens who had more consistent sleep durations.

We know there are many reasons sleep is important, so why do so many teens not get enough sleep? There are three main reasons cited to explain this precipitous drop in adequate sleep for today's teens. Let's explore these.

1. Excessively early school start times

Prior to the 1970s, elementary, middle and high schools all started about the same time, around 8:30 or 9 a.m.[5] Then in the '70s, districts began to make start times earlier for a host of reasons, especially school buses. School busing increased around this time as baby boomers meant more students in schools, along with more people living in spread out suburbs and a fear of allowing kids to walk to school. Schools were hit with financial issues, like the energy crisis of 1973. To cut back on spending, they cut the number of school busses and had the buses pick up kids at different times. Not wanting the youngest kids to be out in the dark of the morning, the teens were picked up earliest and the youngest kids were picked up later.

And yet, the data show us that of any group, high schoolers should have the latest start times of all students. Researchers have discovered that there is a biological shift in the bodies of teenagers that results in them not starting to feel tired until after 10 p.m., on average. What is so fascinating is that this shift in naturally feeling tired later in the night is seen in most mammals as they mature.

Researchers have found that levels of the hormone melatonin, which causes feelings of tiredness, start to rise later in the evening for teens than they do for children or adults. This shift means that teens want to go to bed later and wake up later.

When my son was attending a New York State public school, he had to get up at 5:45 a.m. each day so he could get to the bus on time and travel 30 minutes to get to the school by 7:25 a.m., the official start time.

As his mom, it pained me to see him scurrying around in a daze in the morning. He told me how he hated the painful feeling of sleep deprivation — that it made him feel angry about life and that he didn't want to have those angry feelings at school. Chase would do all he could at night to get to bed earlier, but for many reasons, he would always get to sleep later than he wanted, dreading his alarm clock in the mornings.

We are talking about biologically-driven circadian sleep patterns that are hard-wired into teen's brains. Early school start times punish them for their biology, and it's inhumane.

2. Academic workloads and out of school activities push out sleep

The Monitoring the Future survey has surveyed eighth, 10th and 12th graders every two years since the early 1990s on a host of topics, including daily homework.[1] Over the years, the average daily time spent on homework for 10th graders has varied. But important for our discussion is that in 2009, it began rising yearly from 56 minutes to 65 minutes in 2014. In 2006, 12th graders reported an average of about 52 minutes of homework, and this went up and down over the following years, landing at 56 minutes in 2014.

While these numbers do not seem like such a big rise, (i.e., less than 10 minutes) we have to remember to take into account that a percentage of teens take far more demanding class loads now than many did in the past. Some teens take three or four AP classes a semester now, compared to one or two in the past. In addition to the added stress and workload of additional AP classes, there is also the relatively recent trend of studying for tests such as the ACT or SAT during the school year. The bottom line is the demands of school work and test prep have increased and can contribute to shortages in sleep.

Apart from the demands of homework, some teens spend additional time before and/or after school participating in activities like sports, clubs, community service and jobs. Overall, the data shows that having such opportunities is a good thing for teens' well-being and personal growth, but some teens are stretched too thin by all these demands — leading to sleep deprivation.

3. Frequent screen time use

As would be expected, investigators have found an association between teens who have more screen time and those who report less sleep. The endless pull of entertainment, games, social media, Tik Tok and YouTube videos can result in hours and hours of consumption.

Meanwhile, many teens are allowed screens in their bedrooms all night, and this can make unplugging from screens less likely. There are two problems with this. First, having all the temptations of the screen right beside them while they lay in bed means they can keep scrolling or playing a game, which is harder to resist as they become more tired. The data is clear about how fatigue decreases one's will power. A vicious loop ensues.

Second, even when the teen decides to go to sleep, data shows that having a cellphone in the room often leads to interrupted sleep. Research shows that many teens wake up in the night to check their screens if they receive a notification or if they can't fall back asleep.

While I have just been reporting on high schoolers here, I want to say that it turns out that the majority of tweens are also not getting the recommended amount of sleep.

I suggest sharing the above research with your kids and engaging them with important questions on this topic. In the next section, I propose ways to delve further into solutions, but here are some conversation starters regarding the ideas above.

IDEAS FOR CONVERSATION STARTERS:

1. Are you surprised that so many young people report being sleep deprived?
2. What do you think are the biggest downsides you experience when you are sleep deprived?
3. What of the three explanations regarding sleep loss do you think caused you to get less sleep than you would like?
4. A high schooler explained how her social studies teacher gave out so much homework that she and many of her peers failed to complete it all. The teacher was adamant that the problem was the students' cellphone use. Have you experienced anything like this? What can be done to improve such a situation?

• • •

Have Kids Think Like Public Health Officials and Devise Solutions

So, what are possible solutions to this public health crisis regarding chronic sleep deprivation? Let's ask our kids — let's get them to think like public health officials. Why do I recommend this exercise? For two reasons: First, sleep is a great topic to get their problem-solving skills flowing, since most kids have experienced sleep deprivation. Second, I'm often frustrated with the fact that most students in our country have very few opportunities to learn about how policies are made at the local level, and even less about how they can make change locally. Think about how much of our news is a bombardment of coverage on federal-level actions and policies, rather than on school counselors, actions by the city council or the local mayor. Kids learn very little about public health and how policies to keep the population safe and healthy are made and enforced at different levels.

Also, we want them to think about advocacy and activism, and know they can be change-makers. We need to communicate that we see in them the potential to change things in society that don't serve their well-being. It's important for them to know that they can work to advocate for change. They won't always be successful, but knowing that they can work to change things that are important to them is key. Even if their advocacy includes pushing back on our tech rules — yep, we still want them to question, self-advocate and be able to practice acceptance when things can't go their way.

So, let's get our youth to come up with ideas and policy-type solutions around the three key reasons youth get less sleep.

1. Addressing early school start times

Despite the science, the push to change middle and high schools to start at later times has been slow in coming. So how does one actually change this? Some have argued that if the school starts later, teens will just stay up later. Fortunately, we have data that proves that argument wrong.

In 2018 in Seattle, new policies were adopted in high schools throughout the city — including the high school my daughter attends — to change the start of the school day to 8:45 a.m. Researchers at the University of Washington collected data on the students before and after the policy change. They found that overall, students got 30 more full minutes of sleep after the change was adopted.

In 2019, California was the first state in the country to pass legislation requiring all middle schools to start no earlier than 8 a.m. and all high schools no earlier than 8:30. This state-wide approach is what we need across the country, and the sooner, the better.

Your child as a public health official:
- Ask your child what ideas they have to persuade school districts to change their start to the recommended time of 8:30 a.m. at the earliest.

2. Finding solutions to heavy academic workload and out-of-school activities that push out sleep

I learned from the college counselor of an elite private high school that she is working with other counselors in other districts to lobby colleges to do away with "early decisions" — the practice whereby kids apply for colleges earlier than usual so they can hear back earlier. She said that this trend forces teens to start stressing about college applications much earlier and more intensely than counselors saw in the past. Should there be a policy around this?

Other schools are working to strongly recommend that teens not take too many AP classes. The schools see that the pressure students feel to take so many AP classes can cause more harm than good by giving them unnecessary stress and burdening them with an untenable workload.

Coaches often expect very long and late practices, and sometimes games go until well into the night. Teens can have games that are far away and do not end until 8 or 9 p.m. Often, team members are told that if they miss just a couple of practices, they can be dismissed from the team.

Your child as a public health official:

- Ask your child what policies they would want in order to help them not be up late with homework.
- What do they think about in-school policies that try to have the teachers coordinate to prevent different project deadlines and tests from happening at the same time?

3. Addressing how screen time use habits can affect sleep

I wish there were major public health campaigns created with teens' help that raised awareness about technology's impact on sleep. Reversing the sleep crisis means improved physical and mental health — it's a fact. So, why don't I see that happening?

What if there was a national public health campaign with the slogan: "Away For The Night"? I can imagine showing a kid playing a video game with the clock displaying 1 a.m., and then flashing to their alarm going off at 7 a.m. Or a teen on the phone at midnight and then again at 3 a.m., and then a shot of the alarm going off at 6:50, followed by shots of the sleepy faces of teens who were up all night on their screens.

The next scene could show iPads, phones and other electronics left outside of the bedroom. A clock reads 11 p.m. and the teens are asleep. And then, as the morning alarm goes off, we see the faces of more rested teens.

What if there were campaigns geared toward parents with the message:

"Away for the Night: Let's work together to help youth get the sleep they deserve. Many parents already ensure that screens are out of the bedroom at night — visit our website to learn how they do it."

A lot of teens have the best intentions and want their phones in their rooms for well-meaning reasons, such as to support a friend who is going through a hard time. But what if it became the clear norm that phones and all other tech were turned off in the night? When I propose this to teens, many like the idea — they know they would get better sleep and not feel guilty about not being available to their friends throughout the night.

One idea to suggest to a tween — let's call her Sarah — who is worried about her friend Paula, is to give Paula her parent's phone number (with permission of course), and make it clear that if Paula ever really needs to reach Sarah, she can call that number.

Your child as a public health official:
- Ask your child what ideas they have for ending sleep deprivation among today's youth.
- If they were tasked with reducing the percentage of young people who had devices in their bedroom at night, how might they go about it?

IDEAS FOR CONVERSATION STARTERS:

1. If you were the head of the government's public health agency — the Center for Disease Control (CDC) — would you make the sleep deprivation of today's youth a major focus of the organization?
2. Which of the three explanations regarding sleep loss do you think caused you to get less sleep than you would like?
3. What other explanations can you think of regarding the causes of sleep deprivation?
4. If you were going to take on one of the issues discussed, which one would you be most interested in taking on?

. . .

Why Screens and Smartphones in the Bedroom is a Risky Act

I interviewed a sweet 12-year-old girl who told me what she likes doing on her phone at bedtime. She said, " At night, I'm like, on Instagram or like, texting people."

The American Academy of Pediatrics (AAP) recommends that children not have any screens in their bedrooms, including phones, computers or TVs. They are actually saying not just at bedtime, but not at all. But for now, let's focus on bedtime.

I completely agree with the AAP's recommendation to keep devices out of the bedroom at night. All the time, I hear from other parents who want this as well but either their kids or teens insist on having devices in their rooms, or the parent is not able to enforce the rule.

Having devices out of the bedroom at night is hard, but not impossible. Let's start by sharing two key studies with the youth in our life about the realities of screens in bedrooms at bedtime.

FIRST STUDY ON BEDTIME ACCESS TO MEDIA DEVICES BEING ASSOCIATED WITH POOR QUALITY AND QUANTITY OF SLEEP

In a landmark 2016 paper that analyzed dozens of studies on the association between portable screen-based media and sleep outcomes for youth ages 6 to 19, the authors found that,

"Bedtime access to and use of a media device were significantly associated with the following: inadequate sleep quantity, poor sleep quality, and excessive daytime sleepiness."[6]

Even children who had access to but did not use media devices at night were more likely to have worse sleep. The mere presence of media devices in youth's bedrooms negatively impacts their sleep.

But how can this be if the kids report not using the devices they have access to? It was data based on self reports, so maybe they were using them at times, but reported that they weren't. Another possibility is what I have seen with my daughter, particularly when she was in the eighth and ninth grades. She was so eager to check her phone in the morning that she would come to my room — where I kept her phone at night — much earlier than her wake up time, just because she was eager to check the phone. She gave up sleep to do so. How much greater is the pull if the phone is right next to your pillow?

The authors referred to this effect as "psychophysiological arousal." Another kid told me that just seeing the device lured her awake. She described it almost like sleep-walking — like she was on autopilot reaching for the device.

SECOND STUDY ON YOUTH CHECKING DEVICES THROUGHOUT THE NIGHT

In 2019, Common Sense Media oversaw a nationally representative sample of 12 to 18-year-olds regarding phone use during night time.[1] They found that of the teens who reported having a phone in their bedrooms during the nights, 36% self-reported waking up at least one time per night to check their phone. This is a huge percentage of teens! On top of that, we can assume many of them checked their phones more than once during the night.

Many younger kids do follow rules and don't use devices in their bedrooms. Setting up a healthy norm that technology will stay out of their bedrooms is key as their social situations change. I remember when my son's best friend, Ben, had a flip phone when they were all the rage. He was in ninth grade, and his mom talked to me about how they had learned he was up late into the night texting. How had she found out? She got a huge bill. Why was he texting through the night now and not before? He had begun seeing a new girlfriend a few weeks back.

When tweens and teens learn the stats about phones in bedrooms, many tell me they had no idea. They start to think differently once they learn this. A few have even told me that having learned this data, they have, on their own, decided to stop having devices in their bedroom when they go to sleep.

Many teens tell me that they feel torn because they want their phone in case a friend needs to reach them, but at the same time, they know they would sleep better without it in their room. Ideally, it would be the agreed-upon norm that no phones were allowed in bedrooms, so that tweens would not have to feel the guilt and responsibility to be reachable all through the night. What if teens could provide parents' phone numbers in case a friend had to reach them? OK, maybe far fetched, but in some homes, this has actually worked.

PARENTING WITH INTEGRITY

Parents come to me all the time saying things like: "My 15-year-old has her phone in her room at bedtime, but it has been that way for one year. I can't go back now."

My response is that as a parent, my chief goal is to parent with integrity. This means parenting in line with what I believe, which is first and foremost to impart unconditional love to my kids. Also, to use science whenever possible to help guide my parenting decisions — including family rules, such as screens out of the bedroom.

To learn about really important science and then not work to put it in place can make many parents feel pretty lousy. They are not parenting with integrity in the way they would want to. I counsel parents to say to their kids:

> *"I want to parent with integrity when I learn. For example, I feel it is key that I tell you about research that I think will help you in your development. I realize I need to advocate for a change. When we see change is needed, I want you to also change paths. For example, I am advocating for screens to be kept out of the bedroom to ensure that you get better sleep. We can talk about the specifics, i.e., what time and such."*

But I must say, many parents who have made this pivot have told me that it was hard for the first week or so. But after that, their teen seemed a bit relieved.

As I kept interviewing the sweet 12-year-old girl, she told me:

"I used to be able to have my phone on my nightstand in my room. Maybe like a month or two ago, my mom wanted to become more conscientious, so now I have to put my phone in the hallway at 10 o'clock. I think it does help me get more sleep."

IDEAS FOR CONVERSATION STARTERS:

1. What do you think about the studies cited here?
2. In what ways could having a mobile device in the bedroom all night be useful?
3. What are the possible downsides?
4. What policies would you have for kids younger than yourself?

. . . .

Creating Healthy Sleep Habits in Younger Kids

Remember what it was like trying to get your toddlers to shut off their little brains for the day and go to bed? It was that magical time of life where they still adored you and were curious about everything around them. They were excited and didn't want the day to end.

Just one more story? Can you check under my bed again for monsters? Can you sing to me until I fall asleep, please please please, Mommy?

But you instinctively knew how important it was for them to get a good night's sleep.

It could be a real struggle at times, getting them to develop consistent, healthy sleep patterns. It was hard then, and now with the existence of screen-based interactive goodies, it can be that much harder.

I remember one mom telling me that when her 1 1/2-year-old wakes up in the crib, his first words are "iPad, iPad."

Getting kids to relinquish a tech device, particularly interactive ones, can be met with much dismay starting from a very young age. Dr. Dimitri Christakis, a researcher at Seattle Children's Hospital told "60 Minutes" that interactive apps are such a draw for toddlers because at that age, making something happen is so gratifying.[8] His lab conducted a small study in which toddlers were given three toys at different times: a plastic guitar, an iPad that showed a guitar playing notes, and an iPad with an interactive app that produced lights and sounds when they touched it. After an allotted amount of time, the research assistants asked the toddlers to give back whatever toy they were playing with. They found that the toddlers gave back the little guitar and the iPad that was playing music with about the same willingness. Yet, Christakis reported that, "With the more interactive iPad app, the percentage of kids willing to hand it back to the researcher dropped from 60% to 45%".

So often in the evening, parents are tired, kids are wired and getting them off devices and to bed can be a really hard job. I used to call this "Bedtime Madness". In part, I was referring to how frustrated I would be trying to get my kids to sleep, and this was even before they had the enticement of the types of devices and engaging content that exists nowadays.

Establishing healthy sleep hygiene in elementary school-age kids is key. You can get extra motivation from knowing that recent government data revealed that a whopping six out of 10 middle school aged kids do not meet science-based recommendations for at least nine hours of sleep.

SOME STRATEGIES TO PUT AN END TO THE "BEDTIME MADNESS"

Read to younger kids with paper books
If you are reading to young kids, I recommend reading paper books for a few key reasons.

First, a study published in the official journal of the American Academy of Pediatrics, "Differences in Parent-Toddler Interactions With Electronic Versus Print Books," states that a good old-fashioned paper book is better than an e-reader because parents and toddlers didn't collaborate as much while reading electronic books.[9]

Second, when a child gets to the stage where they are reading alone in their room, the goal is to let them focus on their paper book without the pull of games, internet and beyond.

Also, I know from my kids that e-readers have all sorts of excerpts from sample books and if they get to a slow point in their current book, it is really tempting to begin reading samples of others.

If an e-reader is used, choose the type that does not allow access to the internet. It will still have sample books that may tempt your kids, but it won't have the pull of the internet.

Finally, modeling going to bed with a book in hand is a great way to increase the chance that your kids will do the same when they are older.

Consider making bedrooms tech-free both day and night

When bedrooms are fully tech-free zones, it can make transitioning into sleep more easy. Getting them to unplug at night is that much easier because they are conditioned to think of their bedroom as a place to unwind and sleep. Even if a device makes it into their room during the day, there are fewer struggles when the device is removed at bedtime. For our kids, we kept all screens (computers, iPods, phones, etc.) out of the bedroom both day and night.

Just as I would not keep a bag of Oreos by their beds at night, I would not want to leave a device with its immersive games, YouTube videos, etc. — all the "sugar" of today — by their beds either. Even if now they go right to sleep and resist the "Oreos," at some point, they most likely will not.

Talk about the bedroom as the place of "you time"

I found it helpful to really promote the idea of them getting their own time when they go into their screen-free room. They get to write down ideas, reflect on the day, write a story in their head. So much of any day is responding to requests from others like teachers, parents and friends. So much is responding to things at the moment — grab this, find that — that it's a big deal when they get time to be alone with their thoughts! What a gift. Their creative thoughts, their deep thinking can all get buried by the hustles of the day, and who wants that to happen?

Sherry Turkle, the author of "Alone Together," was the first to point out to me that with screens ever-present, youth might need time to learn to "self soothe." Winding down before bed is a great time for self-reflection and for thinking about life's questions, like "How many stars are there," or "How I could have handled a conflict differently?"

Tessa has loved to journal in the evenings before bed and to read paper books. Chase also enjoys writing down his thoughts and reading books before falling asleep.

Avoid tech dependency

There is no doubt that tech can do cool things like read to a child at night via a "book on tape" or play soothing music — but this comes at the risk of dependency.

I am cautious of anything that can create dependency when it comes to sleep. Yes, there is the idea of a teddy bear that they may want for sleep early in life. But as they get older, the goal is not needing anything to aid in sleep.

In medicine, we see so many people who become dependent on pills to sleep. This is a major health issue. These medicines have risks and often as the body becomes accustomed to them, it requires higher and higher doses to fall asleep.

My jaw dropped the first time I saw a Procter & Gamble ad marketing melatonin gummy bears to help toddlers "sleep naturally." No, they have it all wrong. Natural sleep does not require any pills of any kind. When we train toddlers that they need a pill (or gummy bear), then as they get older and face life stressors, the urge to find a quick fix with a pill will be that much stronger.

It might be that a screen-related tool is what you do need to help your child fall asleep. If that is the case, consider having the device out of the bedroom, such as at the door, so the pull to play with the device through the night will be less strong. Also, consider trying nights without it to see if it is really needed. Let them know that it will be helpful to not be reliant on the tool in the future when they go to sleep at a friend's house and they can't have access to music, for instance.

IDEAS FOR CONVERSATION STARTERS:

1. What are some of your favorite things in your bedroom?
2. What are the things you think about when falling asleep?
3. Could you write down some reflections from your day in a notebook?

• • • •

How To Help Safeguard Sleep for Teens

Every parent I know wants their tw/teens not to sleep too little, and not to sleep too much (i.e., on weekend mornings), but to sleep a healthy amount. The truth is, we only have so many ways to help ensure a healthy level of sleep.

There are two key ways we can influence healthy sleep and both require effort. First, set times where tech goes off for the night and second, eliminate the temptation of screens by keeping them out of the bedroom at night.

These are both much easier said than done! I completely get it, I have been there. Here are the suggestions I have learned along the way.

START WITH WHY "SLEEP IS SUPREME"

Science has a long way to go to unravel why certain animals sleep. After all, it is a risky endeavor. Think about how an animal becomes such easy prey while sleeping.

Researchers have discovered that sleep helps cement learned knowledge. In general, if a student learns something one night and then sleeps on it, they are better at retrieving and manipulating that knowledge than if they had not slept on it. Sleep is also known to help with problem-solving.

Meanwhile, a lack of sleep causes many problems. For example, it is associated with an increased risk of uncomfortable feelings, such as anxiety, sadness, irritability and anger. Also, lack of sleep increases the risk of obesity, diabetes, accidents, academic decline and impulsive decision-making that often leads to regret.

The bottom line is sleep is supreme.

COLLABORATE TO CHOOSE A TIME
WHEN DEVICES ARE TURNED OFF AT NIGHT

It is key that teens feel that they have a say in when their tech gets turned off. Having their buy-in makes it easier for them to cooperate. For example, Tessa really wanted to retrieve her phone and have it with her in the bedroom first thing in the morning to connect with friends about clothes and school events. We allowed it. Showing her that we listened to what was important to her made it easier for her to agree on an acceptable time to turn the tech off at night. Compromise is key.

BUT I STILL HAVE HOMEWORK!

Yes, they will say this in the beginning. But once it is established that screens go off at a particular time, they will need to become more efficient at getting school work done earlier. So much of school work is computer-based, and it's asking a lot for anyone to stay on task when there are 4 million fun diversions just one click away.

Having clear times when screens are away means that kids have to manage their time and not keep distracting themselves from getting their work done.

When they don't get their work done because of their electronic curfew, they can finish the work in the morning, at lunch or take an academic hit for it. Natural consequences are a vital way to learn, and the goal is that they improve by being less distracted while getting school work done — a great skill for them to harness as a result of our efforts to set a limit.

PUT IT IN WRITING

It is funny when a time finally gets set and then a week later, everyone is genuinely confused about what that time was. This has happened to my family many times. I say something like, "Wait, I thought the phones went away at 9." My daughter then says, "No, Mom, we said 9:30." Then we ask my husband, Peter, and heck if he knows.

Hence, the beauty of writing it down. Perhaps you have a contract about all screen time rules or maybe you just create something about sleep time.

I recommend that when you write things down, also write down exceptions. So, perhaps you decide, "If a school project is taking longer and he/she needs the phone to communicate with friends, then the phone can be turned in later once a week."

Another thing to write down are the consequences. So, for example, if the phone and/or other tech is found in the teen's room in the morning, they might get one warning, but the next time it happens, they will lose the device. Then, if it happens again, they will lose it until 5 p.m. that night.

AUTO-OFF

We all know that kids do not always do as asked. To eliminate the nagging and arguments about getting them to turn off their devices, use the technology available to you. For example, Apple's Screen Time app can be used to shut down apps on your child's phone at a certain time. Circle Home Plus allows you to control all of your family's connected technologies from one device. Xfinity customers can set controls on content and internet access via the Xfinity Xfi app.

HAVE A SCIENTIST'S MINDSET

My father-in-law is a scientist and is one of the most patient and giving mentors I know. I have gone to him for some support over the years when I have felt stuck while making a documentary. I would tell him how sad I felt that there were so many things I filmed that would not be used in the final film, and that it just felt like such a waste. Or, I would tell him how I was unsure if a story was coming together, even though I had put in countless hours working on it.

I remember the moment precisely when he told me the following:

"This is what scientists do all day, every day. They know that not only is it possible, but it is very likely, that all the work they are doing on an experiment will not work. And yet, they keep doing it.

Then they learn things and try a different way of doing it. We scientists don't see it as wasted time — it is just part of the process."

That advice really helped me push through hard times in filmmaking, as well as parenting. Trying to make a rule work can be taxing and I have had to regroup, talk more with my family and try different approaches.

For so many parents trying to keep tech out of the bedroom at night, there can often be reasons they want to give up. Do any of the following sound familiar?

> *"I go to bed before my teens, so there is no way for me to make sure they turn them in, so I have given up."*
> *"They sneak in screens, so why even try?"*
> *"They have to do homework late into the night, so why even have a rule about this?"*

Yes, these and many other obstacles can arise. But with a scientific mindset, seeing these pushbacks as challenges to analyze and work through — and doing so with a curious attitude vs. acting like a ranting, angry scientist who runs around smashing her graduate students' Petri dishes — is a useful mindset.

IT IS RARELY TOO LATE

I strongly believe that it's a gift to be able to model for our kids how we handle things when we realize we are not happy with our choices. For example, if we learn about research that makes us rethink how we have been parenting, then we can discuss how important it is to change our approach when science gives us new insights. We are modeling a growth mindset. As a parent, I want to keep learning so I can parent in the best way possible.

This applies to any parent who has allowed devices in the bedroom, but now feels that they are ready to re-address the situation after reading the data. I understand that for older teens, this might feel impossible. It might be the case that the hit to the parent-teen relationship would be too great to enforce such a rule at this point. If that is the case, sometimes trying to get them to put screens away even for a night or two can be a win.

For example, I was visiting my friend whose son was a junior in high school, and I asked her if he had his phone in his room at night. To her chagrin, she said yes, he did. Her son entered the kitchen where we were talking, so I started to ask him about how things were going with having his phone in his room at night. He gave the common answer that he liked having it as his alarm clock. He said he wasn't up on it "that late" at night. I asked how it might be to try to live without it at night, just for a few days. He said, "Nah, I don't think I could do that."

A few weeks later, I was talking with my friend on the phone and asked what was happening with her son and his phone. She said: "Oh yeah, it is really great. He did take you up on trying a few nights without his phone, and now he keeps it out of his room at night. Thank you!"

IDEAS FOR CONVERSATION STARTERS:

1. How good do you feel when you get a good night's sleep? How bad do you feel when you don't?
2. How many hours of sleep do you think is optimal for you?
3. What time do you think would be a good time to take all of your personal devices out of your room?
4. Where might be a good spot in the house to deposit the devices?

. . .

People Share Their Rules for Sleep Time

A woman who had heard me give a talk came up to me and said:

> *"Bedtime is so hard. My daughter is in middle school and she tells me that every single one of her friends is allowed to have their phone in their room all night. She says it would be absolutely unfair of me to not let her do the same. She knows I have not felt good about her phone in her room. What should I do?"*

I told her how often I hear some variation of what she is saying — that all other parents don't have such and such rule. My kids also would say that to me.

It makes sense that kids believe this. How many of them are standing around saying, "My parents have x, y or z rule." It would be socially uncool to say that.

An important start in countering this myth is for parents to talk more openly about the rules we have.

I asked our *Screenagers* community — those who have seen the films, who subscribe to my weekly Tech Talk Tuesday blog and those on our social media — the following question: "Do your kids' devices come out of their rooms at bedtime? If so, what is the routine? Where do the phones, tablets, and computers go?"

Here are some of the responses.

> *"We have a docking station in the living room where all the phones go. They stay docked until the morning. My boys are 11 and 14."* — C. C.

> *"All of it charges in my room at night. We use Bark monitoring."* — E. F.

> *"[The] school laptop stays in the dining room (homework zone) charging, the phone stays on the kitchen counter charging, Kindle can be in bedrooms because of reading!"* — K. M.

> *"We have a pretty strict no-tech rule for kids' bedrooms. The only things allowed are kindles and mini Google home (that they use for music or alarms). Computers and laptops are in common areas."* — R.H.

> *"Our 13-year-old's iPad charges overnight in our room starting at 10 p.m."* — M. M.

> *"The devices never go in their rooms for starters. They charge in the kitchen and stay there unless they need it for researching something, or they are going somewhere."* — A.B.

"We only have Kindles, and yes, once their screen time amount is used up, they go at the top of my closet :)" —S. W.

"All are charged in the home office. No devices are being charged in bedrooms." — G.A.

"We set up a charging station in our kitchen. Our 14-year-old checks in her devices at 9 p.m." — S.C.

"Mine are in high school. They use alarm clocks. No phones in the bedrooms." — M.M.

"Our 13-year-old's downtime starts at 9 p.m. on weekdays (which has been a lifesaver). He charges his phone and iPad on a shelf right outside of his room, and while he doesn't necessarily like it, he gets it, and having it close to him has made it easier. Admittedly, he is annoyed that we (his parents) aren't doing the same practice. We are going to reorganize our lives so we'll do it too." — M.M.

"We turn on Screen Time so they can use the phone for alarms. All apps are turned off. They don't like alarm clocks ... too loud." — L.F.

"We have a charging station on the main floor and at the end of the day, all devices (including parents') are docked to charge for the next day. We use old fashioned alarm clocks to get up for school/work." — E. F.

"Everything is in the office. It's charged overnight and ready for the next day. No matter how much they complain, it's the rule." — J.R.

IDEAS FOR CONVERSATION STARTERS:

1. What time do you think is reasonable to turn off all electronic devices?
2. What is the number one reason you want your devices in your bedroom at night when you sleep?
3. Where would you suggest devices go at night if they are not in the bedroom?
4. When devices are in your bedroom, do you ever check them in the middle of the night?

Chapter Five:

Essential Preparation for Screen-Related Conversations

I titled this chapter "essential preparation" because this is where I share some of the things that have helped me the most in finding my way through crucial conversations related to screen time.

One thing that has helped me is having little reminders about why it is so important that we do the work to create the times and places where screens are put away. The following is one such reminder.

In 2018, "Good Morning America" ran a story called "48-hour screen-time experiment," showing what happened when a couple let their four children, ages 6 to 11, have as much screen time as they wanted over a span of 48 hours.[1] The intense desire for endless amounts of screen time unfolds. The total time spent on screens over the two days for each child was 16, 29, 35 and 46 hours. Keep in mind, the hours relate to all media seen, so the producers counted three hours with two screens as six hours. The kids often used more than one screen simultaneously, but the sum total was still huge. On Sunday night, when the experiment ended and the parents took their devices away, the kids had major meltdowns.

Our kids need us to help them sort out a plethora of screen related issues and limits, but it is challenging. Often, it just feels much easier if we give in. We all know that with younger kids, it is tempting to hand them a device when they are whining, particularly when you want to get things done. The sad fact is that this often does stop the immediate pain that their begging causes. One saying always comes to my mind, "Pay now a little or pay later much more." In this case, the saying means that the more we give in to the immediate, easy approach by handing our child a screen, the harder it will be to say no when they are older.

As kids get older, screen time issues get harder and harder to manage, particularly starting at age 10 or 11. In general, setting rules around screen time with kids starting at age 11 or onward is much harder than setting rules with kids 10 or younger. Exceptions to this rule exist, of course. I know that an individual child can be wired very differently than the majority of kids in their age group, but this is the general rule. There will be times when teenagers dismiss, eye-roll, or even put us down. A psychologist, Dr. Laura Kastner, once explained such teen behavior in this way:

> *"Think of the parent as this big tree and the teen as a person standing under the tree, and all they want is sunlight. The teen doesn't think twice about cutting down the branches of the tree to be able to see the light — hence, the teens can cut us down at times and not even be remorseful about it."*

Parenting now is incredibly challenging. Before getting into a chapter on setting specific guidelines, I wanted to discuss guideposts and also a frame of mind that has proven to be really effective in my life and in other parents' lives as well.

My Roadmap for Productive Conversations

To have more calm and productive communication about screen time in my family — including deciding on rules and getting them to actually work over time — I developed what has become my roadmap, which I call the "3 V Approach." I like the letter V because it creates a peace sign when you make it with your fingers. Who doesn't want to have more peace and love in their homes or classrooms?

Each V stands for an anchor that I come back to when faced with screen related issues, which still happens often. The three Vs stand for: Validate, Values and Village.

THE FIRST V IS FOR "VALIDATE"

Communication in our home greatly improved once I understood that many of my statements regarding screen time were negative and shut down the conversation. I needed to learn the art of validation — the skill of truly appreciating what my kids enjoyed about their screen time and what they felt needed attention. Starting by validating their feelings allows us to talk more positively about the role of tech in their lives, as well as all the great things about the tech revolution.

I started, for instance, joining my son at times when he watched comedians on YouTube some mornings. I wanted to let him know how I could see why he found them so funny. To validate Tessa, I explained how I could see that watching YouTube could be helpful at times. She often watched people her age for information on how to curl hair or how to pick a college. I might pass by her and say something like, "What that person is saying makes a lot of sense."

THE SECOND V IS FOR "VALUES"

As a family, talking more about our values and the things that really matter to us has helped in our discussions and in our decision-making around screen time and non-screen time. For example, one thing I really value is doing things in life that promote physical and mental health. Science and experience reveal the importance of adequate sleep for both of these areas of health, particularly for young people. My kids often hear me say, "sleep is supreme," and so it was no surprise to them that we developed a house rule preventing devices from being in bedrooms during sleep time.

Another example of a value that my kids have grown up with, and that has helped us sort out tech etiquette has to do with valuing spending quality time to get to know people of different ages and backgrounds. In particular, I want my kids to grow up having many experiences of getting to know other adults.

My husband and I value our kids' input on all sorts of topics, and that includes thinking about how screen time fits into our home and all of our lives. We want their input when we are working out the right times for tech to get put away and other issues around tech time.

Our discussions around values, of course, go beyond just those related to screen time. Our youth are inundated with society's strong messages of valuing academic success far above other forms of success — and that concerns me.

A good example of this can be found in a 2017 study, where researchers surveyed more than 500 middle-school students from a high-achieving school and asked them to rank values their parents prioritized.[2] It was found that adolescents who believed that both of their parents valued character traits as much as or more than achievement exhibited better outcomes at school, greater mental health and less rule-breaking behavior than their peers who believed their parents were primarily concerned with academic performance.

I also remember talking with Jessica Lahey, who wrote, "The Gift of Failure." She told me that she is amazed how over half the hands go up when she asks groups of middle and high-schoolers which of them think that their parents love them more when they get good grades.

I work hard to make sure we talk about all sorts of values in my house — far beyond valuing just how a person performs in school.

THE THIRD V IS FOR "VILLAGE"

I realized early on that trying to police screen time alone was extremely difficult and not the best thing for my kids. I noticed that when other kids came over to our house, or my kids went to other homes, someone in the group would immediately get on a device — causing a ripple effect where everyone else would partake. "Free time" became "screen time."

I needed other parents to talk with about how we could work together to ensure that devices didn't monopolize our kids' time together. One example of how I broached this was when my daughter was in middle school and the kids all had mobile devices and phones. I asked the other parents how they would feel about having a screen-free carpool. I distinctly remember how self-conscious I felt when I brought it up to the first person I called. To my relief, the mom I spoke with was equally concerned about screen time and loved the idea.

We implemented that rule in our carpool and believe it or not, the kids thanked us. They ended up chatting together instead of spending time on

their screens, and I loved hearing them discuss different life situations.

Meanwhile, I also needed ideas from other parents about screen time limits that worked in their homes, as well as successful parenting strategies around screen time in general. I found that sharing things that worked well in my own home was appreciated. It was also helpful to share and hear about the things that have not worked. It's good to know when a parent finds a new tech system that seamlessly turns off their kids' tech at a certain time at night, or when someone has figured out how to make a "no screens one day a week" rule stick. Perhaps many of the parents in your kid's friend group don't allow violent games in their homes.

Whether it's the school setting boundaries for its staff and students, parents creating a tech-free carpool, or a sleepover event that calls for all phones to go into a basket, working together as a village made up of caring, strategic and vulnerable individuals can make things better for everyone.

HERE ARE SOME SPECIFIC WAYS TO BUILD YOUR VILLAGE

1. Reach out to the parent of one of your child's friends and ask if they are interested in sharing wins and failures as a way to help you both improve screen issues in your respective homes.

2. Explore the best way to connect with your child's school community on these issues. Is there a staff member or task force assigned to set limits for the school community? Can you get involved? Perhaps the PTA has a group that convenes to share ideas about navigating these issues at home.

3. Work to set up specific screen-free opportunities for your children and their friends when they are together (ie., tech-free sleepovers) and be sure to share these trials with the parents of the friends, so that they feel empowered to try things themselves.

IDEAS FOR CONVERSATION STARTERS:

1. Do you feel like I focus too much on the negatives of screen time?
2. Do you feel like I fully understand the importance of your screen time?
3. What are some of your core values?

. . .

We Worry Our Youth are Losing Communication Skills, Let's Help Them Gain Them

As you prepare to negotiate tech time issues, know that it is not just the final product you are working toward, but that the process of negotiating and talking about all the issues in this book will also help foster your child's communication skills.

I commonly hear sentiments expressed by parents and teachers worrying that our kids are losing their communication skills.

When people say this to me, I think they are often surprised by my response:

> *"I can relate to your concerns. But let's also think about Aunt Jane or Uncle Joe, who didn't grow up with a lot of screen time, and boy, do they struggle with effective communication."*

My point is that there are many things that factor into whether a person develops good communication skills.

However, it is true that screens can be a hindrance. Now more than ever, youth can hide behind a screen if they are uncomfortable with face-to-face communication. This can indeed impede acquiring ease in talking to others.

Let's look at the data on this for little kids. We know that excessive screen time for little kids can delay speech advancement, as shown in these two studies:

In a study of babies, researchers interviewed 900 parents of 18-month-olds and learned that 20% of toddlers spent time on mobile devices and 80% did not.[3] The toddlers on mobile devices had significantly more delayed language development than the 80% who did not interact with screens.

In a study of children ages 2 and 3, researchers found that those who were on screens more often were significantly more likely to struggle with language and communication once they entered school.[4]

But how about for tweens and teens? Well, I will be the first to say that there is very little data on how adept they are at eye contact and how comfortable they are with talking to people of different ages and backgrounds. (This extreme lack of research indicates how behind we are in appreciating communication as a science and as worthy of studying and teaching with more intention.)

We know that developmentally, it's natural for many to become more self-conscious as they enter their early teen years. It's normal to feel slightly uncomfortable when meeting new people, talking in groups and having vulnerable conversations with people who are close to you. But for youth who have elevated levels of social anxiety, this feeling of discomfort can be exacerbated during this time in their development.

Screens are now very easy to turn to and often allow people to "look busy in awkward situations," as Tessa said in *Screenagers*. Anxiety levels go down the more times you go through awkward situations, but when these situations are never faced, it is hard to reduce the anxiety for future awkward moments.

I was once talking with my son when he was 17, and I asked, "What things have I taught you that you can recall and what lessons have I imparted to you about communication skills?" He thought for a bit and said:

> *"Well, you have always told me that people are doing the best they can with the tools they have and that has always helped me to remember that when I have an issue with someone, I give them the benefit of the doubt. And the other thing you have always said is that when I am having a hard conversation with someone, to always talk about how I am feeling, so the person will be less defensive."*

Schools are also finding ways to teach more active communication skills, like how to communicate online and offline, and how older teens can help younger people with communication. In one program, high schoolers came to a middle school and did a presentation recreating a situation where a girl gets left off of a Snapchat group chat where her friends are talking about going to get ice cream. The program then has the students and the peer leaders meet in little groups to discuss. In *Screenagers NEXT CHAPTER*, high schooler Vanessa explains what she has found helpful in handling such a situation:

> *"Something I found, because I have the same issue. When you're in high school they don't go away, you're still not gonna get invited to everything. And I found out when I would go and have that conversation with someone and say like, 'You did this.' They would get really defensive and say, 'Well, I didn't mean to do that.' So something more effective that I found was saying, 'I felt bad. I felt left out.' You're not putting them down for doing that. It gets a lot further."*

Vanessa was teaching the same key point my son had recalled. The communication skill of using "I" statements is one of the most valuable skills we can teach our kids starting in elementary school. It is important that we not only explain the idea, but also help them put it into practice. So if they come to you when they are fighting with a sibling and say, "he did this, he did that," you must work to calm them down. Have them explain the facts — what happened and then how THEY feel vs. what HE did, or how HE made them feel.

Using "I" statements is key to keeping the other person in the conversation from becoming defensive. Then, there is the work of learning to avoid defensiveness — to listen actively and not barge in.

In *Screenagers NEXT CHAPTER*, we see an older teen explain to a group of middle schoolers:

> *"I was so nervous. It's one of my best friends. And it was so hard to sit there, her say, I felt this way about something I did and then have myself not jump in and say, well, that's not right. I had to sit there and think about what she was feeling, and remember not to just defend myself the first chance I got."*

A 12-year-old boy in the group learning from Vanessa told me after the group session ended:

"I remember Vanessa talking about when she had the situation with her friend and that was a better way of communicating because if not, how I would usually do it by barging into a conversation. We really never get the point across and it just ends up me defending myself."

Finally, as we worry about the loss of communication skills, I would argue that teens have many deep conversations about hard-to-discuss topics. Things like sexual consent, sexual identity and mental health are all being discussed more so than in the past. There are an array of reasons for this. One of which is that kids, young adults and older adults are all sharing the same platforms, like Facebook and Instagram, so more adult-type themes are around younger kids in a way that was not the case in the past. Also, the shows youth watch today deal with much more intense themes than in the past.

On a positive note, it is great that schools have things like mental health clubs that teach peers how to have more meaningful conversations. Meanwhile, parents are more likely than ever to talk to their kids about all sorts of topics that were considered out of bounds not that many years ago.

WHAT PARENTS CAN DO:

- Ask your child if they have heard people say that kids are not able to communicate like they could in the past. There is a good chance they have heard this, and we want to let them know that there is no evidence to show this. In fact, there are many ways that kids are stepping into more challenging conversations with more skills than in the past.

- Make sure to validate all the ways your child is a good communicator. Hold up specifics. We want to make them see communication as a skill that can be improved upon.

- Discuss all the ways communication savvy comes into play in relationships — negotiations, helping someone who is going through a hard time, working out boundaries in a home (like screen time), keeping a house clean when they go off and live with others in the future and the list goes on.

IDEAS FOR CONVERSATION STARTERS:

1. Can you think of any concrete communication skills you have learned?
2. Can you recall a challenging conversation with a friend and how you think you handled it?
3. Have you heard about using "I" statements, and do you do it?
4. Can you think of any interpersonal skills I have overtly taught you or that you have picked up from the way I interact with others? The way I try to resolve conflicts with others?

The Four Key Cs

"What's the problem with my kids being on screens for major chunks of days? Why should I care?"

I wanted to try to answer these questions that I started asking myself early on in our screen time struggles. I also needed to stop and answer the following questions:

"Why do I care what my kids choose to do when they are on screens? Why should I care?"

I came up with four main categories for why I wanted to help ensure that they had time off screens and that they had some guidance and insight when it came to things they did on screens.

Sometimes I call them "My Four C Values." I love that this sounds like my "force-y values" — it's good to laugh at myself and I know that, in their eyes, I can be a bit "force-y." Though I am by no means a "tiger mom," I am on the more directing side of the parenting scale, and I may be a lioness at times (my zodiac sign is a Leo after all).

My 4 Cs are creativity, competency, connection and compassion.

1. CREATIVITY

We are all born with the ability to be creative — every day we are creative in the broadest sense of the word. We create our day as it unfolds by making different decisions.

The data tells us that by far, the number one thing youth do today on screens is consume. They consume other people's shows, other people's video games and the list goes on. Very little time is spent creating their own works during their screen time.

As a parent, I want my children to have plenty of opportunities to utilize their imaginative and unique selves while on screens and to ensure that they have plenty of time off screens to do creative things.

- **On screens:** When my kids were young, I got them the video game Contraption, where they made — yep, you guessed it — contraptions. Chase had GarageBand so that he could make music, and I still recall the hip hop song he decided to incorporate into a school project. They also had software to help create online albums of family photos.

- **Ensuring time off screens:** To make sure my kids had plenty of time to be creative offline, I made sure they had opportunities to do things like build, paint, design a scavenger hunt, help neighborhood kids create skits, try to reassemble a bike or build a balsa wood model, to name a few.

2. COMPETENCY

Gaining competency in different aspects of life is a key to a more fulfilling life — it is a crucial step in fully "adulting" and a vital part of gaining a stronger sense of self.

- **On screens:** The letters you will draft to a teacher explaining a situation that needs explaining. Or using computer tools to help organize an educational brunch you are throwing for your mental health club.

- **Ensuring time off screens:** I encouraged my kids to get comfortable taking various types of public transportation alone when they felt ready to do so. I've also worked to ensure they gain competency in cooking. All these things required not being glued to a device.

3. CONNECTION

Another of my core values is connecting with people. This means deep connections with friends and family all the way to the little connections with a store clerk. This means making an effort to connect with people from all different backgrounds and ages.

- **On screens:** Texting relatives or using Skype to share what is happening in each other's lives is a great way to do this. In the 11th grade, my son started volunteering for an organization that used Skype as a way for students in the U.S. to tutor Syrian refugees living in refugee camps.

- **Ensuring time off screens:** I ensured that they had plenty of time and opportunities to have conversations with people from all over without devices. This could mean having time when we walked through our neighborhood, when we got to know the local barista or when we had tea with a relative in her nursing home.

4. COMPASSION

While it is innate to be caring and to have the desire to help others at times, this is also something that can be fostered in our children through the way we raise them.

- **On screens:** My kids were raised on a serious dose of meaningful documentaries, such as "Spellbound," "First Position," "That Sugar Film," "Street Fight" and "Mai's America." We also watched TED Talks by people who created programs to make a difference, such as ones by Muhammand Yunus, Jacqueline Novograntz and Marcus Bullock.

- **Ensuring time off screens:** Ensuring time off screens for things like volunteering and planting in the natural area near our house are things Tessa and I have done. We create time for undistracted talking with the people who sell the *Real Change* newspaper which has been a significant part of my family's compassion-building. People who are dealing with issues such as homelessness sell this paper and get to keep most of the profit and my family really enjoys the conversations we've had with these people. So many of them are appreciative that we stop to have a conversation with them. My kids have had a deeper appreciation of their humanity and injustices in our society through these ongoing, small but meaningful encounters.

Here is a pretty wild example from my family's attempts to make something creative that was both screen related and born from compassion. When my family and I lived in India, we created a project where we worked with local kids to organize a flash mob for Tuberculosis awareness. We put it on the internet to raise awareness further (you can find it on YouTube if you look up "India's First Kids Flashmob Dance").[5]

IDEAS FOR CONVERSATION STARTERS:

1. Which of the 4 Cs do you think you engage in the least when it comes to your screen time?
2. In what ways are you creative with your screen time? What about when you are off of screens?
3. Do you have feelings of competency during your screen time? In what ways do you feel competent off of screens?

Working To Prevent
Emotional Dependence on Tech

For many teens, being without a phone can cause difficult emotions. I will discuss some of the research around this, and most importantly, what can be done to try to prevent and overcome this reality.

A Pew Research Center survey of US teens in 2018 found that:[6]

> *"Overall, 56% of teens associate the absence of their cellphone with at least one of these three emotions: loneliness, being upset or feeling anxious. Additionally, girls are more likely than boys to feel anxious or lonely without their cellphone."*

In *Screenagers NEXT CHAPTER*, we hear from one of my favorite researchers in the field of screen time and psychology, Larry Rosen. Rosen discusses a study where college participants were asked to hand over their phones before a class. He says:

> *"So imagine that I'm in a big lecture hall and I bring in students to the lecture hall, and I tell them: 'Please give us your phone. We'll give your phone back when we're done with the study.' We measure their anxiety. 10 minutes later we measure their anxiety, 20 minutes after that we measure their anxiety, 20 minutes after that we measure their anxiety, right? So what do we find? If you split people up into those who use their phones a whole lot, all day long, and those who use it a moderate amount, those who are moderate users show an initial increase in anxiety but then they level off. Those who are high users, even 10 minutes, in they're already more anxious and their anxiety keeps going up, and up, and up. The longer we don't let them use their phone the more anxious they get."*

When my teens got mobile devices — starting with flip phones, on which they could only text — it was important to me to foster in them a mindset of enjoying the world without their phones. So when we would go out as a family, for example, we would talk about leaving their devices at home. They were able to do this and be content.

Even in his older teen years, at ages 16 and 17, my son Chase would be fine with leaving his phone at home. And Tessa, now a senior in high school, can still go to school without her phone. She sometimes even leaves her phone at home when we go on day outings as a family. That said, she prefers to have it and most of the time, she does have it with her. Chase, now in college, also always prefers to have his device with him.

Chase tells me that many of his college classes require tech to be put away. He sometimes sees students going on their phones, but not often. And since laptops are not out, students are taking notes with paper and pen.

I think it is important that our middle and high schoolers know that some college classes will have such rules — and that rules like these also exist in workplaces. For example, sometimes it will be expected that phones get put away during long meetings.

The goal is to help your kids feel as comfortable as possible when they cannot be on their phones. Even when they have their device on them, can they feel emotionally OK without constantly checking it? Many teens (and many adults as well) can't stand to be away from their phones. I believe that practicing little challenges around breaking free from devices can lead to long-term benefits.

Start off by explaining your expectation that there must be times when your kids go out into the world without their device so that they can decrease their emotional dependence on it. Doing something together where the whole family decides to leave their devices (except maybe one parent for directions, etc.) helps break this dependency.

Setting up the challenge with a reward is also an effective strategy. So, for example, a parent may let their kid know that phones are not allowed on an outing, but also that they recognize that this will be a challenge. As a reward, the parent may let the kid pick out a special ice cream, or a card game to play or YouTube videos to watch when they get home.

IDEAS FOR CONVERSATION STARTERS:

1. What are the positive emotions you experience when you have a mobile device with you out in the world?
2. What are some of the hard feelings you experience when you can't have your device with you?
3. When are you naturally off of your device and not missing it?

. . .

"I Hate that I Wasted the Day Away"

I am impressed by the number of tweens and teens who tell me they feel bad about spending a lot of time on screens. These young people say things like, "I hate that I wasted the day away." I ask if they ever talk about this feeling at home. Generally, they say, "No" because they don't want their parents to say something like: "Yeah, see? I told you so" or "Well, you should have known and just gone outside."

Helping youth identify the feelings of "time wasted" can help them learn how to resist the urge to be on screens. If your child does not openly say they feel like they are wasting time, now is a great time to have a conversation on this topic, because it will surely come up in the future. For example, during the school year, they might be trying to finish their homework, but the urge to check social media or watch a YouTube video keeps them from reaching their goal. Suddenly, homework is not done, and it is already 10 p.m. or even later. Many kids struggle with this.

Here are ways you can share your time-management strategies to help kids foster their own

1. Talk about times you choose to indulge in technology for entertainment. Maybe it's when you finish a big project for work, or the one night in a week when you watch extra TV. Your kids might be surprised that you have thought this through. Modeling this idea is essential.

2. Share how tempting it can be for you to avoid doing something challenging with doing something that feels like "wasting time" — like watching way too many movie trailers (i.e., me) instead. Give examples of challenging tasks you have avoided — like calling a friend you need to resolve a conflict with, calling your tax accountant or calling HBO (to yet again cancel your online subscription. They always say they will have someone call you, but they never do).

3. Talk about the idea of a "pre-commitment strategy," a term coined by Nobel Prize winner, economist Thomas Schelling. His concept was to organize things to ensure success by setting up systems that make it difficult to back out later and fail at a goal. For example, if you know you waste time to sleep by bringing your screen into your room at night, the pre-commitment strategy would be to set a rule that the screen must be left outside of your room. That way, you will not have to deal with the dilemma of going on your screen and then telling yourself to stop.

4. How do you forgive yourself when you end up feeling like you "wasted time?" This act is important to identify because when we beat ourselves up for doing what we set out not to do, we often react by continuing to do the activity that made us waste time in the first place. For example, wasting time through watching yet another "Black Mirror" episode might make you upset that the bills did not get paid. Then, to soothe yourself from the stress and self-deprecation this choice has brought on, you continue to watch more episodes. Instead, if you can stand back a moment, breathe and use your self-compassion and resilience tools to say something like, "I needed to watch all those for a reason." Or, "I am not sure what that choice was, but I am going to let this pass and not get anxious over it." Or, "I will begin again," or "I will try tomorrow." Whatever you say to yourself, share this with your kids.

IDEAS FOR CONVERSATION STARTERS:

1. Do you ever feel like you've wasted time on a screen?
2. Do you have any strategies to help you manage your screen time?
3. How do you forgive yourself when you feel like you have wasted too much time?

. . . .

Setting Boundaries is Hard for Many of Us, Including Me

There are a variety of reasons why screen time for many youth has outweighed activities and interactions that would benefit them. In other words, there are reasons for why kids are indulging in excessive amounts of screen time.

One of the reasons is the inner discomfort that many parents and teachers feel when they must say "no" to their children and teens. Saying no and being able to tolerate the myriad emotions that can arise — such as guilt, self-doubt and sadness — is challenging for many people. On top of that, the child may react to the "no" with their own negative emotions, like anger and disgust. It is a major undertaking to tolerate any one of these emotions, let alone several of them at one time.

It has been hard for me when my kids are upset with a rule I enforce. I just want them to be happy and hate to see them upset. It is difficult when I see that I'm to "blame" for their negative feelings. Hundreds of studies show that having some boundaries with our kids and enacting them lovingly in ways that ensure they are heard and participating has the best outcomes, as opposed to what is called "passive" parenting. So, I continue to work on tolerating my emotions when I stick with saying no or ensuring a consequence is met. But it takes work.

I have thought long and hard about how challenging it is to tolerate the discomfort of setting boundaries and saying no, not only from my viewpoint as a mom, but also from my years of practicing medicine.

One of the hardest times to say no that health providers are confronted with over and over, is when a patient requests opioids when the provider does not think the opioids are in the best interest of the patient.

When the physician denies the patient's request for opioids, the patient can become angry and begin to attack, or become sad and start to cry. A whole range of reactions can be unleashed. The physician saying no to the prescription will, therefore, have to prepare and have their own emotional reaction to the patient's feelings and behaviors. A physician can feel scared, guilty, sad, angry or any combination of emotions at the same time. It can be a lot easier to write the prescription instead of saying no and working to change the conversation so that it focuses on why you are worried about a patient's opioid use.

In medical school, students learn next to nothing about addiction medicine. This amazed me since so many of the patients I saw in the hospital during medical school were there due to addictions — a lung disease caused by tobacco use, a liver disease caused by alcohol and so on. I decided to take an elective in addiction medicine and got an incredible mentor, Dr. Barry Rosen. He always told me, "That while a surgeon has her scalpel to heal, a primary care physician has her words."

Watching Barry lead complex dialogues with his patients, who were laden with intense emotions such as shame, denial and hope, was watching true mastery in action.

I went on to do research and create short films on doctor-patient communication, opioid requests and recovery. In the films, I talk about a powerful way to stay compassionate when setting boundaries. It is always important to remind yourself that it is the addiction talking (or crying or yelling), and not the person. That person at, say, 15 years old (or any pre-addiction age), would never have thought to themselves: "I would love to be a slave to heroin, wouldn't that be great? And how cool to know that I could die each time I use it."

The real skill of a health provider is effective communication that allows them to maintain a connection with the patient, so that along with a "no" comes a discussion about why the answer is no. This is important in opening up collaborative decision-making for alternatives and at times, conversations about recovery treatment. Daily, my heart hurts when I think of all the people and families dealing with any form of addiction.

Saying no to addicted patients who want opioids takes skills, strategies, experience and compassion. Helping our kids maintain a healthy balance with screen time may not seem so scary in comparison, but it can still make parents feel uncomfortable and can pose a challenge for many of us.

Perhaps you have wanted to set new limits, like saying no to screen time in the car, no to screens in the bedroom at bedtime, or no to screens at the dinner table. There are some tips below to help you be successful.

1. In preparing to set a screen time limit, spend time writing out why you want to set this limit. This will help you feel confident that it is an overall positive thing for your child — something that will provide undistracted time for better sleep or for them to build in-person relationships.

2. Remind yourself about the studies that show parenting with love — but with boundaries — leads to the best outcomes (vs. command and control parenting or a passive parenting style).

3. Baby steps are key. Just pick one thing you have wanted to say no to and work on that single challenge. Start with the easiest one.

4. Know that you are modeling to your children, students, girl scouts, etc., the deeply important skill of acting with integrity. If you believe, as I do, that having device-free time is good for youth (and all of us), then you are showing them that you are willing to act in line with your beliefs, even if it means stepping into discomfort.

5. Achieving greater autonomy as one enters adulthood is a primary human need. Whenever possible, give your child some agency around the "no." For example, you think that it would be beneficial to your 13-year-old if devices, including the phone, were no longer present in her room at bedtime. You do the steps above and now want to appeal to her need for some control. Ask her something like: "What time do you think the phone should get put away? Should I come and get it, or should you give it to me at that time?"

6. Remember, it is a gift to hold people accountable. This shows we care. The opposite is just ignoring whatever they decide to do, which can send a message that you don't care. In fact, one of the problems of passive parenting is that researchers have found that kids with these parents often say they feel like their parents don't care about them. So know that as you do the work to enforce the "no," you are giving a gift — one of energy and deep care.

IDEAS FOR CONVERSATION STARTERS:

1. Saying no to people can be really hard. Can you think of a situation where you had to say no recently? How did it go?
2. Are there people you feel like you need to set boundaries with, but find it hard to do?
3. Do you feel like you are listened to when we come up with screen time rules?

• • •

The Science of Creating New Screen Time Habits

Researcher Wendy Wood designed a series of studies to examine how our habits persist even when they are in conflict with our true desires. In one of the studies, people were invited to watch movie trailers in a movie theater, and were told that the purpose of the study was to get their opinions on them.[7] The participants were offered free popcorn in the movie theater. Unbeknownst to them, their behavior with the popcorn was actually the main focus of the study. The popcorn was extremely stale because it had been made a week earlier.

The researchers found that people who had the habit of eating popcorn when going to a movie theater were significantly more likely to eat the stale popcorn than those that did not usually buy popcorn. They had such a habit of getting popcorn at the theater, that they automatically ate the popcorn even though it was awful. When these habit-eaters were asked if they liked the popcorn, they said things like, "No way, it was really bad!"

There was a twist. In a variation on the study, they told participants to eat the popcorn with the hand opposite the one they usually used. This small change had a big effect. Fewer of the habit-eaters ate the bad popcorn. Changing the circumstances a little helped awaken the part of the brain that got them thinking: "Should I really keep eating this bad popcorn? No, it is not worth it."

I get two main lessons from this study. First, given how strongly habits pull us along in life, the more we work to create habits in line with our goals, the better off we will be. Second, when we have habits we want to break, little ways of switching our brain out of automation can be a smart move.

Regarding raising kids, the big question is, how do we help them establish habits that can serve them long into life and how can we help them better understand habits so that they can make and break them in their own lives?

I went through long periods of time growing up without doing much regular physical activity, including during college. After college, I moved to Washington, D.C. with a high school who was an avid runner. I started running and soon, I was hooked. It got to the point that missing a day of running made me so irritable that it was far better for me to run than to miss running — even when it was 100 degrees.

What about the hard work of trying to start a new habit? I went into primary care medicine because I know that changing our behavior is the hardest thing we do as humans. Doing things differently than we normally do is incredibly challenging.

Researchers used to think that the key to adopting a new behavior was simply will power. Say a person wants to swap out 30 minutes of YouTube scrolling with 30 minutes of working on wood models instead, in order to start a habit of doing creative projects. To predict the success of making this change, we would need to know how motivated the person is. If the motivation is strong enough, it can be one of the main elements to promote change.

And yet, while important, motivation does not predict successful habit formation as much as one would think. As a physician, I have worked with many people in the hospital with profound lung diseases who are extremely motivated to quit smoking, but have not been able to break the habit.

Researchers have found that productive people who stick more to their positive habits do not have oodles more willpower than the rest of us. Instead, they set up systems that lower the barriers that might keep them from doing the desired behavior. Eventually, it becomes a habit this way.

Let's talk about the science of creating new positive habits related to screen time — for kids and adults alike.

1. KNOW THAT WITH ENOUGH REPETITION, A NEW HABIT WILL FORM

It is impossible to say exactly how long it takes for something to become a habit. It depends on the person, the behavior and a host of other factors. To give a sense of the time frame, here are some things I have gleaned from studies. Adding something to one's day, like drinking a glass of water, takes around two months to become automated to the point where you don't have to make decisions about it. Something like going to the gym could take three or four months of going every day before it becomes really habitual.

Perhaps a parent wants to get into the habit of always putting their screen away when they first see their child after school or after work, for that initial reconnection. They start to do it with reminders, and maybe after three weeks, they no longer need the reminders because it has become a habit.

Maybe a preteen who has the habit of going on YouTube every morning to watch sports scores or updates on a video game decides instead to make a habit of walking the dog for 10 minutes. This might take two weeks of daily dog walking before it becomes a habit.

2. KNOW THAT REWARDS ARE A KEY PART OF MAKING HABITS STICK

We have quickly gotten into the habit of checking screens all the time because we get rewards — new little entertaining bits of information or connections to friends are all hugely reinforcing.

To form a new habit of practicing piano for 10 minutes for four days a week instead of watching TikTok videos, for example, consider a small reward for the new behavior. Of course, we would all want the fun of practicing to be the reward, along with the reward of seeing improvement — that is ideal. Yet, in the creation of habits, external rewards may need to be put in place at times. Ideally, once the habit gets formed, internal rewards will kick in.

3. ARRANGE THINGS IN ADVANCE

If you want to change a habit that is not serving you, such as going onto TikTok for an hour after dinner rather than using that time for something more productive, maybe try putting your phone in a new location before dinner. That way, after dinner, these little changes can wake your brain up to remember, "Oh yeah, I don't really want to have that feeling of regret I have after sinking into TikTok, so I will resist the urge to go on it."

4. HELP YOUR KIDS SEE THE UPSIDES
WHEN THEY PUT THEIR SCREENS AWAY

For example, if they are not on a device but are playing with a younger sibling, point that out. You could say something like: "It is so great that Mattie had your undivided attention. Our greatest gift is our attention — and what a lucky little sibling to get some of that."

IDEAS FOR CONVERSATION STARTERS:

1. What are some examples of the daily habits we do that we don't even think about?
2. What habits do you feel have a hold over you even though you wish they didn't?

· · ·

When They Know They are
Being Manipulated — It Can Help

Research and experience show us that as kids mature into their teen years, they become more prone to experiencing adverse feelings towards signs of injustice and to the adults who they feel are causing the injustice. So, how can we use these facts to better help adolescents make healthier screen time choices?

As adults, we are well aware that manipulation and deception are rampant in marketing. In my area, health, I am constantly appalled by the claims that are made on supplement products, including "fights cancer, " "promotes longevity," and "strengthens the immune system" — all without any scientific proof.

We know that tech companies work hard to keep our kids (and us) glued to their screens. For example, psychologists come up with new ways to manipulate youth so they will stay on social media for longer. It is important to note that manipulation is not always used for nefarious purposes.

One example of this is called "Snapchat streaks" or "streaks" for short. A streak shows up on Snapchat when a user has communicated with someone consistently for a consecutive number of days. Many youth have streaks that are 100 days long or more, often with dozens of their peers. They say some of the reasons why they like having unbroken streaks are bragging rights and the ability to show friends that they really care. This is an ingenious system the company created to keep youth on their app for longer.

We know that Netflix no longer releases one episode at a time, and instead releases whole series at once to promote binge-watching. Another example of manipulation is the practice used by YouTube to harness data from millions of people in order to suggest videos that they will most likely find appealing.

Do you think all teens are aware of the fact that some form of manipulation can explain why they are on digital devices for as long and as often as they are? Well, a study in 2018 asked a nationally representative sample of 13 to 17-year-olds to rate how much they agreed or disagreed with this statement: "Tech companies manipulate people into spending more time on devices."[8]

They found that 72% agreed with the statement and this was reported in the news. To me, the real headline should have been the fact that 28% of teens were not aware of this manipulation. And here is the important piece. When they are aware they are being manipulated, there is evidence that this will influence them to make healthier choices about screen time. Let me share some research to explain why I think this.

Behavior change experts have tested to see if decision-making is impacted when teens are informed that they are being manipulated.

They decided to look at decision-making through junk food. Public health officials have long known that it is hard to get teens to stop eating junk food and that campaigns created to change this behavior have often proven ineffective. But researchers wanted to test a new strategy using the points I mentioned above.

Not too long ago, researchers David Yeager, Fred Steubinge and others conducted a study in which they divided eighth graders into two groups.[9] One group was given traditional materials explaining how sugary snacks are unhealthy and the other group was given information about how the sugar industry often relies on manipulative and unfair practices to attract kids to their products — for example, by purposefully making junk food more addictive and by marketing it directly to young children.

The next day, all the eighth graders had snack time and were offered different food choices. They had no idea that this snack was related to the study. The students were offered healthy food options along with traditional sugary junk food options and were free to choose what they wanted. Students who had received the information on the manipulative tactics of the food industry were significantly less likely to eat junk food than those who had received the lesson on the health consequences of junk food.

Now, let's look at an actual public health campaign that used thinking similar to the researchers in order to see if they could elicit change in the behavior of teens based on tapping into their interest in justice and their dislike for adults and companies that are manipulative. Legacy, a group dedicated to decreasing smoking rates in this country, came up with a campaign called "The Truth Initiative."

They created ads showing body bags being dumped outside the Philip Morris headquarters to illustrate the large number of deaths caused by tobacco use each day. These ads seemed to motivate youth to reject the manipulative tactics of the tobacco industry. Research has shown its impact. For example, one study published in the Journal of Adolescent Health found that greater awareness of the anti-smoking Truth ads among 15 to 21-year-olds strengthened their anti-smoking attitudes and increased their support for a social movement to end tobacco use.[10] From the results of the study, researchers extrapolated that the

campaign was directly responsible for keeping 450,000 teens from starting to smoke during its first four years.

I think sharing these studies with our kids and teens is a great way
to get them thinking about the ways tech companies work to keep our
attention. This is, after all, truly an attention economy. How much did
your teen pay to use Snapchat? Nothing. Facebook for us? Nothing. The
way we pay is with our attention — that is the currency that business
models depend on.

Fortunately, many teens are indeed aware of the manipulation. 72%
in the survey above did agree that tech companies manipulate people
to be on their devices longer. This statistic includes 23% of participants
who "strongly" agreed with that statement. Respondents in the survey
said the following:

> *"Instagram doesn't care how you use their app, they just care if
> they're getting used. If you're posting and being active, that's all
> they care about"* — 15-year-old.

> *"The companies that own these social media should stop scam-
> ming teenagers into spending the majority of their time on their
> sites"* — 16-year-old.

I want to share something Tristan Harris said in 2020 when he was asked
to share his views with congress in a hearing regarding tech and manipulation. Harris worked in tech, including having been a design ethicist at
Google before leaving to co-found the Center for Humane Technology.

A congressman asked Harris if marketing is really that different
than it was in the past, giving an example of how items in a supermarket
are placed in specific ways to compel customers to buy them, especially
at the checkout line.

Here is part of how Harris responded to him:

> *"... in the case of technology, we have a super computer pointed
> at your brain, meaning like, the Facebook news feed sitting
> there and using the vast resources of 2.7 billion people's behav-
> ior to calculate the perfect thing to show you next and to not be*

discriminate about whether it's good for you, whether it's true, whether it's trustworthy ... And the degree of asymmetry is far beyond anything we've experienced."

IDEAS FOR CONVERSATION STARTERS:

1. How much do you agree or disagree with this statement? "Tech companies manipulate people into spending more time on devices."
2. What do you think about the study where eighth graders were taught about the manipulations of junk food companies and how they made their food choices the next day?
3. In what ways do you see things happening online that might be influencing your behaviors?
4. Should there be more laws to regulate tech companies in this regard?

• • •

Family Meetings Replace Family Fights (The Inspiration Behind Tech Talk Tuesdays)

Many years ago, my friend Patricia, who is about 10 years older than me, told me that from the time her kids were in middle school to when they were in high school, they would have "family meetings." She would light up when she told me what a powerful tool this was for improving all sorts of issues in their home.

Here is how it went: There was always a piece of paper on the refrigerator labeled "Agenda," and if anyone was bothered by anything — like if her kids were mad at each other — they would write it on the Agenda. Or, if the dad was frustrated by the dishes left in the sink, he would write it down.

Then, about once a week, they would have a meeting. It always began with going around the table and having each person give a compliment

to at least one other family member. Then, they would discuss whatever was on the Agenda.

For each meeting, one of her two kids got assigned as the scribe. Patricia told me that this would lower tension levels because she would say to them, "OK, just write that down."

Meetings were always ended by one person, (this honor rotated each session) who got to pick something fun to do with the family — like a game they wanted to play together that night or maybe an outing to the zoo that coming weekend.

The meetings worked incredibly well in fostering calmer conversations and working through conflicts. They even motivated Patricia's kids to resolve disputes on their own outside of the meetings. That happened because if one of her kids put something on the Agenda, the other sibling would want to immediately take it off. No one really wanted to have to discuss it at the weekly meeting, so writing it on the refrigerator often sparked the siblings' ability to sort it out themselves so they could erase it from the Agenda.

Because having these family meetings worked so well in her home, Patricia often told her friends about them, and several of them started to do the same thing in their own homes.

Looking back, I think hearing about these meetings planted a seed in my brain that subconsciously inspired my Tech Talk Tuesdays weekly blog.

Patricia's family set such a great example of procedural justice. And indeed, one central element of my blog has been to discuss rules around screen time. And the ability to do this well requires procedural justice with all of the young people in our lives.

David Yeager, a growth mindset researcher, introduced me to the concept of procedural justice as it relates to parenting around screen time. Here is a good definition of procedural justice:

"Procedural justice is based on four central principles: treating people with dignity and respect, giving citizens' voice during encounters, being neutral in decision-making, and conveying trustworthy motives."

Procedural justice's four main principles include:

1. Being fair in processes
2. Being transparent in actions
3. Providing the opportunity for voice
4. Being impartial in decision-making

A study explored procedural justice in families with older teens concerning disputes.[11] One of the findings was that in the families where procedural justice approaches were used more often than in other families, they were positively associated with a teens' psychological well-being and negatively related to deviant behavior. On the flip side, the researchers found that "... disrespectful treatment was the best predictor of deviant behavior."

As I got better at working with my kids to decide upon the tech rules we have in our home, I realized that this procedural justice approach makes all the difference. As parents, making sure their voices are heard, being flexible and incorporating some of their concerns is essential. While we aren't impartial to the decision-making, which is one of the criteria in the classic procedural justice model, we have tried to stay very calm and not too opinionated when it comes to choosing rules.

IDEAS FOR CONVERSATION STARTERS:

1. What do you think about having family meetings like the ones described here?
2. Do you think it would be easy or hard for you to write down a problem and have to wait a few days to have it addressed, as opposed to resolving it right away?
3. Do you think we do a good job of applying procedural justice in our home? Do you feel that your input is listened to and respected?

Chapter Six:

Contracts and Family Rules

When my daughter Tessa, who is in *Screenagers*, saw the completed film, I was shocked by one of her first reactions. She said, "I didn't realize so many other kids are dealing with all this rule stuff like we are." She had been with me over the years as I was making the film, and yet somehow, she did not know how common it is for families to struggle with setting limits. She went on to tell me how her friends rarely talk about their rules around screen time.

I knew this was also the case with parents because I seldom heard any of them talking about the rules they were trying. We would all gripe about the stress of screen time, but when it came to specific rules, I found people were pretty quiet. This was, in part, because so often, what we try does not work. And also I think parents don't want to be judged. At the same time, all of us really wanted specific ideas for rules. Parents were starving for insight into how to set limits and what these limits should look like.

Knowing which rules, limits and guidelines to have can be confusing for parents. And then comes the work of implementing them consistently, which can be exhausting. While filming *Screenagers*, I learned how reticent parents are to share their screen time rules. The fear of being judged as "lazy and too lax" or as "overly controlling" prevents many of us from telling others the rules we are trying (I count having no rules as a type of rule-setting).

This backdrop helps explain why a Facebook post by Janelle Hoffman went viral. She had posted the contract she wrote up for her son, who she was giving a smartphone to for Christmas in 2016.

Frankly, it was really brave of Janelle. When we share our rules or attempted rules, we risk feeling judged — are we too controlling? Too lenient?

The reporter for a Good Morning America story, Becky Worley, wrote an accompanying blog to the segment she produced.[1] I mentioned this segment in a previous chapter. It involved a family who gave their kids unlimited screen time for 48 hours. Worley wrote:

> "I have been covering and studying this issue [tech] for a long time. As a result, I am super strict with my 10-year-old twins: No screens at all during the week and only TV shows on the big screen on the weekends. No YouTube, no tablet games, no Xbox or PlayStation in our house. My two exceptions are planes and hospitals."

And to my point, she adds:
> "This is the first time I'm writing about what our family does because I don't want to seem judgmental; there are a million different types of kids, family situations, and techniques for parenting."

This chapter is full of ideas for creating workable family rules and includes sample contracts, such as one we did with our daughter, parts of Janelle's original contract with her son and a more recent one she created with her daughter.

Some families, of course, do not have contracts, which is perfectly fine. Dr. Cliff Sussman, a psychiatrist who works with teens around screen time issues, says he never uses the word "contract" with his families. In his opinion, "contract" implies an "all or none" approach — i.e., either a contract is valid or it has been broken. To me, a contract is just written goals and a few clearly stated rules. I don't see it as being "all or none," but his point is a good reminder that there are different connotations of the language we use.

Some will have a less formal written agreement or a non-written understanding of screen guidelines. Many families start one way but then change to a different strategy.

No matter the name, the goal is that there is some clarity about what the rules are. I know firsthand this is easier said than done. On more than one occasion, my husband and I would become frustrated seeing one of our kids on a screen at night. We would ask each other, "What is the darn rule?" Then inevitably, one of us would bark back, "I don't know, you're supposed to know!" And then we would ask our kid what the rule was, and they would shrug. Ergg! So we would go back to the drawing board. In a few days, we would reconvene to sort this out.

In addition to giving ideas for screen limits, I also give examples about how we can use technology to help limit tech use. This can help, but comes with a fair load of complexities. I must say that it has been frustrating for me that tech companies have not done a lot to create systems that help parents set healthy limits. For example, it took many years for Apple to finally incorporate Screen Time into their iPhones — a system that helps parents set limits on their children's phones. Not only did it take Apple way too long to provide that tool, but the tool also has issues. It can be tricky to pair the parents' phones to the children's phones, which is required to make it work. There are also ways to get around the Screen Time limits by changing the time on the phone's clock.

I await the day when everyone's homes will have systems in place that automatically and seamlessly shut off technology at a specific time, as well as ensure that the content used is appropriate. But of course, even if this were to happen, it would never replace the conversations we have with our kids that are just as important in our ever-changing digital landscape.

* * *

Four Steps Before Making or Revising a Screen Time Agreement

My initial foray into having clearly defined rules by creating a contract was not only a major flail, but millions witnessed it. On Tessa's 13th birthday, though I was super reticent, my husband and I decided to gift her what she wanted SO MUCH — an iPhone. I hadn't planned to film it, but as we were giving it to her, the filmmaker in me grabbed my cellphone and started filming — hence, the very grainy footage in the actual film. Tessa started to sing with delight and my son took the phone from me to capture my nervous face.

A few days later, I gave Tessa a contract with cellphone expectations, goals and rules. I used Janelle Hoffman's contract — the one that went viral on Facebook — as a starting point.

My intention was that Tessa would work with us to refine the contract and feel at least some buy-in to the rules. But that is not what happened.

The moment where my husband and I give her the contract is captured in the film. Tessa reads from the contract:

> *"Phone must be kept in the office when at home. There will be days when the phone will stay at home, certain family days, et cetera. You will make mistakes and there will be consequences. We will deal with that together."*

Tessa looks up from reading the contract and rolls her eyes.

I respond: 'That's exactly it. That's what we're trying to help you do, find the balance, because you don't wanna live life where you're just constantly online or a life where you're not online and in despair."

Tessa says: "Can I send this to my friends? Say my parents gave me a five-page contract?"

I respond: "I think it's four pages. How many pages is it?"

Tessa says, "Four, but I exaggerate."

OK, four pages. Let me explain because that sounds like a mini-novel! It had lots of parts about goals regarding screen time, and it was not just four pages of rules. But from my post-embarrassment vantage point, four pages is still way too long.

After giving Tessa the contract, I repeatedly tried to see if she would talk to us about tailoring it with her input. But rather than engage with us, she would clam up every time we asked.

One of the lessons I learned is that it would have been better to start with the steps you read in the previous chapter — i.e., doing prep work like spending time talking about all the positives of screen time and shared values — rather than presenting a written document to start.

From there, we could have discussed with her the elements that might go into a contract, without even getting into the details. Here are two ways that I think can help with such an approach. First, I want to recommend the "Family Media Plan" that can be found on the American

Academy of Pediatrics website. Here, you can see the components suggested for a contract. You don't necessarily have to make these rules binding with your child.

Another approach is to read over the key components I have written below in order to get the conversation going. It can be helpful to have this discussion over a couple of days so that you ease into it — first discussing ideas in general. Eventually, these conversations can build toward deciding the specifics.

To reiterate, it is key to have clearly defined rules. A study that surveyed 7,415 children ages nine to 15 and 5,685 of their parents about rules regarding screen time found, "Rules that were consistent and that were reported by both parents and children were associated with the lowest prevalence of children exceeding recommended screen-time limits."[2]

Here are four key steps I recommend:

1. DEFINE YOUR FAMILY'S GENERAL VALUES

Consider questions such as, "What are the core values we have — each of us individually and as a family?" One's values intersect into many screen time issues: Internet safety, privacy, time management, plagiarism, appropriate posts, online bullying and kindness.

Parents: Think about your "why." Why do you care how much time your kids spend on screens? I wrote earlier about creativity, connection, competency and compassion. Are there any of these that you find particularly important to ensure your child has time to expand off screen?

Kids: You might ask them something like, "What are the main reasons people want to have balance in their lives regarding screen time and other activities?" Help them identify some of their personal goals around things such as family, friends and hobbies. At first, they may just shrug, but with time, hopefully some important discussions will be sparked.

2. TALK ABOUT TYPES OF FAMILY RULES

This is where you translate your values into ideas for "tech limits," "agreements," "rules" — whatever you want to call them. The main focus is to start determining times when screens should be put away, such as during meals, in bedrooms and cars. Here are things you can discuss:

- Bedtime: Is there a time when devices go off? Can devices be in the bedroom? Where do they go in the house if not in the bedroom?

- Homework: Can the child have a computer out while doing homework? Can they have a phone out? Can they respond to texts, messages or Snapchats while doing homework?

- Gaming: Are there rules about the amount of time spent on and/or type of gaming? How about where they can game?

- Social Media: Are there rules about where time is spent? Specific apps they can or can't use? Are there times they can't use social media?

- Passwords: Do parents have passwords to every device and every account? For how long? Until the child demonstrates a certain maturity? Or after a certain period of time?

- Meals: Can they have their device out at meals?

- Other specific times: Can tech be used when guests come over? How about out in the world — such as grocery shopping or pre, post and during school?

3. TOUCH ON INCENTIVES AND CONSEQUENCES

Raising this topic with kids can be a good way to get their brains thinking about this area without choosing specifics right away.

One of the hardest things about parenting is deciding on appropriate incentives and consequences and carrying through on them. All sorts of issues are involved, like when are good times to use positive incentives and what are fair consequences?

4. DISCUSS THAT SOME WIGGLE ROOM IS PART OF THE EQUATION

We all know that real life requires wiggle room. It's important to think ahead about circumstances in which someone will need to use their device despite a rule prohibiting it. Given that the phone is a device with so many functions, there are often very legitimate reasons for these slippages. For example, our daughter recently remembered that she needed to text information to her outdoors club about trails they were considering hiking. So, she came into my room where I had her phone and quickly got that done.

IDEAS FOR CONVERSATION STARTERS:

1. What should we call what we plan to create? A plan? A contract? An agreement? Something else?
2. What things are you concerned about us not taking into account enough when we think of rules?
3. Any new system or plan usually requires adjusting. How will we have regular times to talk about changes that need to happen? (Tech Talk Tuesdays? Hint, hint.)

. . .

Sample Contracts, Including My Daughter's

One day on the news, I saw a story about Janelle, a mom who made a contract for her son before giving him an iPhone. The story showed a clip of the card she gave to her son with the phone:

> *"Dear Gregory: Merry Christmas! You are now the proud owner of an iPhone. Hot Damn! You are a good and responsible 13-year-old boy and you deserve this gift. But with the acceptance of this present comes rules and regulations. Please read through the following contract. I hope that you understand it is my job to raise*

you into a well-rounded, healthy young man that can function in the world and coexist with technology, not be ruled by it."

Her post included all the details of the contract she gave to her son, and it went viral instantly. It dawned on me that the reason it went viral was that there really wasn't a person out in the world who was openly sharing family rules. I wanted to meet Janelle, so I went to her home, bringing along my video camera of course.

As we sat in her home with four of her five children running in and out of her kitchen in Sandwich, Massachusetts, she told me:

"I wanted to be thoughtful and I wanted to be deliberate in giving this technology, and I had a lot to say. I wanted to protect his sleep and remind him of those human experiences, like ordering a slice of pizza while looking into somebody's eyes and being in the movie theater without checking text messages. So I decided to compile my intentions for giving this device and I put them to paper in an 18-point iPhone contract also known as our family iRules."

I want to share with you some of this contract, as well as one she made later on with her 13-year-old daughter. I will also provide you with the contract we created with Tessa when she was in eighth grade — after I learned ways to get her to help modify it and have some buy-in.

EXCERPT ROM JANELLE'S CONTRACT WITH HER 13-YEAR-OLD SON, GREGORY

- If it rings, answer it. It is a phone. Say hello, use your manners. Do not ever ignore a phone call if the screen reads "Mom" or "Dad." Not ever.

- Hand the phone to one of your parents promptly at 7:30 p.m. every school night and every weekend night at 9:00 p.m. It will be shut off for the night and turned on again at 7:30 a.m.

- It does not go to school with you. Have a conversation with the people you text in person. It's a life skill. (Half days, field trips and after school activities will require special consideration.)

- Do not use this technology to lie, fool or deceive another human being. Do not involve yourself in conversations that are hurtful to others. Be a good friend first or stay the hell out of the crossfire.

- Do not text, email or say anything through this device you would not say in person.

- No porn. Search the web for information you would openly share with me. If you have a question about anything, ask a person — preferably me or your father.

- Turn it off, silence it, put it away in public. Especially in a restaurant, at the movies or while speaking with another human being. You are not a rude person; do not allow the iPhone to change that.

- Do not send or receive pictures of your private parts or anyone else's private parts. Don't laugh. Someday you will be tempted to do this despite your high intelligence. It is risky and could ruin your teenage/college/adult life. It is always a bad idea. Cyberspace is vast and more powerful than you. And it is hard to make anything of this magnitude disappear — including a bad reputation.

- Leave your phone home sometimes and feel safe and secure in that decision. It is not alive or an extension of you. Learn to live without it. Be bigger and more powerful than FOMO — fear of missing out.

- You will mess up. I will take away your phone. We will sit down and talk about it. We will start over again. You and I, we are always learning. I am on your team. We are in this together.

OUR REVISED CONTRACT WITH TESSA

Tessa's contract changed from the four-page contract that I initially presented to her to something more effective. From the ages of 13 to 16, the contract was revised on four different occasions. This is the fourth version from when she was 16.

EXPECTATIONS OF TESSA

- Parents will know the password for this phone. We plan to ask you to show us at times how things are going on different apps. We don't plan to randomly search your apps, given your maturity level. There could be a rare situation where we insist that you show us something, but only if we have reason to be worried. But truly, our goal is to have you drive and show us things and to know that you can come to us and talk about issues as they arise.

- Remember the goal for all of us is not not to email or say anything to someone that you would not say out loud to them or their parents.

- Since the phone is permitted at school, you will aim to use it according to their rules and consistent with the principles of this contract.

- If something happens to the phone, depending on the situation you may be responsible for the replacement costs or repairs.

- Remember that the internet is forever. You will be tempted to do something questionable or risky. Know that what you do on the internet can impact your life today and well into the future. If you don't want to explain it to a stranger, your grandparents or future boss, don't do it.

EXPECTATIONS OF PARENTS

- First and foremost, we trust that you will make good decisions about what you do on this phone and with screens in general, and we want you to be able to come to us if things are not going well.

- We will respect your privacy when you are talking or texting on the phone.

- If we have a concern, we have the right to read text messages or review call logs without telling you first — but our goal is to always have you in the driver's seat when we look at your social media.

- We will pay the standard monthly fee for the cellphone.

SPECIFIC USAGE

- You will not use your phone during mealtimes and focused family time. (Of course now and then there will need to be exceptions and we understand that. Communication is the key.)

- When it comes to doing homework it is about working together to find study habits that foster focused concentration/attention span to improve the quality of work done. Currently, you will put your phone in the other room while you study for 20 to 30 minutes, and then you can enjoy a 10-minute phone break.

- The phone may be used in the morning, but you are expected to be ready for school (breakfast eaten and cleaned up, and your personal responsibilities).

- You may use the phone responsibly at any time, but every weekday, put the phone away at 9:45 p.m.

- On weekends, it is expected that you will have periods of one to two hours when you are not on your phone. Sometimes, we may have family days without phones.

- Screens are kept out of your bedroom, including your phone but on the Friday through Saturday night you can have your phone and a laptop in partly during the day and night but all must come out of the bedroom when you go to sleep.

- You will make mistakes and there will be consequences. The standard consequence will be loss of the phone for at least part of the following day.

The more that a child is involved in creating a screen plan, the better. Some parents try to get their child to write an initial draft of a contract, and it's wonderful if your child will do that. Two years after Janelle wrote the contract for Gregory's iPhone, her 13-year-old daughter wrote up the first draft of her own contract, while Janelle wrote out parent expectations for her phone use. Then, they all came together and went over things and modified as needed. Here is an excerpt from each of their final versions.

EXCERPT FROM JANELLE'S CONTRACT FOR HER 13-YEAR-OLD DAUGHTER, LILY

Lily is Gregory's younger sister, so her contract was created a few years after his.

Lily's iPhone contract — Lily's section

- Phone must have a password. Mom and Dad must know it.
- If I see anything bad, I will say something about it.
- Always ask if I'm not sure if I should post.
- I can't have it in my room when it's time for bed.
- I can bring it to school, but it's turned off unless a teacher says it's OK or we're allowed to have it out.
- Ask permission before getting apps or purchases.
- Turn off at 8 p.m. on school days. Except if I have soccer until late.
- Turn off at 10 p.m. on weekends.
- Post positive stuff and don't be rude to anyone.
- No inappropriate pictures of people, places, etc.
- Remember to take in everything around me and to not always be with my head down.

Lily's iPhone contract — Janelle's section

- You must sleep when it's time to sleep and eat when it's time to eat. Screen free. Always.
- There will be things you have to do — study, solve, practice, prepare — with a full heart, mind and focus. If your screen is not an aid, it's away.
- Your device is public space. It is a billboard outside of your school. A message to the world. A true group convo. Don't say it, share it, like it or look it up if you don't want all eyes on it.
- Here's the thing about jerks — you are not one. Devices disappear if this should change.
- It may become harder to just breathe and be, sit with yourself and others. But you must. Do not give this up for anything.

- You are a child. A beginner. New. I am old and wise and on your side. I like it here. Use me up. Put me to work. You are not alone.

There will be plenty of kids that do not want to take the first stab at creating rules. Maybe they do not want to take a first stab, but are willing to write things down as you all talk, and to write them from their perspective. The bottom line is that there are many ways all of these things can happen. I always remind myself that this process of negotiation is important — a lot of learning is going on, for the child and the care providers.

At Janelle's website, you will find the full contracts for Gregory and Lily, as well as contracts of her other children.

IDEAS FOR CONVERSATION STARTERS:

1. How do you feel about the word "contract" vs. another word?
2. What are some of the expectations that make sense for kids and screens? What about teens and screens?
3. What are some of the basic expectations that parents should have?

. . .

Our Family's Tech Rules — Always a Work in Progress

Family rules or guidelines can be about things concerning only family time and home spaces, or they can include things specific to the kids. When *Screenagers* came out, we found that having three categories for rules really helped us: family time, study time and sleep time.

Before I go into more specifics, let me be the first to say that there are always hiccups.

Any family that proclaims they have a set of rules that ALWAYS gets followed perfectly is either a family of one, or "always" actually refers to most, but not all, days.

Here are the details of these three rule areas and how they have changed over time for us.

FAMILY TIME

In the home

- First and foremost, we have devices put away for all mealtimes together. This includes resisting the urge to look things up on devices when a question comes up. For example: "What movie was he in? What is that flight again that monarch butterflies do that is so impressive?" By not grabbing a device, we stay connected. The main goal is to be undistracted together, and this trumps the desire for instant answers to specific questions.

- Other device-free times in our home include when we watch a movie, do a puzzle, play a board game or are on a call with other family members. Also, when we are in the kitchen setting up for dinner and cleaning up after dinner.

- Devices are out of the bedrooms, even during the day. The main purpose of this rule has been to increase a sense of connection with our kids. It gives us a bit more insight into what they are doing and allows for small interactions between us even when they are on their screens. I have been in so many homes while filming for *Screenagers* where parents lamented that their kids and teens spent hours and hours in their rooms. This solidified my goal to not let this happen in my home.

- Eventually, at some point during his junior year of high school, we said it was fine for Chase to be in his room to do homework with his computer. Had he wanted to earlier, we would have said yes then too — after all, we know space is a key need of teens. Luckily for us, he had not asked before then.

- Even now, as a senior in high school, Tessa still spends most of her time out of her bedroom when she is home. We have adjusted rules on Friday and Saturday nights and she can use a laptop and phone in her room, but needs to have them out of her bedroom when she goes to sleep. There are some times on weekend days that she will have a device in her bedroom to do homework or socialize. We are fine with that, since she spends plenty of time in our home's public spaces and we all get to connect in little ways often.

Out of the home

- We have had a policy that either the teens leave their phones at home or if they have them, to mainly keep them out of sight. Keeping them out of sight also applies to us parents. Even as high schoolers, our kids would leave their phones at home on many outings. And Tessa, who is now a senior in high school, still does this at times. Chase, who is now in college, does not want to leave the house without it when we all go out. That is fine for us because he still tries not to be on it too much.

- What I have really advocated for is that when we have to look at our phones, we try to say why — I see this as good digital citizenship. So it might be something like, "I just have to let this person at work know something," or, "I have to tell my friend we are running late." There are times when we all start checking our phones, and allowing some of that works for us, but when our teens were younger we really discouraged it.

Study Time

- When our kids first had phones, we had a rule that phones had to be put away during study time and checked during break times. They would leave their phones in the other room for chunks of time while they studied. It might be about 20 minutes of studying and then 10 or 15 minutes on the phone. It was never that regimented. They both also try not to go on social media or YouTube during study time.

- When they were younger, I would sometimes find the phone by their computer or I would see them switch tabs to check social media. When this happened, I reminded them not to do that. It was about mentoring and helping them to be mindful of their goals rather than enforcing consequences. They knew all too well that homework would just keep piling on and on if they didn't use some self-discipline to get it done. Now that they are older, they are better at self-policing because they know how much their phones can distract them. They still struggle and do have plenty of time when they go down a screen time rabbit hole.

Sleep Time

Our rule has always been that all devices, including phones, stay out of the bedrooms during sleep hours. Now, when Chase visits from college, he still puts his phone out of his bedroom at night. He has that habit from growing up with this rule and still finds that it means that he sleeps much better when he follows it.

For a while, Tessa charged her phone in the office, but it became clear that she would at times check it before going to bed — which was after her tech curfew. Also, I felt it was such a temptation for her to keep checking, particularly since the office might be empty and there was no oversight.

We realized it made more sense to have her charge it in our bedroom. I also charge my phone in my room. At times, Tessa pops into my room to check something on her phone, which is fine because it generally doesn't happen more than a few times a week.

I have always adhered to a strict rule that I am not on my phone in my bedroom. I also keep my laptop out of my room about six out of seven days a week because I just like to read a book before falling asleep, rather than bringing work into my bedroom. I am happy Tessa sees me modeling this, and I know that she will realize this is an option when she is living on her own and is in full control of all her screen decisions.

PUSH BACK IS NORMAL

None of these rules are hard and fast. Life has its surprises and being flexible is a mindset that we want our kids to develop. For example, in our family, we have a "no cellphones in the car" policy, but there are times when something important comes up and someone has to do a quick check. The kids know that I appreciate it when they tell me why they are breaking the rule. They might say, "I am telling Ben that we are late to pick him up." I also follow the same etiquette, so if my son Chase is driving and I have to do something quickly on my phone, I tell him what I am up to.

And there are of course times when teens push back against rules. In these moments, tension mounts and an argument can happen. What has helped me in these moments is to adjust my consideration of "fighting" as a bad thing and to remember that studies show that there are some upsides to arguing with teens. I reviewed some research around parent-teen conflict and found some "silver linings."[3] They are:

- Teens consistently report feeling much less stressed about arguing than their parents do. So how about we decide to be less bothered by it too? After all, fair is fair.

- Research shows that teens benefit from productive arguments with parents, and vice versa. Healthy, productive arguing, from the teen perspective, is when the parents listen to their claims and adjust the rules based on their input.

IDEAS FOR CONVERSATION STARTERS:

1. What do you think of the family rules discussed here?
2. How would you feel about trying a phone-free outing with only one phone on us for directions and emergencies?

• • •

People Share Their
Summer Screen Time Rules

Here are some rules that people generously posted on Facebook in response to this question we posted: "What are the summer screen time rules in your house?"

1. *"The rule in our house: No reading, no screen time. I've let up on some time limits over the summer, since we're pretty strict during the school year about it. However, they still need a time limit, or they would literally spend all day staring at a screen. It's getting tough to limit screen time, though, because there are so many devices! Phones to Chromebooks, iPads, Kindles, Xbox to TV. They device hop. I'm ready to lock them all up for the summer!! We use Circle to limit screen time and keep them safe online."* — Pamela O.

2. *"All chores must be done daily in order to keep the phone."* — Debbie K.

3. *"Summer is no different than the rest of the year for us. iPad is for math drills every day (less than five minutes) and that's it. Maybe an occasional movie on "Friday Family Fun Night." I do this with my kids 7, 8, and 10 years old, but not with my 17-year-old, as he's practically out of the house by now."* — Raina J.

4. *"For my 9 1/2 and 4 1/2-year-olds, we are doing one hour of screentime Monday through Wednesday and on Friday with a family movie on weekends. Saturday and Sunday mornings, screentime is fine for one hour or so. We are camping a lot this summer, so there is no screen time then either. It sucks to be the screen police, but is all for the better!"* — Penelope S.

5. *"They need to have their room picked up, bed made, eaten breakfast, brushed hair, read (basic morning routine), and then can have 30 minutes of screen time. I made a list of things they could do to earn more than 30 minutes*

screen time — up to two hours per day. But while we are traveling, we have to adjust." — Natalie P.

6. *"We have a 13-year-old and we just started no phones or screens of any kind from 9 a.m. to 3 p.m., which was based on the fact that usually, she is in school from 8:30-3:30, so this is better. This applies to everyday. Yesterday, exactly one week after school got out, she asked to play pingpong during the day with us and cards at night. She is starting to get bored. After those hours, she's allowed one show (they range from 20-40 minutes). She's allowed a maximum of 30 mins on Instagram, but can message her friends to chat the rest of the day, except from 5:30-7:30 p.m., when the whole family has no screen time allowed. Complicated, huh?!"* — Linda C.

7. *"One hour of TV is allowed daily; one hour of video games on Friday, Saturday and Sunday AFTER lunch and after 30 minutes of reading and one hour outside. He can do extra chores to get more video game time. We took the iPad away last year — best parenting decision we've ever made. Our son is 9 years old."* — Holly W.

8. *"We have an 8 and a 10-year-old and allow them 40 minutes of screen time Monday, Wednesday and Friday, and then they can earn more from reading after they do their list (instrument practice, exercise ideas, chores, playing with baby brother). Tuesday and Thursday, they get 30 minutes maximum screen time that is some sort of school/educational app. Saturday is kids' movie night. Sundays are screen-free."* — Rebekah K.

9. *"When my kids were young (they are grown now), I made them punch cards. Every Sunday, they received a new punch card with eight punches. Each punch was worth half an hour of screen time. They could use their punches whenever they wanted (for approved shows). When the punches were gone, they were done for the week. When they gave their cards back to me the following Sunday, they received a quarter for each unused punch and received their new card. Worked great!"* — Mary K.

10. *"My kids are older—13 and 15 years old. Especially for my oldest, I believe in self-regulation. But that is what works for us, she doesn't really care about*

technology. I also think parents need to be accountable as role models. That being said, our Google Wifi is awesome because you can pause devices. We paused screens in our house from 9 a.m. to 9 p.m. That only works for devices without a cellular plan, but for my younger child, this means he has time to decompress before bedtime and time away from screens when he gets up. He spends most of his day at the pool or with friends, but I don't micromanage the rest of the time." — Melissa F.

11. *"My 15-year-old is working at a summer camp for six weeks ... phones are kept in the office except for free time, which is limited!"* — Aline C.

IDEAS FOR CONVERSATION STARTERS:

1. When you think of summer, what off-screen activities do you like to do?
2. What rules should we consider having in the summer to keep screen time from preventing those things?

. . .

Creating Consequences Is Hard But Necessary

Setting rules and fair consequences for when they are violated, ideally in collaboration with our tweens and teens, is a gift we give our children. It is a lot easier to check out and just let kids and teens sort out for themselves what, when and how long they want to use screens. But having a few key rules and enforcing them strengthens executive functioning and self-control.

Enforcing rules is by far one of the hardest things we do as parents, especially with teens. There is so little guidance to help with consequences out there. A key point is that we don't want to over-punish. I explain this more later on in the chapter.

My husband has helped me learn the value of having our kids brainstorm with us about fair consequences. I remember a conversation I had with Tessa as I employed this interactive process that Peter had advocated. Tessa hands my husband or me her phone, or plugs it in to charge in the corner of my bedroom on Sunday through Thursday nights at a time we agreed upon.

I asked her for ideas for consequences if she did not turn in the phone at the agreed-upon time. Her first suggestion was that if she broke the rules, she would not have access to her phone for the entire following day. I responded, "Really?" with a tone that implied that maybe that would be too severe. She then quickly came up with something a little less harsh: "I can't bring it to school the next day." We agreed that it made sense.

Next, we started brainstorming ways she would succeed with the rule. I asked if she thought it would help her to set an alarm on her phone for the time it is supposed to be put in my room. She said: "Yep, that makes sense. I will set it for five minutes before to help remind me."

We asked several parents for examples of their rules and consequences. Below are ideas based on their answers.

Rule: The phone gets handed over to a parent at 9 p.m.
Consequence: If not done, a parent takes the phone at 8 p.m. the next night. Then, the night after, the original rule where the child hands it over at 9 p.m. applies again.

Rule: The iPad (or other portable screen) is not to be in the bedroom and must stay in the office or another family common space.
Consequence: If brought into the bedroom, the iPad is put away for the rest of the day and is not used the next day at all.

Rule: No video games on Monday, Tuesday and Wednesday.
Consequence: If found to be playing video games, they lose video game time for one day.

Rule: While doing homework, the phone is kept in another room and the child takes scheduled phone breaks.
Consequence: If they are found with the phone while they work, it gets put away for the rest of the day.

Rule: Provide a specific, limited amount of time that the child/teen can play a video game.
Consequence: If the child does not comply when the time is up, the time allotted is shortened by 10 minutes next time.

Rule: No use of a personal device at certain events, such as a family gathering.
Consequence: If they use a device at the event, they cannot use it after the event and the following morning.

Rule: No use of the phone in class.
Consequence: If the phone is used in the classroom, it must stay home the next day. If it happens again, it stays home for the week.

Rule: No internet or video games during the school week, and if the child needs to check something on the internet, they must first ask a parent.
Consequence: If they are found doing this during the week, then they lose some of their Saturday computer time.

Rules and consequences are a gift we give our kids, especially when both parties participate in establishing them.

IDEAS FOR CONVERSATION STARTERS:

1. What can be done to increase the chance that rules will be followed (such as visual reminders, timers or even tech solutions such as apps that turn things off automatically)?
2. What are the consequences, or what should they be?

. . .

Using More Positivity
To Get More of What We Want

During the early days when I was first struggling with my kids over screen time, I found that when I saw my kids on a screen when they weren't supposed to be, I would react quickly from a place of frustration. I would grab whatever device they were using and glare at them. Eventually, I realized this approach was not how I wanted to be handling things and it was not working. That is when I started to look deeper at the research about what works best for shaping behaviors we want our children to engage in.

Tammy Fisher Huson, Ph.D., is the author of "Fearless Parenting," among other books, and has fortunately taught me about the power of the Nurtured Heart Approach. This is a method of working with kids, developed by psychologist Howard Gasser. He realized that children so often get attention when they are acting up, but adults often ignore them when they are doing things as they should. Children subconsciously want attention, even if it is not the best kind, and so often continue the more disruptive behavior. What if adults started directing their energy toward the behaviors they want more of, rather than the undesired actions? When this gets employed, research shows we get more of the behaviors we want. Let me break it down.

The Nurtured Heart Approach is based on three principals, which are like three legs of a stool: Absolute No, Absolute Yes, and Absolute Clarity.

The idea of Absolute No is that the parent does not get energized and mad if a child does not follow a rule, or does a behavior that you do not want them to be doing. Let's say your child is supposed to stop playing their video game on time, but they come to the dinner table late. Rather than putting your energy toward getting mad at them — by saying something like: "Hey, that is NOT OK I kept yelling for you to come and that took way too long!" Instead, you should take a few deep breaths and when the child does come, you employ the next step: Absolute Yes.

Absolute Yes is about recognizing the good choice your child made by validating why it was not easy and what it says about the strengths they have. Howard Glasser called these strengths "Inner Wealth," which I think is an awesome phrase. So when your child finally comes to the table, you might say something like: "Hey, I see you left your game and you got to the table, and I know that was not easy. You love that game, and disconnecting is really hard. You could have just kept playing, but you didn't. It shows a lot of will power and respect for us. And it shows that you know our dinners are important."

There's a good chance the child will still be a bit grumpy, but often, you will see their face light up a bit because you have held a mirror up showing them the good things about them and their behavior.

In that setting, the child was pushing a boundary. Let's take another situation. Two siblings prone to fighting are in the kitchen talking about things, joking around and having fun. As a parent, you enter the room. With the Absolute Yes approach, you might say something like: "It's so fun to see you being pals, I love how you make each other laugh. What a great quality in both of you." Then, when the siblings are fighting later on, you want to say calm and give their argument very little energy. You might need to intervene and if you do, do it with low energy. The point is that it is easy not to point out the times when they are making each other happy or when they are working together to clean the kitchen, which is why it is even more impactful when you do point it out.

Tammy once said this to me in an interview for *Screenagers NEXT CHAPTER*:

> "What do I really want to build in my child? Maybe it's resiliency. I need to be more resilient under challenge. Maybe it's persistence. And you choose that idea and then you're going to look for it. And then you're going to name it. I need to reset myself. I cannot call my kid lazy because if I continue to put voice to that, he will be. He will rise to whatever we name. Whatever you name, you get more of. So I decided to name greatness. Decide to name something you want more of that's powerful and positive."

Absolute clarity is about being clear with expectations and working for consistency in the home. First, the family has to come up with a few rules around screen time, ideally with the youth involved. Then, let's say a child breaks the rule by playing Fortnite on their father's computer after their screen time for the day has ended. The child had already played their two hours for the day on Saturday, yet the parents discovered he went on his dad's computer to play longer.

The reaction to a situation like this should be calm. This is not about getting angry or trying to make your child feel shame or less than because they broke the rule. Tammy has often told parents to remember that kids' behaviors are not about the parent. When a kid breaks a rule, many parents take it personally. We do not consciously feel this way, but on a subconscious level, we think, "If you really respected me, if you really cared about this family, you would not break the rules." It is crucial to work against this mindset and remember that this is not about us.

In this state of absolute clarity, the next step is to say to your child, "We have a family rule, and it was broken. So, as you know, tomorrow you can't have your Fortnite time." It's best to make the consequence short in order to give our kids the chance to shine as soon as possible. So you might say: "The day after, you will have your time back, and I know I have raised a responsible child that can stick with the rules. Life has lots of rules, and I know it is not easy to follow them. But you are capable, I know it."

So often, it is easy for a parent to want to do the other extreme — to say no to video games for a week or something like that. We are angry and as I mentioned before, we may feel a personal affront, We may feel like if we give a big punishment, this is more likely to get them not to sneak around and break the rules in the future.

Tammy told me this one important thing: this is not about you, the parent. So when a rule is broken, do not take it personally. Do not put a lot of energy toward the fact that the rule was broken, so as not to show lots of disappointment in them.

Research tells us that when there are really long punishments, kids do not focus their energy on the poor decision they made and how they can learn to do better, but rather on their anger toward the parents. In addition, this can make them more prone to wanting to sneak, break the rules and work at getting better at not being caught.

This might sound like a funny comparison, but not long ago, we got a dog for the first time and the whole dog training thing was completely different than I had expected. When the dog peed on our rugs, I thought I was supposed to get mad at him and rub his nose in it, but trainers told me that this approach would not work. What!?! I was shocked. They all told me we had to enact a reward approach. We needed to focus on taking him out and rewarding him when he went where he was supposed to go.

Our kids are not dogs — I know, I know!!! For our kids, some negative consequences are indeed valid at times. It is hard to decide what the appropriate level of consequence should be for rules that are broken. That is for sure. Yet, keeping all of this in mind can help to ensure that our consequences are not too extreme.

What I love about this technique with teens is that this focus on making them feel positive about their good choices is right in line with what is happening in their brains. Science shows that something fascinating happens in the developing brain's reward center, starting in the early tween years. During this time, it becomes significantly more sensitive to positive reinforcement than anytime before or after. As psychologist and researcher Lawrence Steinberg, Ph.D. stated in *Screenagers*:

> *"There's more dopamine activity in the adolescent brain's reward centers than in the brain's reward centers at any other point in development. Good things feel even better when you're a teenager."*

When Tammy told me about the Nurtured Heart Approach, I worried because it reminded me of the "everyone gets a trophy" idea. In fact, it is nothing like that. The whole point is to hold up a mirror and point out to kids very specific things they do that are worthy of noting.

The Nurtured Heart Approach also works for teens and, frankly, for all ages and all relationships. I now use this approach not only with my kids, but also with my husband. I take more time to point out things he does that I appreciate, and try to be much calmer when talking about things that bother me.

TAKE-HOME POINTS FROM MY PERSONAL EXPERIENCES

1. I started to point out positive behaviors with my teens more often. For example, if Tessa regularly put her phone by my bed on time to charge at night, I might say something like: "Hey, hun, I just want to say that I have been really impressed by how on top of it you have been with your phone at night. That shows a lot of responsibility on your part, and a lot of respect for yourself to make sure you are getting the sleep you deserve."

2. I have also started doing this more in other areas of my teens' lives. Not long ago, I was driving Tessa home from school, and she talked about a social conflict she was having with her friends. While she talked, I consciously looked for the parts of what she said that I could reflect back to her. I said: "So even though you were angry, you were able to act calm and you went and talked with her. That is not easy, you could have just avoided it all. And instead, you stepped into the challenge and that shows real grit and courage." I saw Tessa's face light up. The best part about that was that some days later, she mentioned how much she enjoyed hearing me say that.

3. Another example is with my son. I asked him to help around the house, but I kept having to remind him. He was getting frustrated with me, and I was working hard not to get frustrated with him. Instead, when he finally did his chores a couple of hours later I said to him: "Hey, the kitchen looks great — I know you had a lot more fun things to do than that. I know it was not fun, but you did it anyway and it really shows you are a good team player, thank you."

WHAT PARENTS CAN DO

At this point, you might worry that your child (especially if you have an adolescent) will roll their eyes at you if you engage in the Nurtured Heart Approach.. The good thing is that when you actually follow these steps, it will happen far less than you would expect. The key is how we do it. It is a combination of three steps that make all the difference.

First, describe the facts (i.e.: you turned in your phone, you resolved with your brother who gets to use the Xbox).

Second, let them know that you recognize the challenge they faced in doing what they were doing in order to follow the rules (i.e.: you finally turned off TikTok, and I know how hard it is. You laugh a ton when watching it and having to stop is not easy). This step of validation gets teens to listen without rolling their eyes. They (like all of us) love to feel like someone really gets what they are going through.

Third, give them specific examples of the positive things their action shows about them (i.e.: you left your phone at home during our outing today, and it shows that you value undistracted time with your family. That is such a great quality in you).

I want to end with this quote from Tammy that drives all of this home:

> *"We ask a lot of challenging things from our kids and they don't have to do them gleefully. When kids do things they don't want to do, and they do it anyway, that's powerful gritty stuff. That's perseverance. That's their ability to manage challenges. How often are we really calling kids out for that? And how powerful is that for the kid to hear that you recognize the challenge that they're facing."*

Tammy's books are great resources to learn more about the Nurtured Heart Approach. And if you are a teacher, check out her book, "There's Always Something Going Right." Howard Glasser, father of the Nurtured Health Approach, has a website with many resources as well.

IDEAS FOR CONVERSATION STARTERS:

1. Can we, as a family, describe some positive behaviors we see each of us doing to manage screen time? What do these actions say about each of us?
2. Absolute No is about not putting energy toward what is not going right. Do you put a lot of energy toward things when they are not going right?
3. Absolute Yes is about putting energy toward what is going right. Can you think of examples for when I have done this?

4. Absolute Clarity is about not being confused about what the boundaries and rules are. It is about having clarity and consistency. Do you think we have that in our home? If not, where can we work to make things clearer?

• • •

Ideas To Help When Struggling With Screen Time Rules

As parents, we are up against a technology revolution that is so strong that it can genuinely overpower all aspects of our lives, and can make having just a few rules extremely hard. Here are some tips that can help if you are feeling a little or very frustrated about limit setting.

Baby steps: Maybe the goal with your teen, for example, is to step back from trying to make certain limits happen and to focus instead on baby-step goals. For example, asking your teen, "What if we focus on arguing less and just work together to find one short time when we are without screens — maybe 10 minutes in the car or ... ?"

Excessive but accountable: During a school break, you might ask them to pick the number of hours they would like to be on screens per day for just for a few days or weeks of the school vacation. The condition is that they are then accountable to whatever number they choose. They will need to agree to check in with you every few days or to tell you the amount of time they have spent online at the end of each day. Consider asking them to use an app like Moment to track the time spent on their phone and video games. This approach often shows teens how much harder it is to limit their time than expected, even when they pick the number of hours they spend online themselves.

Work on you: It feels clichéd, but the only real control we have is working on ourselves. This is how we get better at recognizing when our teens trigger us and how we learn ways to handle it skillfully. For example, you might want to talk to your teen at the very second they are disrespectful or inappropriate, but you know that this type of conversation doesn't generally go well in the heat of the moment. Instead, go outside, mark down the date and the time, write something in a journal, take a breath, and then plan to bring up the situation later. When you bring it up later, try to use "I" statements such as, "I feel XYZ when you do XYZ." This is a much more effective way to get your teen to talk with you than if you said something like, "When you do XYZ, it really is disrespectful."

Join them: If the screen time issue has become too toxic, you might want to abandon talking about it for a while. Instead, dive into an in-depth empathy exploration by asking if you can join them in doing something fun on screens together like playing their favorite video game. After doing this a few times, you may clear out some of your anger and you'll likely have more capacity to say something like, "Wow, I can really see why you love these games so much."

Reverse it: When you find yourself having a good moment with your teen, see if you can engage them in a short role-reversing exercise. Ask something like this: "Can you humor me for a moment? I am going to play you and can you play me." If they say yes, you might continue with: "Look dad/mom, I love my phone/computer time and I want to be on it at least X numbers of hours a day." Hopefully, they will engage and act as if they were you. Try to keep it lighthearted.

Back Peddle: Consider starting a conversation with: "Hey, I want to talk with you about screen time and given our past conversations, I realize that no matter what I do it's tricky. If I don't try to talk about screen time, I feel pretty crappy as a parent because I think my job is to make sure you have lots of different experiences and opportunities. But if I do bring up anything, you might feel judged or angry. Is there a way that we can discuss this that might make it go better?"

Get involved outside the home: I know how much this has helped me. When I feel stuck in my personal and family life, I refocus my energy outside the home. I find that when I take my foot off the gas pedal at home and apply it to a related but outside situation (such as mental health advocacy), I start to feel much better. You could consider checking out our initiative to address cellphones in school at AwayForTheDay.org.

IDEAS FOR CONVERSATION STARTERS:

1. How would the family feel about taking a non-judgemental tech time inventory? This would just be a way to gauge what the average daily time on different apps and screens is for each of us.
2. How about an experiment? What if we download and use the app Moment to calculate the time spent on phones and compare it to what Apple's iPhone Screen Time feature reports?
3. How about a role-playing exercise? Kids become parents. Parents become kids. See if the conversation provides new inroads into better understanding and a calmer home.

* * *

Co-Parenting Tech Time: Working Through Differences

Co-parenting screen time can be a real source of stress for parents who are married and even more so for those who are divorced.

I've come across several divorce lawyers who have included screen time in their co-parenting contracts. It's no surprise. Being the more lenient parent to curry favor with the child has been used for eons in divorced couples. Now, more often than not, the goodies are screen-related.

Most psychology frameworks emphasize the importance of parenting as a "united front." This is when parents come to a consensus behind closed doors and then present the agreement to the child. Here, I provide communication tools that can help parents find a compromise when they do not see eye to eye.

First, let me share what my husband and I have experienced, and continue to experience, when it comes to our different views on screen time rules. We have disagreements about how to best handle screen-related conflicts with our kids. The techniques I bring up below are ones that we have found helpful over the years.

GROUND DISCUSSIONS IN SCIENCE

First and foremost, try to ground your screen time conversations in data. For example, you and your partner can agree to read about recommendations regarding sleep and youth and why it is so important for physical, mental and academic well-being. Once you both know 36% of teens report waking up to check their phones at night, you may decide that your own childrens' phones should stay out of the bedroom.

CONSIDER SPLITTING THE DIFFERENCE

Adolescent and family psychologist, Laura Kastner, says that when parents are really divided about screen time rules, they split the difference. So if one parent is saying that four hours on the weekend is fine for video games and the other parent is set on just one hour, can they compromise at two and a half hours?

EMPLOY COMMUNICATION SKILLS

I have three communication skills that you may already use, but if you are like me, you will appreciate being reminded of them. The more I am reminded of communication tools, the greater chance that amid a conflict, my snappy lizard brain won't spout off, and instead I will pause and strategically employ my wiser wizard brain — which increases the chance of the conversation going smoothly.

1. So often we use "you" phrases — such as, "You let them use too many screens," "You don't understand how it's impacting them," "You are too lenient," or "You are too strict." This, of course, usually just makes people defensive and the conversation often goes nowhere. Rather

than this approach, try instead to lead with how you are feeling and explaining what you think should happen.

2. When parents disagree about screen use, the conversation about the rules and consequences can escalate quickly into the red zone. I've found what I call the "I Heard You Say" method to be extremely effective in helping all parties involved get a positive result.

   Ask the other parent to explain something that has been a point of conflict in parenting. Such as, "Can you help me understand why you believe Timmy does not need a set time for game-playing during the week?"

   Before they start to explain themself, let them know that you will repeat what they are saying back to them in order to ensure that you understand it correctly. Then, a few sentences in, try to repeat back as accurately as you can what they have just said. It is actually much harder than it sounds.

   When they seem finished, ask, "Is there anything else?" The goal is for them to feel heard. So calmly invite any more points they want to add.

   See it from their perspective: Say something like, "I can see by what you are saying why you feel the way you do." Hopefully, you can get a tiny bit into their shoes this way.

   Saying that you understand their perspective does not mean you agree with it. The magic is how much calmer and agreeable the other person becomes when they feel like they are really being heard. A therapist I once had told me, "People often want to be understood more than they want what they think they want." This might be true, but I think it is also true that people often want to be understood as much as they want what they think they want.

3. Psychologist and researcher Marcia Linehan developed an approach that I love. It is in the section of her work related to interpersonal relationships and has to do with asking for what you want. It is called the "DEAR MAN" method.

   D — Describe the situation, just the facts. For instance, "Timmy is having a hard time waking up in the morning because he is playing video games late into the night."

E — Express how you are feeling and your understanding of it. Use "I" statements. For example, "I am worried and concerned about him being able to pay attention in class."

A — Assert yourself by expressing what you do or do not want. Be direct. You might say, "I want video games to be off by 9 p.m. each night."

R — Reinforce how the change you are proposing can benefit everyone involved. Like: "I think Timmy will do better in school and we will have fewer fights in the house if the games are off at 9 p.m. I think this can also help our relationship because we get so angry about this most nights."

M — Stay mindful by staying on course and not bringing up other issues.

A — Appear confident. Doing so makes it harder for the other person to dismiss your request.

N — Negotiate with the goal to make both parties as satisfied as possible. If you want Timmy to turn the game off at 9 p.m. but your husband thinks it should be 10 p.m., why not 9:30 p.m.?

I use this method fairly often in charged situations at home and at work. I tend to use the DEAR part most often. For example, if I am about to enter the room of a patient that I know is going to ask for something that I do not think is in their best interest, like opioids, I will do a quick DEAR in my head and feel much more prepared when I enter the room.

Interestingly, teens who have learned DEAR MAN often use it for things they do NOT want. For instance, they might let someone know that they do not want them to text them all the time, or do not want them to write teasing comments on their posts.

GETTING OUTSIDE HELP CAN BE KEY

At times, parents will be in such conflict over tech time that trying to present a united front will be impossible. Kids are perceptive. It can be confusing for children and teens if parents try to pretend they are united, and yet all sorts of clues point otherwise. When this is happening, ask for help. Professional counselors can be essential when things have become especially toxic.

In some homes, managing screen time is the source of a lot of stress and tension. It can often be downright toxic. My friend Laura Kastner, author of "Wise Minded Parenting," always asks the parents she works with, "You may be right, but are you effective?"

No, sometimes we find that nothing we try to do works. We get stuck, and getting outside help is a great step. As mentioned earlier, I was happy to film the grandmother and caretaker of 12-year-old Chris as she worked with the counselor to help her to set effective boundaries and find ways to connect with her grandson. Eventually, Chris became more engaged with his pets and in *Screenagers*, we see him going with his grandmother into the pet store and having a good time.

One of the most common concerns I hear from parents is how they feel stressed about setting screen time limits for video games and trying to understand if there are underlying issues that things like gaming might be masking.

Set up a visit with someone who can mediate a talk with you and your teen — or even the whole family — by using some of the techniques in this book. Consider a grandparent, a counselor, a college advisor or a person the family admires who is a skillful mediator with their own children. Or, how about a leader from a religious center? The ideal situation is to work with a trained counselor, but they can be expensive and hard to find — particularly if school is out and you can't see a school counselor.

The intensity of the struggles, the fights and the rifts in relationships can be painful. If you are at your wits' end about screen time issues, seeking the help of a professional coach or counselor can be beneficial. Professionals can provide ideas on how to rethink strategies, which in itself can be valuable. They can help you adapt more effective communication skills, create systems that will work for your family and teach you tools for maintaining them. Counselors can help you think through whether a behavioral, emotional, or learning assessment of your child might be helpful. You might go with your child, by yourself, or just with your partner. A professional can be an incredible mediator, helping everyone to feel heard, which is KEY to resetting entrenched patterns.

Check with your child's school, or talk with your pediatrician or your own doctor to find such people. Insurance company websites also list providers. Counselors you seek do not need any special training around screen time issues in order to be effective mediators.

The painful truth is that finding a coach or a counselor can be hard. Many insurance companies only cover a minimal list of providers who may have very long waitlists. Many mental health professionals do not take insurance. This is partly because insurance companies grossly undervalue mental health care and reimburse at a very low rate. If the provider only accepts direct payments, they will give you a bill that you can submit to your insurance — assuming you have insurance. Hopefully, the insurance will help cover it, but there is often a significant deductible and other barriers. Erggg, so frustrating, I know. In the clinics where I see patients in Seattle, many do not have insurance, are unemployed and suffer from homelessness or other challenging situations.

Remember that coaching does not have to come from a professional. Consider reaching out to an insightful friend, a counselor in your religious faith, a support group and/or a trusted relative.

Does managing screen time in your house turn into shouting and slamming doors?

- Is there a specific issue regarding screen time where family members have a hard time budging from their own perspective on the matter?

- Can you recall a person who helped smooth out a misunderstanding between you and a friend when you had an argument — perhaps a teacher? What skills did that person have?

- Many influencers and celebrities talk openly about getting counseling. Do you know of any?

IDEAS FOR CONVERSATION STARTERS:

1. Do you have a friend who asks for things in a way that annoys you?
2. How about a friend who asks for things in a way you appreciate?
3. Think of someone who you feel really listens to you when you talk about anything emotional. What makes it clear that they are listening and caring?
4. Could you see yourself using the DEAR steps before asking something of someone?

. . .

Tech Tools To Help With Screen Time Limits

Rather than constantly repeating, "Time to shut it off," why not have your WiFi at home automatically turn off at a specific time? Fighting fire with fire can be helpful when it comes to technology. Using tech to manage tech for things like having an app automatically turn off at certain times, blocking inappropriate content on your devices, or, receiving helpful data on use activity can be really helpful. There are myriad apps and tools that can help you set up systems that reduce anxiety and struggles around screen time.

Many families have made these tools work for them and it is definitely worth a try to see if any may work for you and your family goals. However, there are sometimes issues with these apps and services that you should keep in mind. The biggest defense against the following shortcomings is continuing to have the types of conversations covered in this book so that children internalize the "whys" around having balanced and healthy screen time.

1. Setting up a new tool may be challenging. Roll up your sleeves and take a big breath because some of them can take a bit of work to set up. Remember, there are usually videos that can help with the process.

2. You are risking a cat-and-mouse dynamic, as some youth will look for ways around blocks.

3. You might gain a false sense of security. It is so tempting to want to believe things like, "Oh, I have a Net Nanny, so I don't need to talk about porn with my 11-year-old." Kids get information from screens in all sorts of places, so relying too heavily on any tech blockers is not smart.

4. They are far from perfect. For example, apps that measure time spent on devices use their own parameters to calculate time and usually, they do not explain their algorithms. For example, an app might

round up their calculations for use. I have done experiments with apps and recommend you do this with your family. For example, I record how much time I am spending on an app or on texting, and then I compare what I recorded to what Apple's Screen Time feature tells me. Times recorded are often quite different. Apple consistently calculates higher usage than I do. For instance, if I read a text on the phone for three seconds, the app might measure it as one minute. Apple does not report how it makes its calculations.

Here is a list of several systems that manage screen time, with brief descriptions.

Apple's Screen Time on iPhone and iPads
- Shows you how much time you and your kids spend on apps and websites
- Provides usage reports
- Sets limits on overall time
- Sets limits on specific apps
- Sets "downtimes"

Screen Time Parental Control — Parental control for Apple devices and Androids
- Sets time limits for enrolled devices
- Sets bedtime and school time restrictions for specific apps
- Pauses a device or gives bonus time
- Blocks all apps at lights out

Meet Circle WiFi router
- Connects with your WiFi router to manage every device on your home network and manage mobile devices everywhere
- Customizable settings for each family member to block content, set content filters and time limits on apps like Instagram, Snapchat, Fortnite, Netflix and more
- Pauses the Internet at the press of a button
- Finds balance by setting recurring Off Time and Bedtime schedules for your kids' devices

- Ability to give rewards for more screen time
- Checks activity by looking through usage and even tracks the location of your family's mobile devices

OurPact

- An app that parents put on their phone and their childrens' phones
- The control phone can block other phones for any period of time and unblock at any time
- Ability to set a recurring device schedule
- Ability to block specific apps

Moment

- Signature function on this app is the "Moment Coach" that provides strategies to help users reimagine their relationship with their phone
- Sets limits on screen time
- Tracks how much you use your phone during the day
- Gives usage reports

Pocket Points

- Provides incentive to to be off of the phones
- Used by colleges and high schools
- Gain points when you keep your phone locked while on campus
- Points can be used to get discounts and coupons to participating businesses

Bark

- Monitors social media
- Monitors texts
- Monitors emails
- Parental alerts
- Works with schools

unGlue

- Sets limits on screen time
- Sets a recurring use schedule on each device
- Provides usage reports

- Remotely turns off the internet to an individual device or to all devices
- Blocks adult content

Mobicip
- Sets limits on screen time
- Sets a recurring use schedule on each device
- Sets content filters
- Blocks apps and internet usage

NetSanity
- Available for iPhone and Android
- Remotely turns off the internet for an individual device
- Sets recurring device schedule
- Blocks adult content

Net Nanny
- Available for iPhone and Android
- Filters out adult content such as pornography
- Parents can put time limits on certain online activities
- Daily screen time usage stats can be viewed

FamilyTime
- Available for iPhone and Android
- Geofences locations
- Tracks device locations
- Provides usage reports
- Sets recurring device schedule
- Blocks adult content

Mobile Fence
- Parental controls
- GPS tracking for Android devices

Verizon Family Base
- Monitors wireless activity
- Sets usage limits

AT&T Secure Family
- Manages internet and email activity on computers

T-Mobile Family Mode
- Manages minutes, messages and downloads on phones

XFINITY TV Online Parental Controls
- Restricts what children can watch online

IDEAS FOR CONVERSATION STARTERS:

1. Do you think it will be easier to turn off certain tech at certain times in the future? Or since it does not behoove tech companies to have their apps turned off, might it not change that much?
2. How could such a tech tool help in our home?

· · ·

How to model improving screen time balance

Over the years, many parents have come up to me at screenings and said in an exasperated tone, "I just know I am part of the problem ... I should be modeling screen time better."

They are often surprised by my response. Rather than say something like, "Yes, yes, I know we all need to do that better." I step in with a concrete suggestion for an action they can take right away. Here is what I suggest.

As a physician working in behavior change for 25 years, I know that the most effective goals are small and well-defined. When I hear a patient say something like, "My goal is just to eat better." I know that it is a doomed plan. A well-known fact about behavior change is that choosing a clearly defined goal and using resources to set it up for success increases the chance for change that is noticeable and sustainable.

So rather than have a vague goal like, "I should model screen time better," pick a specific goal and then model how you are going to reach it. I believe this is an extremely valuable gift — helping youth learn how they can change their behavior.

Let me give an example from my own life of what I mean. I had the habit of reflexively going onto my laptop to work after dinner. Did I really want to do this almost every night of the week? No, I didn't. Furthermore, I did not want to model this behavior for my kids.

I decided I wanted to change my behavior. I decided I was going to try not to log on to my computer after dinner on Tuesdays, and instead treat myself to a creative and relaxing time. I wanted to make earrings and be more available to the family. Sure enough, I failed miserably for the first few weeks. On the first Tuesday, I completely forgot and automatically went on my computer. The next Tuesday, I did not do enough prep, so that night I still had a bunch of emails I had to send.

The key part of my failures is that along the way, I told my kids what was happening. I shared with them my setbacks and what actions I was going to take to prevent further failures. After the first week, I put a big reminder for myself on the refrigerator. After the second week, I put a note on my to-do list for Tuesday mornings so I was sure to be done with emails pre-dinner.

I also used this opportunity to talk about one of my favorite models of behavior change found in Joshua Klapow's book, "Living Smart." It goes like this:

S — Set a goal.

M — Monitor progress by making a note on a calendar each time you succeed.

A — Arrange for success. For example, I put my beading tray out on the kitchen table on Tuesday mornings so that I would know exactly where it is when when my screen-free night arrived.

R — Recruit people to help you or hold you accountable. It would have been fun if I had found a friend who also wanted to go screen-free on Tuesday nights. I didn't do that, but I did tell some friends my goal and ask them to hold me accountable. Wanting the ego lift of being able to report successes to them gave me some extra motivation. Honestly, though, knowing my kids were witnesses to my attempts was the strongest motivation. When I had slip-ups, I would ask them for their suggestions of what I could do, and they loved giving me advice.

T — Treat. My favorite part! Choose a personal reward you value, like having a special dessert or going to see a movie.

Using this model, I set my goal of not going on screens after dinner on Tuesdays, and I got my things out.

My suggestion is to pick one thing you want to change about screen time use and share that with your kids.

Here are some examples of behavior changes with tech that I have heard from parents, and the first one is my very own experience.

- Can you share one of your own screen time goals with your children or students? And then can you commit to checking in and updating them on the goal (being accountable) in the near future? Remember, it is just as important to share your failures as it is to share your successes because the message is that behavior change is hard, particularly when it concerns the constant enticement of screens. The important thing is that you share with your kids how you are learning from your failures, such as by modifying the goal or setting up reminders, etc.

- Here are some examples of behavior-change goals with tech that I have heard from parents: "After checking my email, my goal is to turn off the WiFi on my computer for one hour each weekday morning so I can get my writing done and not be tempted to check my email." And this one: "I am going to try to resist checking my phone when we are setting up for dinner and at the table so I get to talk with my family in a more connected way."

Talk openly about the goal you are working on. Even ask for your childrens' help. Kids want to feel like they matter, so they love it when we go to them for advice or help. Most importantly, we are modeling that behavior change is hard and that we often need other people to help us.

- Now, all this is not to say that our day-to-day modeling of screen time use is not important, it is! When I ask students of all ages at assemblies who think their parents are on their devices too much anywhere from 50% to 75% of the hands go up.

Interestingly, I have been surprised by the data I have seen in two surveys showing that over 70% of parents feel they are modeling screen time just fine. The American Psychological Association's 2017 Stress in America survey found that 72% of parents somewhat or strongly agree that they model a healthy relationship with technology for their children.

First, a moment of validation to all the great modeling adults do all the time. There are lots of ways we model good tech behavior — I see it all the time when I am out. People make eye contact and talk to the cashier at a store; families share a meal with no devices in sight.

But it is true that for kids and teens, experiencing what they see as hypocrisy is hard for them. There is a good chance you have heard statements such as these from your child, "Well you are always on YOUR phone," or "You watch a lot of shows, why can't I watch more?"

I have three final suggestions regarding our use of tech and the issue of modeling to our kids.

POINT OUT WHEN YOU ARE ON SCREENS FOR WORK

Getting in the habit of saying out loud what you are doing on screens can help your kids see that a lot of what you do is work-related. Perhaps you have to respond to a work colleague or a PTA planning question. You might say something like, "Excuse me for a second, work needs a response." This not only reinforces that you are on your device for work, but also models the great digital etiquette of explaining why you have to excuse yourself rather than just "disappearing" into your device, oblivious to those around you.

POINT OUT THE THINGS YOU CONSCIOUSLY WORK TO DO TO HAVE A BETTER BALANCE WITH YOUR TECH TIME

Rather than assume they see you doing things, you can actually point them out by saying things like, "I just put my phone on do not disturb mode now that we are all going for this walk." Or, "I took two game apps off my phone today because I found that I was playing them during break at work and I realize I feel better if I walk around for a bit instead."

ASK ABOUT THEIR FEELINGS

Asking our kids how they feel about our current screen time is key. Asking them about what ways they feel we aren't available to them, screen-related or not, is such a powerful way to express we care. There is a moment in *Screenagers* when Tessa tells me, "Anytime I come in and you're near the computer or trying to multitask, you seem pretty distracted when you have your computer with you."

This motivated me to be more aware when she entered my office. Whenever possible, I would try to look up and say, "Hi," with real acknowledgement. There is only so long that Tessa will be living at home and walking into my office — the more I can be present when she wants my attention, the more she will know I am available.

Discussions are so important, particularly in light of research that consistently shows that there are a large percentage of kids who say they wish their parents were on screens less and paid more attention to them. For example, in a survey of 8 to 13-year-olds, 54% of them felt that their parents checked their devices too often and 32% felt unimportant when their parents were distracted by their phones.[4]

IDEAS FOR CONVERSATION STARTERS:

1. How do I model screen time? What messages do my actions with my devices signal to you?
2. Have you seen me try to change a habit, screen time or not?
3. What do you think of the "SMART" approach to behavior change?
4. Is there anything about my time on screens that you want me to try to change?

Chapter Seven:

Challenging Conversations

Who feels completely confident talking to their kids about online pornography or sexting? These are just a few of the challenging topics that our tech revolution has brought to the table.

I recall a couple of years ago when my son Chase showed me the Discover feature on Snapchat, which grabs content from sources like Cosmopolitan and BuzzFeed and makes it accessible to anyone. Some of it, particularly content coming from Cosmopolitan, contains sexually explicit material. One story entitled, "Sex Positions & Kama Sutra" had how-to illustrations of threesomes, phone sex and positions that "pair really well with weed."

Needless to say, I was pretty shocked and upset — many youth have Snapchat, and I learned that the app makes it pretty hard to turn off the Discover feature.

Meanwhile, how do we talk with them about their social lives when they feel like we don't understand their new social world, including social media?

I am the first to say I still have a long way to go to figure this all out. Take flirting, for example — it is more complicated for teens to navigate now that social media plays such a big role.

According to a study by the Pew Research Center, "Teens, Technology and Romantic Relationships," 6% of teens with dating experience have sent flirtatious messages to someone they like.[1] Thirty-five percent of teen girls surveyed had blocked or unfriended someone who was flirting in a way that made them uncomfortable — which is double the 16% of boys who had reported doing this. 10% of teens in a relationship reported that their partner used the internet to pressure them to engage in unwanted sexual activity.

Often, teens will make comments on people's posts, saying things like, "You are cute" and other compliments. Teens tell me that they would not say these things face-to-face, but it is fun online. Meanwhile, they can often tell if someone is interested in them just based on whether they send a Snapchat or a direct text (a direct text carries more weight). This is confusing!

There are times when things go really wrong, and this is something all of us parents worry about. I interviewed a high school girl who I will call Emma. She shared her story with me. In middle school, a boy she liked kept asking her to send a "pic" on social media. She felt conflicted, but eventually she sent him a picture of herself in her bra without thinking about it very much. Immediately after sending it, she felt regret.

Unfortunately, the boy decided to share it with a few friends and from there, it started to spread around to the other students she went to school with. When Emma went to school, she was mortified. She thought that everyone was looking at her and she felt incredible shame. She developed significant depressive thoughts that became stronger and stronger over the next few weeks.

Here is the part of the story that really impacted me. She told me that she desperately wanted to tell her mother what was going on, but at the same time, she was terrified her mom would be mad and disappointed in her. She was also worried that her mom would take away her ability to contact her friends by confiscating her phone and computer.

Finally, she told her mom. Emma's mom told me how incredibly sad she felt hearing that this happened to Emma and that she didn't feel safe enough to come and talk to her. She said she felt awful that Emma had to "carry that around by herself" for so long. With her mother's love and support and professional counseling, Emma got much better.

We want to do all we can to increase the chance that our kids will come to us with issues. We want them to think of us as their allies. When we talk about challenging topics with our kids, such as pornography and sexting, we convey to them that we can handle these topics. It is not our goal to overreact and invoke punishments that cause social isolation. When we hit this balance, they trust us more and more.

Parents sometimes say to me: "Why even bother? My kid would never come and talk with me about these types of topics. I would never talk with my parents about these things."

But if you work hard to stay in a non judgmental head space and have short, caring conversations, there is a good chance your kids will talk with you about things you did not feel comfortable talking to your own parents about.

Drugs, Alcohol and Social Media

Police in Marin County, California arrested a person who was selling drugs. What made this 2019 arrest different from most other drug busts is that this person was selling drugs through Snapchat. Yes, the same Snapchat that our kids use to send selfies to friends. It's happening on Instagram, too; dealers use code words, hashtags, emojis and display actual pictures of what they have to offer.

"Drugs on social media are incredibly prevalent," said Josie Sanguinetti, school resource officer for the Marin County Sheriff's Department.[2] "Every high school and some middle schools in the county have been touched by this."

A San Rafael Police Department's narcotics officer told me that he could find marijuana, Xanax, prescription painkillers and Molly (MDMA) within an hour of searching on social media.

Simple searches with hashtags like #weed4sale, #oxy or #painpills will pull up story after story on Instagram or Snapchat with pictures of drugs, cash and emojis. According to law enforcement officials, the Christmas tree, fire, and the dollar sign emojis are codes for drugs for sale. Requests get left in comments or you can direct message the dealer. With the right language, you can receive a response. Dealers often request that the conversations about price, quality and delivery happen on encrypted messaging apps like Kik or WhatsApp. Deals are executed through electronic payment apps like Venmo or PayPal, and then the product is mailed to the buyer, or it gets delivered in person and paid for in cash.

Although Instagram and Snapchat have made some efforts to ban certain hashtags and search terms, they cannot flag all posts.

"We're not yet sophisticated enough to tease apart every post to see if it's trying to sell someone illegal drugs or they are taking Xanax because they are stressed out," Carolyn Everson, Facebook's vice president for global marketing solutions, told The Washington Post.[3] "Obviously, there is some stuff that gets through that is totally against our policy, and we're getting better at it."

Facebook (which owns Instagram) created a blog post listing of the steps they are taking to combat the sale of drugs on their platforms.[4] It is interesting to learn what they are doing. For example, Facebook is developing technology to recognize hidden words in images — a technique sellers use to pass on information without being detected.

Here are other examples from the Facebook blog post of how they are working to stop online drug transactions:

"We block and filter hundreds of terms associated with drug sales. People mostly find this content by searching for it. So we prevent these terms being suggested in search as well as limit the discovery of hashtags related to drug sales on Instagram. If someone begins to type a hashtag that might be related to drugs, we block the remainder of it."

"We've made it easy for people to flag bad content so we can quickly review and remove it."

"We're working to ensure that our services are also used to help educate people about the risks, prevent drug misuse, and raise awareness of the opioid epidemic. We work with the Substance Abuse & Mental Health Services Administration to provide addiction support when people look for help or try to find drugs on Facebook and Instagram. We also work directly with law enforcement and/or emergency responders, routinely responding to valid law enforcement requests for information, and we notify them of emergencies whenever someone may be at serious risk of harm."

So what can a parent do? Talking calmly about drugs and alcohol sold online is important for many reasons. For one, bringing up these topics signals to your child that this is something they can and should ask you about. Research demonstrates that in families where these topics get discussed, youth are less prone to risky behaviors with drugs and alcohol.[5] Here are some suggestions for talking about drugs and alcohol.

GIVE A "PARENT POP QUIZ"

In terms of talking about drugs on the internet, one suggestion is giving a "parent pop quiz." Giving short pop quizzes is a technique I use with my teens sometimes to start a conversation about a challenging topic. When asked in a lighthearted way, I find this really helps with their engagement. The following is an example:

Question: True or False? If someone starts to type a hashtag on Instagram that might be related to drug sales, Instagram blocks the remainder of it.
Answer: True.

Question: True or False? When sellers of drugs try to hide words in images to advertise their activities, Facebook is very good at finding those words.
Answer: False, the Facebook algorithms are not great at finding hidden words in images, but programmers are working to improve it.

REMEMBER TO TALK ABOUT THE "WHYS" OF SUBSTANCE USE

When it comes to talking about drugs and alcohol in general, make sure to not just give all the negatives, but also include a few of the"whys" around substance use. As a parent, it is so tempting to avoid mentioning the "high" feeling and the decrease in anxiety that often comes as a result of drug use, because we do not want to act like we are promoting it. I know this has been true for me. We get more buy-in from our teens when we discuss a fuller perspective. If we come from a place of "just say no" rather than having fuller, more in-depth conversations, we risk limiting later conversations or hindering their chances of coming to us to talk about issues they or a friend may be having.

DISCUSS THE MESSAGES AROUND SUBSTANCE USE IN MEDIA AS A WHOLE

Another important topic to raise with your youth is how drug use gets portrayed in the media. When my son was in eighth grade, he watched a show about a superhero called "Arrow." I remember watching an episode with him where the characters were drinking alcohol in a bar. There was tension in the room and they were doing shots. I was so upset that this show, geared towards tweens, included this. It led to a conversation I had later on with my son about how males on screen rarely talk about what they feel, and how they are often shown drinking alcohol in scenes where they are angry.

I have also reinforced with my kids that even if they do not think portrayals of alcohol and drug use impact them, research shows the opposite. For example, in one study, middle schoolers were asked to carry handheld devices for 14 days and to log ads they came across about alcohol.[6] They were also questioned at various times throughout this study about their pro-alcohol beliefs. Indeed, their views were more positive after viewing the ads.

DO SOME "NORM-SETTING"

It turns out that youth tend to significantly overestimate the percentage of peers who use drugs and alcohol or engage in risky sexual behaviors. Studies find that when youth learn true percentages, the chance of them partaking in these activities are lowered.[7] Providing accurate data is referred to as norm-setting.

Ask your tween or teen what percentage of high schoolers they think have never consumed alcohol. In a recent study, it was 44% of high schoolers. I bet your child thought the percentage was much lower than this. Public health initiatives teaching students real figures have been shown to reduce drinking rates.[8]

DISCUSS THE RISKS OF SUBSTANCES

It can be very effective to start by asking your youth to list the risks they are aware of. It is particularly important to discuss the new distressing reality that fentanyl can be mixed into any pill, and that a very low dose of it can be lethal. I am pleased that college students tell me there is a growing awareness of this issue and that many students have no interest in ingesting a drug in pill form because the risk is too great.

When it comes to alcohol, one of the things I have wanted my kids to know is the fact that alcohol dramatically impairs decision-making skills and intoxicated sexual encounters can be regrettable and even dangerous. I know from research that when surveyed, less than half of teens say that their parents ever discussed this topic with them.

My kids often hear me talk about the fact that it is common for girls to hope to win the attention of boys they like by engaging in sexual acts, only to feel used afterward. Being under the influence of marijuana, alcohol and other drugs can increase the chance that such a situation will occur. Feelings of being used can negatively impact a girl's feeling of self-worth and can also be long lasting. Of course, these scenarios can happen to boys too, but they are far less common.

Another point I have repeatedly discussed with my kids is that just one alcoholic drink can make the rational, decision-making part of their brains — the prefrontal cortex — switch off. And then, the emotion center of their brain will start to run the show, saying things like, "Have another drink, and why not another?" I often suggest that if they or their friends choose to drink, it is wise to have safeguards in place so that the emotional part of their brain does not wreak havoc. For instance, work out a buddy system with a friend to keep tabs on each other to prevent this. Or, wait a significant amount of time after one drink before considering another.

IDEAS FOR CONVERSATION STARTERS:

1. The internet can be a tool for spreading important public health messages. Have you seen anything about the risks of drug use?
2. Have you seen drugs advertised for sale on social media?
3. What ways are drugs or alcohol displayed in photos of people you know? How about in photos of people you don't know? What are some of the risks of such posts?
4. If you were to create a PSA or meme discouraging drug use, what might it be?

• • •

Talking About Sexting
With Non-Judgemental Curiosity

It is natural for young people to want attention and to be intrigued by bodies and sexuality. With all this exploratory sexual behavior, there are risks, and parents like me often find ourselves asking, "What if?"

> *"What if my kid or teen sends a picture? What if their picture gets shared without consent? What if their picture ends up in the wrong hands or the authorities find out? What if they get sent one?"*

With the natural anxiety that parents have, it is no wonder that youth clam up so often when we approach this topic.

So let me offer some new ways to consider approaching it.

When talking about sexting, it is key to not shame sexual feelings. There are many developmentally normal reasons youth will want to send or ask for images — having this desire does not make them a bad person. It can also be equally normal to not have that urge. For example, many teens say they have had no interest in posting or sending anything that looks sexy.

As always when talking with your kids, let them talk first whenever possible. Tossing some of these ideas into a conversation in a matter-of-fact way can be a great approach to the idea of risk without getting into a judgmental place where your child may shut down.

"Sexting" has become a word that many parents dread, but we must face it. It is a reality that some teens, and even preteens, send sexualized photos, videos or messages.

Having productive conversations about sexting with our kids or teens can be challenging. For one thing, they feel like we just "don't get" their world, so why should they talk with us about it?

Given that there is some truth to this, (we did not grow up with sexting) one approach that I find helpful is to bring up the subject with a truly curious, matter-of-fact type of attitude.

Useful, curious questions include, "What is your understanding about sexting?" or, "What things get tossed around about the topic of sexting?" When you give information, such as mentioning results from a research study, a useful follow-up question is, "Does this ring true?"

Here are questions you may find helpful in talking with the youth in your life about sexting. These conversations may start at around age 10 or so, but of course, you need to decide what age is best. If you have already discussed this topic with your teen, some of this can still get used in order to readdress it.

WHAT DO YOU THINK ABOUT THE WORD "SEXTING?"

Just asking them to express their views on that word can be a neutral starting point.

Personally, I have never liked the word "sexting." It feels like too-strong a word for a lot of what is actually going on these days. When we use the word "sexting" to describe certain images, I worry that we get into a blame-and-shame mindset that can prevent constructive conversations. Some images that we label as "sexting" could more appropriately be referred to as simply "physically revealing."

HOW SHOULD RESEARCHERS DEFINE SEXTING?

Definitions of sexting are all very similar to this one:

> *"Sexting is the sharing of sexually explicit images, videos or messages through electronic means."*

HOW COMMON DO YOU THINK SEXTING IS?

Different surveys report varying prevalence data. One group of researchers combined 38 studies on sexting and reported that about 30% of teens had received some type of sext, and that 15% had sent at least one.[9] It especially concerns me that 10% say they have shared with others the sext they received without the consent of the person who sent it.

WHAT ARE REASONS PEOPLE WOULD CHOOSE TO SEND A SEXT?

Sexting can be a form of flirting. Sexting can be about wanting to attract attention from someone attractive. It may be done in hopes of seeking approval to gain self-confidence. With older teens, sexts are often sent between people in a committed relationship.

WHAT ARE THE REASONS PEOPLE WOULD CHOOSE TO ASK FOR A SEXT?

It is more common for a boy to ask a girl to send a sext, but it can be the other way around and also can occur between kids of the same gender. There are many reasons kids ask for sexts. Here are some of the main ones: A person may ask because they are attracted to the other person and really want to have such an image. They may believe that by asking, they are complimenting the person. A girl may want to be flirty and ask a guy for a sext. A guy may ask a guy for a sext if they are in a relationship and want this type of intimacy. There are times when groups of tween or teen males will ask girls for these images in order to collect the largest number of sexts among their friend group. It is a sort of contest, and they use the acquired sexts as bragging rights.

WHAT WOULD MAKE SEXTING NOT RISKY?

One way to get the conversation going — rather than to scare them about the riskiness of sexting right away — is to flip it around and talk about how to ensure that sexting is not risky.

- **Complete trust** — One needs to be 100% sure that there is trust in the relationship before sending a sext. According to a 2016 survey from Statistics Brain, "48% of young adult women and 46% of young adult men say it is common for nude or semi-nude photos to get shared with people other than the intended recipient."[10]

    Can the person sending the photo fully trust that the other person will not share it with others?

If the two people involved are dating, that sense of trust is most likely high. But what happens if things go south?

What relationships have you witnessed where things were so close and then completely changed? How could a person be 100% sure that their partner would not share the photo with someone else in the case of a messy breakup?

- **Consent** — If a person is being pressured to send a photo and they finally do, have they done so with their full, legitimate consent? What happens if a person sends a photo to someone who wasn't asking for it? For example, some boys will send girls photos of their penises without asking if the girls are OK with it. I have heard girls say how this makes them feel shocked, angry and some they even use the word "disgusted." They say if they never asked for the photos, they definitely did not want them. It is incredibly important to receive enthusiastic consent before both sending and asking for sexts.

- **Chance** — What if, by chance, someone gets into a person's phone that has sexts saved in the camera roll. In many states, it is illegal for teens to send these types of photos to other teens, and if the phone is hacked, the teen could get in serious trouble. Even if the teen doesn't get in trouble, the person who hacked into the phone might begin to circulate the photo. This is a factor that is very hard to control, so people involved should try to work out a system to lower the chances of a third party discovering sexts.

What I find so useful in this type of conversation is that ultimately the risks of sexting will come up but it is not the entry point.

IDEAS FOR CONVERSATION STARTERS:

1. Why would people send a sext?
2. Why would people ask for a sext?
3. What would it take to make sexting risk-free?
4. Can you imagine some of the risks of sexting? What could happen with those photos?

. . .

A Confusing Legal System and Sexting

We want our kids to understand the potential legal problems and consequences that come with sending or receiving sexual images. Talking about the quirks and faults of the legal system can provide a good inroad.

Consider starting this conversation with this approach that I have found surprisingly useful when talking about things like sexuality with my teens. I call it the "Painless Parent Pop Quiz Approach." I say to my teen, "Hey, time for a quick Painless Parent Pop Quiz", and then I ask them a few questions. I call it "painless" because they will not be graded or judged poorly in any way if they get answers wrong. So here is a Painless Parent Pop Quiz that you could try:

Question: "Do all states have laws about sexting?"
Answer: No

Question: "In which states is it riskier to engage in any type of sexting behavior — a state that has specific sexting laws or ones that do not?"
Answer: It is riskier in states that do not.
Explanation: When they don't have specific laws, it is actually more concerning because the state can treat the situation as a child pornography case, where the consequences can be much more severe.

A REAL-LIFE EXAMPLE

A few years ago, two 16-year-olds from North Carolina (a state that didn't have sexting laws in place) were arrested and charged with multiple felony counts of sexual exploitation of a minor under the state's child pornography laws.[11] Their crime? The boyfriend and girlfriend sent nude photos to each other via text. They were charged as adults, could have faced four to 10 years in prison, and, if convicted, would have to register as sex offenders. The kids agreed to plea bargains that reduced their charges to misdemeanors. Still, a very scary situation. The teens had no idea of the risks they were taking in exchanging these photos — the last thing they wanted was to get in trouble and to break a law.

In this instance, if the couple had been in a state with sexting laws — such as Arizona, Florida or Arkansas — they would have most likely been charged with a misdemeanor and given the chance to prove that their intent was not criminal. Sexting legislation is designed to deter teens from sexting with consequences including education and less severe sentences.

It turns out that about half of the states do not have sexting laws, so child pornography can be claimed. Examples of states that do not have specific sexting laws include California, Virginia, Oregon, Wyoming, Montana and Mississippi. You can go on this website: https://cyberbul-lying.org/sexting-laws to see what is happening in your state. Looking at this site with your child is a good way to start talking about these issues.

ANOTHER REAL-LIFE EXAMPLE

I discovered the website www.sexetc.org, which is full of lots of import-ant information and videos created by teens and experts that teach sex-related topics.

On their site, they provide a student's email that I want to share. In a post about sexting, an 18-year-old writes in about how his 17-year-old girlfriend sent him a naked photo and asks if it's true that he could be charged with child pornography. The website answers their question and makes suggestions of what to do:[12]

> *"Yes, what your friend told you is true. Naked pictures of people under the age of 18 are considered child pornography. When people hear the words "child pornography," they may think of small children who cannot give permission to have their picture taken and might not understand what is happening. People may not think of someone who is 17 as a child. The reality is that, legally, the picture can be considered child pornography. There can be legal consequences for showing such a picture to someone else or for having possession of this kind of picture. The best thing to do is to delete the picture and talk with your partner about why*

you think taking and/or sharing nude photos might not be such a great idea anymore."

Do laws influence behaviors? Understanding current policies are important, but how does understanding translate into less risky behaviors? Talk with youth about whether they think all these laws and policies are making an impact and decreasing risk.

What seems to peak teens' attention is when they hear about how it is common for people to regret sending a sext after doing so. This is what research by Dr. Elizabeth Englander uncovered. She told me:

> *"Most kids have friends who have sexted but legal consequences are so rare that it's likely this will strike them as a scare tactic. Instead, parents can emphasize that kids who send these photos often regret it, feeling scared, depressed or even traumatized. That's more likely to ring a bell and feel truthful to them."*

IDEAS FOR CONVERSATION STARTERS:

1. Are you aware that it is against the law to send and receive nude pictures, even if they are from your girlfriend or boyfriend?
2. If you were creating laws on this topic, how would you do it?
3. If you were to write a letter to a younger student, what advice would you give them about issues surrounding the taking and sharing of revealing and suggestive photos and videos?

· · ·

Girls Feeling Pressured Online

Sexual exploration is a natural part of growing up, which is so much about being seen as cool and desirable by peers. Girls get a lot of attention for their looking "sexy." Now with social media, they can also get unwanted solicitations.

I hear from some preteen and teen girls that they or their friends have been asked by boys via social media to send nude pictures, also called "pics." Before we delve more into this, I want to say that there are also many tweens and teens I talk to who say they have not encountered this, like this high school senior who told me this:

> *"With regards to sending 'pics' and all of the stuff along those lines, my friends and I have been extremely lucky with nothing bad happening to us. For me personally, I never ever wanted to send anything because I was always taught 'post with a purpose.' I think it can be super easy to think that by sending a photo to one person, it will stay with that one person. And maybe it does, but once the picture is sent, it is thrown up into the cloud of all your social media history. I have always been extremely hesitant about sending anything because if the chance that my social media information was breached and became public, I would never want anything bad to be put out."*

A MIDDLE SCHOOL STORY

The sad reality is that this can and does happen. This is something that a high school girl shared with me regarding her younger sister. She told me:

> *"When my sister was in seventh grade, she was pressured by a guy to send a bare chest photo and the boy saved the photo without her knowledge. Nothing came from it until mid-eighth grade, when an anonymous Instagram account, @hername_nudes, was made. They had posted the photo publicly with her tagged. They then started threatening her through Instagram DM, saying they were going to request to follow everyone she knew so then they would all see. My sister had to get my mom and the school involved to be able to pursue further action in order for it to stop. She has never sent anything since and still feels personally invaded and sad from the situation."*

I feel deeply sad for the few girls I have heard of this happening to over the past years.

When girls get asked to send photos, they can feel extremely pressured, especially when they are being asked repeatedly for them. Also, they may get a threat stating that if they do not send the photo, there will be rumors spread about them. Another scenario is when someone gets an explicit photo of a girl and then uses the image to blackmail her.

A HIGH SCHOOL STORY

Let me share another story about a freshman boy who tried to use a photo as a tool of blackmail.

In this situation the boy (I will call him Jim) asked a girl (I will call her Julie) over social media if she would go out with him. She knew he had a girlfriend, and she was upset that he asked her out. She contacted a friend to talk about the situation and get advice on whether she should tell Jim's girlfriend.

Later, Jim heard that she was asking for the other girl's advice. He was worried that this would get back to his girlfriend. In what I imagine was a poorly thought-out move of desperation, Jim sent a selfie of a nude girl holding her arm over her breasts to Julie. You couldn't really make out the face in the photo. Jim said he would tell everyone it was a photo of her and that he would disseminate it if she didn't say she was lying about him asking her out.

Julie saw that given the strange angle of the photo, it could actually pass as her. She became really upset — she was 100% sure it wasn't her. She had never sent anyone such a photo. She was furious and scared that he was threatening to broadcast it out.

The girl told her parents and they went to the school counselor. The counselor worked with Julie to support her and make sure she felt safe. The counselor and others at the school talked with Jim and his parents. They also spoke alone with Jim so that like Julie, he could open up about his feelings, regrets and so forth. He was suspended from school for a few days.

I share that as an example of a high school story that is not too extreme. There are several stories of situations that are much more upsetting.

Sextortion is when a person has an image or video of someone, and threatens to circulate those images into the public if certain things are or are not done. I know of situations where older teens used images to get other teens to do sexual acts. These situations are rare but of course heartbreaking, and we want to prevent them in any way possible.

WHAT CAN A PARENT DO?

1. Remember that being pressured is the exception, not the norm. Although it happens, it is a small percentage of what actually happens online. — make sure to say that so your kids know you are coming from a realistic viewpoint.

2. We need to arm girls with ways to respond to pressures. Talk about the fact that a study has shown that teens are more likely to do these things from their bedroom and at nighttime — which means that private spaces and sleepiness can both be factors. So talk about that insight. Just having that awareness can lead to the few seconds of thought that can stop them from taking an action they might regret.

3. Be a safe zone — tweens and teens often tell me that they don't tell a parent about any issues such as these because they are so worried their phone and other devices will be taken away for a long time, and then they would feel cut off from their friends. By giving reassurance that you understand their fears before anything like this comes up can make the difference between hearing about a situation and not.

4. Let me share this advice that came to me from the older sister who shared the story of her sister above. Reading this to your child can be a great way to impart ideas without them coming from you. This 12th-grade girl wrote:

> *"I would tell your child that even if whoever they sent it to doesn't screenshot it, that doesn't mean that another picture wasn't taken on another device. I have heard many stories of boys taking pictures of nudes from their iPads, computer photo booths or a friend's phone. My last little bit of advice is that if a girl decides to send them, because we know that what you say won't always*

stop them, NEVER INCLUDE YOUR FACE IN THE PICTURE. If a nude has the person's face in it, then there is no way that if the picture is leaked it can be denied. I can not stress it enough. Do not include your face within the picture because that is only giving more ammo to the person receiving it."

The more we can let our girls and boys know that we want to support and help them first and foremost, the more likely they are to come to us for help when they need it. Rather than allowing ourselves the knee-jerk reaction of a freak out, we will work to stay calm, see things more from their perspective and take a 360-degree view. Sharing our goal to support them several times before an incident ever happens can really help.

IDEAS FOR CONVERSATION STARTERS:

1. Have you heard of times when girls have been pressured into sending sexy photos?
2. What are some of the feelings girls might experience when this happens?
3. What are some reasons guys may pressure girls to send photos?
4. Should health classes discuss these issues, or should they just be for home discussion?

Talking With Younger Kids About Pornography

Of all the topics I have written about over the years, I continue to be incredibly saddened by the guinea-pig position our kids are in right now having access to all manners of pornography. It's not just "sexual content" and it's not only soft-core porn. Hardcore porn is just a click away.

It is so tempting to believe that our kids won't be exposed to porn. It is true that blockers can be installed, but we always have to assume that they won't work 100% of the time. Also, the fact is our kids will be on screens with others in all sorts of settings, meaning we can't control all the devices our kids will come in contact with. Exposure to pornography is always possible.

For her book, "Boys and Sex," Peggy Orenstein interviewed over 100 boys between the ages 16 and 24 and found they were first exposed to porn at around age 9.[13] She writes, " ... often the first exposure was unbidden: older brothers (or older brother's friends) spun around a smartphone screen ... to freak them out." She found that intentional searches for pornography started around sixth to eighth grade.

As Ornstein writes so powerfully:

> *"Porn raises the question about how young people's erotic imaginations get shaped long before they've even so much as had a good-night kiss: the impact it may have on desire, arousal, behavior, sexual ethics and their understanding of gender, race, and power in sexual expression."*

Several years ago, my good friend called me very upset. Her 10-year-old daughter had gone to a sleepover with three other girls, one of whom was a few years older than her. When her daughter came home, she was unusually quiet and withdrawn and stayed that way for two days.

Finally, her daughter came to her with teary eyes and told her how the older girl had shown them videos on her phone of two women taking a shower together, and another of a man and a woman. She was very upset.

My friend said to me, "She was only 10, I didn't know I needed to start talking with her about all this already, and I had no idea what to do in this situation."

Over the years, several parents have told me about their kids seeing porn while on elementary or middle school playgrounds, via other kids' phones.

I found the following exchange so ironic. My friend's twin boys went to their middle school principal one day because they were upset with the school policy that allowed everyone to be on their phones during lunch. They told her they missed having time with their friends, who were now all on their phones during lunch instead of playing. The principal realized that she had been focusing her efforts on the school dress code because she thought that was what was distracting the kids. She realized from this exchange that the phones were causing a bigger distraction. That school eventually changed their phone policy to one where students were required to put their phones away for the day. The thing that got me about the story is that, as a society, we put a lot of energy into dress code issues — especially monitoring and regulating whether a girl's outfit is too sexy for school — and yet intensely graphic videos are readily accessible by kids on our schoolyards.

The bottom line is, no matter what your beliefs and feelings are about pornography in general, porn is not for children. We don't know how their access to these images and videos will shape their ideas about love and sex, but we do know that pornography is readily available to them and that they will likely be exposed to it. Young kids may be scared, disgusted, interested or excited by images of porn. Likely, they will have a combination of these responses. We know for sure that they have no larger context to analyze or even understand what they are seeing — as their parents, we need to help them navigate this. There is no way around it. It's our duty to talk with our young kids about porn.

TIPS FOR TALKING ABOUT PORN WITH YOUNGER KIDS

Knowing precisely what to tell your kids about porn and what age they will be ready for this conversation is impossible to recommend because every child and home is different. The goal is to start bringing it up early, usually when kids are in elementary school, so they know about these issues and that you will be there to support them if they encounter them..

HERE ARE SOME COMMUNICATION APPROACHES
TO HELP YOUR CONVERSATIONS

1. Consistently convey the message that curiosity and wanting to understand people, bodies and sexuality is normal. Let them know that you are available to answer their questions now and as they grow up.

2. Point out the positives in affectionate relationships as your children are growing up. For example, if you see a teenage couple holding

hands and laughing together, consider saying something like, "It is so great seeing people in a fun relationship."

3. Consider reviewing videos that help raise this topic with kids. If you think it would be appropriate, then watch the video with your child and discuss it. For example, Amaze.org's YouTube videos have a video called "Porn: Fact or Fiction" that is worth checking out for this purpose.

4. Be prepared with talking points. Consider having some variation of a few of the following talking points in your back pocket when you find an appropriate time to discuss with your child.

   - When people pay actors to pose for nude photos or have sex on screen, this is called pornography or "porn" for short. It is not meant for kids and yet, now with the internet, kids come upon it by mistake or their peers show it to them quite often.

   - As humans, we have sexual feelings — after all, it is sex that lets us create more humans. Actors are paid to perform sexual acts so other people can watch and explore their sexual feelings, but it is important to remember that porn does not represent real life. Sex is about healthy communication and meaningful relationships, and that is not what the pictures and videos show in pornography.

   - On a phone or computer, someone may show you naked people interacting with one another. Sometimes, these videos and images pop up when you are searching for something else. You might be curious to look more, and that's normal. But the truth is, if this happens, it is better that you shut off the device and come talk with me.

   - If someone ever starts to show you images like the ones I am talking about, it is important that you have some tools so that you are able to stop the situation. Let's practice ways you can do this. Maybe you can say something like, "Yeah, yeah, I'll be right back" in order to walk away and call me or just go into another room or bathroom.

- Remember, please come to me if you see the types of things I am talking about. You would never be in trouble! Kids aren't bad when this happens. So know that, first and foremost, I want to help guide you in this complicated world as your parent.

It is normal that these videos and images can lead to sexual feelings, even in young people. That is normal. We do not want our kids to feel any shame for having sexual feelings.

IDEAS FOR CONVERSATION STARTERS:

1. Some kids who have come across naked people on the internet don't tell anyone. Why might that be? Remember, you can always talk with me.
2. When you are on the internet playing a game or watching a YouTube video, have you ever seen naked people?
3. Do you think that porn shows how sex really is between loving people?

Talking With Teenagers About Pornography

Our kids are just a click away from coming face-to-face with adult content. Porn is not only easily accessible, but it is also normalized in our society. This infuriates me. I think it is unforgivable that porn is not guarded by firewalls. Even with blockers, young kids can be exposed to porn via unblocked computers or phones. We are not talking about the centerfold pictures from the '70s or '80s. Online porn includes many disturbing types of sex acts and sometimes violence against women. Because it is all just a click away, how do we help our teens understand what they might see? Or what they might be choosing to watch?

We help them by having open and honest conversations. I know most of you are cringing at this. There is probably nothing more awkward than talking to our kids about sex and porn.

A parent recently told me that she walked past her 14-year-old son's room and jokingly shouted at his closed door, "Hey, are you looking at porn?" Her husband got upset and told her not to say that. "You might be making him feel bad," he said.

She told me she was just trying to find a way to ease into the subject and realized that making a flip comment through his door was not the right approach. She knew she had been putting off sitting down with him and talking about porn. She also told me that she didn't want to be the only one starting these types of conversations, so she was going to talk to her husband in order to move forward as partners more intentionally.

When I first started talking with my kids about porn, I was surprised by how tongue-tied I would get. In my job as a physician, I have had countless conversations with people about all sorts of topics related to sex — such as erectile dysfunction, pain during intercourse and much more. But my patients were not my kids, and we never discussed porn.

For the record, I am not morally opposed to sex videos, but when it came to my kids, I had a lot of concerns. I wanted to make sure they knew of my worries without cutting off future conversations. If my tone was too prudish or too angry about how women get treated in these videos, it could backfire. So I combed through the research about youth and porn and was amazed at how little there was. I turned to adolescent psychologists, sex therapists and others to come up with conversation points.

HERE ARE SOME OF THE TOP SUGGESTIONS THAT EMERGED, AND THAT HELPED ME

Each parent will approach this topic differently; there is no right way to do this. As adults, we come to these charged issues with very different philosophies and experiences. You may feel differently about how you want to approach this topic with your adolescent.

Put on your "experimenter's cap"
To overcome barriers to starting these discussions, I've adopted the mindset that these hard conversations are really just little experiments. This takes the pressure off having to get it right or wrong. If one technique doesn't work, switch it up at that moment or analyze the encounter

and try a different approach for the next one. Frankly, if our society is doing a mass experiment on the sexuality of today's kids by flooding their screens with freely available porn, we need to be experimenting with healthy conversations.

Address the elephant in the room

Shine light on the fact that this conversation is awkward. Start with: "I know talking about sex and porn is awkward, but it is important. And awkward situations are often the important things to talk about."

Hand the steering wheel to your teens

Your teen probably already has some ideas and opinions about porn. You can say: "I know you probably have opinions about porn, like that it is complete fantasy and not at all like real life." Then ask, "What other messages about porn have you heard or believe?" And, "What do you think about the porn that is out there today?"

Talk while driving

Sitting next to each other in a car — especially if they are in the back seat — will mean less eye contact, which takes the discomfort down a notch. This is a great way to broach uncomfortable topics for the first time, but ideally won't be the only time these topics get addressed.

Talk about what makes for positive sexual experiences

Talk to your kids about what makes a sexual experience positive. Here are a few key points I have conveyed. First, I talk with them about how wonderful it is to get to know someone over time, to feel that attraction and build trust. How exciting it is to move into the physical realm — initially beginning to connect through holding hands and kissing. It might sound old-fashioned to say these things, but they sure aren't getting that message in the media.

Being able to talk about things such as birth control and sexual readiness is hard but important. It is great that so many teens, now more than ever, talk about the importance of consent.

I tell my kids that they are writing their own sexual stories. They will need to make choices about what will make their stories more positive and less negative. I tell them that decisions made under the influence of drugs and alcohol can increase the chance that they will do things that they don't want to be part of their story.

Discuss your concerns about porn

These are some of the main concerns I have around porn that I have made sure to discuss with my kids over the years.

The people who act in porn get paid to do things and act like they are enjoying them, but often what they are portraying is not pleasant, and may even be painful. Women are often treated abusively in porn. They get treated as objects for sex and little to no care or tenderness is portrayed. Porn often shows violence against women, with images of them being slapped, sworn at, tied up and worse.

When someone clicks on a video, they have no idea what scenes will be shown, and sometimes they can be disturbing. It is impossible to unsee such images, though they will fade over time.

Because humans can't control what causes feelings of arousal, a person might see something that logically grosses them out or upsets them, but be physically excited by it. This can make a person feel bad about themself.

Teens who have watched porn are at an increased risk of feeling insecure about their body parts because porn presents the idea that larger sexual parts are key — which is not at all the case.

Boys who watch porn are at a higher risk of being self-conscious of how they perform sexually. None of the important things about being in relationships — like being caring, taking your physical relationship slowly, being able to talk about consent and what your partner wants to do and doesn't want to do — show up in porn. Porn rarely portrays actors using condoms, even though condoms are a necessary way to prevent pregnancy and infections like HIV, chlamydia and gonorrhea.

Studies show that a very high percentage of women in the sex industry have experienced some form of abuse growing up, and many experience harassment and trauma while working in the porn industry.

There is very little role modeling for consent in pornography. Porn generally does not show conversations or actions that convey that consent was given before a sexual act occurs, which is the opposite of what many high schools and colleges are working on teaching in order to decrease problems in sexual encounters.

Some people begin to watch porn compulsively. The urge to look at sexual material builds and even if they don't like how much they are watching, they might find it hard to stop.

IDEAS FOR CONVERSATION STARTERS:

1. What are some of your ideas and beliefs about porn?
2. Do some people think that the sex that happens in porn is just like real sex?
3. What do you think is different about sex in a real, loving relationship?

. . .

Lying About Screen Time

When I am talking with teens about screen time, I often ask them, "What do you want your parents to understand regarding your screen time?" The number one response is, "I want them to trust me." Many of these kids go on to tell me about the ways they sneak tech time from their parents — under the covers, during school days, etc. It took me a while to wrap my head around this disconnect.

I have come to understand how much trust means to our kids. They want adults to believe that they are capable of getting things done and being independent. They need our trust and our confidence to give them the strength to deal with all the challenges they face growing up.

So why lie? Kids and teens lie to us about lots of things, but usually, it's in the form of withholding information. It's not just that they don't want to get in trouble; research shows that one big reason teens lie is that they don't want to be judged poorly by adults.

Developmentally, lying takes intelligence. It's a skill young kids start to explore around age 3, and it increases until they're about 6 years old.

Usually, by 7, it's on the decline. When kids hit preteen and teen years, sensation-seeking urges and the desire for greater autonomy increase; they often will withhold information, and at times they will outright lie.

Sneaking screen time is a common form of "lying" these days. It can cause friction at home and put strife into our relationships. Kids don't feel happy about sneaking — it comes at an emotional cost. They know at some deep level that they are undermining the one thing they want so much from us: trust.

SO HOW DO WE RAISE MORE HONEST CHILDREN? HERE ARE SOME DATA-DRIVEN IDEAS

Try to decrease how often you tell little "white" lies. Kids and teens pick up on the times we tell lies — both small and big. It is funny when I start to break down how many little white lies I told while raising my kids. Sometimes, I didn't even know I was lying. For example, I would say to someone, "I will be right over," and my kids could see I didn't look ready at all.

Once they were teens, I started having more discussions with my kids about the complex nature of truth-telling. For example, at their public high school, excused absences were only offered for medical reasons. Yet, there were rare occasions when something non-medical required that they miss a day. We agreed that there should be other excuses besides medical ones, and we talked about how we make decisions about ethical issues.

Other times, the kids would see me thanking someone for a fun night, knowing that it actually was not fun at all! Sometimes we stretch the truth to provide positivity in the world. (After all, there were a couple of fun moments in the evening and I of course want to thank them for trying to make the night work.)

REWARD TRUTH-TELLING WITH GUSTO

Here is an example of the many research studies that show that when we respond in a positive way to our kids' truth-telling, we get more of that behavior.[14]

Children in the study, who were 7 to 9 years old, overall reported that they thought that better feelings are linked to confession compared to those linked with lying. Children who expected more positive parental responses to confession were reported by parents to confess more in real life than children who expected more negative parental reactions to confession.

PRACTICE THE SKILL OF EFFECTIVE RULE SETTING

Research shows that in homes where parents use certain strategies while setting and maintaining rules, the children lie the least. These parents:

- Are emotionally warm when discussing rules
- Have taken the time to set some clear rules — explaining why they have been set, and listening when their kids disagree with them
- Will, when warranted, make adjustments
- Enforce rules without anger or judgment as much as possible

Here is an example: Tommy, an 11-year-old boy, admitted to me that he would sneak his iPad at bedtime. Even though he used it under the covers, his parents eventually found out. When Tommy got caught, his dad told me he didn't punish him. Instead, he had a conversation with Tommy about why using his device after bedtime was not good for his health and sleep. He wanted Tommy to know that while he understood the pull of the games on his iPad, there were reasons to set limits. After that, his dad started keeping the iPad in his room at night so Tommy would no longer be tempted to get it from the living room. Also, over time, adjustments were made so that Tommy could use the iPad a little longer at night. His dad told me that the sneaky behavior really decreased after all of that.

I know that learning that kids have lied can be emotionally hard for parents. That is why having conversations when we find out about sneaking or lying can be so challenging. If they come forward on their own to admit a transgression, is it right to commend them for their honesty and not actually give them a negative consequence? Each situation is different, but as a parent, I came to realize that at times yes — this was enough. It shows a great deal of strength to come forward. It also shows they trust us. If they thought we were going to get overly mad or have severe consequences, they would do all they could to never admit to sneaking or lying.

Researchers have wanted to understand what increases the chance of a youth telling the truth. The fear of punishment or the expectation of praise for telling the truth have a lot to do with it. Researcher Victoria Telwar and her colleagues at McGill University in Canada have done multiple clever studies looking at children and the subject of lying. One of her experiments was with children ages 3 through 7.[15] Each child would go into a room with a researcher to play a guessing game with toys. After a certain amount of time, the experimenter, before leaving the room for a few minutes, told the child that they should stay seated forward and not peak at a toy behind them. The majority of the children could not resist this temptation and ended up peeking at the toy.

When the researcher later asked the child if they had peeked, the majority of them lied. For some of the children, the researcher did not ask right away, but instead read one of two stories. One was, "The Boy Who Cried Wolf" — where in the end, the boy who lied in the story gets eaten. Another group of children read the story of George Washington cutting down a cherry tree as a young boy and lying about it. After lying, he tells the truth and his father expresses how happy he is that he has come forward with the truth.

Now the question was, how would each story affect the chance that the child would tell the truth? A convenience survey of 1,000 adults found that over 75% thought that the Wolf story would increase the chance that the child would tell the truth. Actually, that story slightly increased the chance that a child would lie!

When a child heard the George Washington story, it reduced the chance of lying in girls by 50% and 75% in boys. Wow!

Talwar believes that the original story about George Washington is effective because it demonstrates "the positive consequences of being honest by giving the message of what the desired behavior is, as well as demonstrating the behavior itself."

Researchers also found that when the parents of first-graders say to their kids, "If you tell me the truth, I won't be mad," some kids confess, but not many.[16] Yet, when the parent says the same thing followed by " ... and I will be really happy if you tell me the truth," significantly more kids tell the truth. The researchers explained this phenomenon with the fact that kids want parents to be proud of and happy with them. Just saying you won't be mad is still far from being happy. It is that extra point, "I will be happy," that makes the kids really respond.

A final interesting perspective is via the work of psychologist Dan Ariely about how one's mindset about truth-telling is a factor in how honest a person will be. When a person testifies in court, they put their hand on a bible and swear to tell the truth, an action that sets their mindset and everyone's expectation. But in so many other situations, it is at the end of a situation — or in most cases, the end of a paper, such as a tax filing form — when a person gets asked to sign indicating that they have told the whole truth.

Ariely wanted to know what happens when the request for a signature comes at the beginning of a form. He worked with an insurance agency. People had to report how much they drove in the last year on a form. He found that when he moved the oath of truth signature from the end of the form to the beginning of it, people reported 15% more driving. In this case, the subjects had an incentive to report low driving numbers to keep their insurance rate higher. But once that they were in the mindset of being asked to be fully honest, they indeed were.

As a mom, I have employed this technique and I am the first to wonder if it makes a difference when I say to one of my kids, "Ok, I am about to ask you a question, but I need you to promise me to tell the truth." I know for a fact it has not prevented all lying, but I think it has decreased some — particularly when I make a good effort to praise their truth-telling.

Finally, I can't stress enough how helpful it is to talk about the topic of lying during a time in life when things are going smoothly at home.

IDEAS FOR CONVERSATION STARTERS:

1. Do you know especially honest people?
2. What are the reasons that people might not tell the truth? Might it be so not to hurt someone's feelings? Or, when rules feel too strict?
3. What are the downsides to not being honest?

• • •

Being Crude and Swearing Online

With all the social media and digital platforms children are exposed to these days, they see and hear swear words like never before. That's where our work as loving adults is required. It is crucial that we take the time to have short, calm conversations about key topics like this one.

I remember clearly when my son had a flip phone back when he was 11, and I let him text me for rides as well as to communicate with his friends. We discussed that since online communication was new to him, I would monitor it now and then to make sure things were OK. I had a bad feeling one day when I saw a fair amount of swearing in texts.

Can you relate? I know I'm not the only parent who feels this way when our kids start using foul language, and when it is suddenly all written out, it can be that much more worrisome. In middle school, it's pretty common.

When I think back, particularly to when my son was in his middle school years, I would feel emotional when I saw swearing and mean remarks on his text feed. Now, many years later, I emailed Chase at college and asked what he thought about swearing during those times.

Chase emailed back:

> *"In middle school, I remember a lot of banter that was crude, rude and sometimes straight-up mean. I think a lot of us were trying to figure out social dynamics. It's classic middle school! I also remember sometimes being the butt of group jokes or making fun of someone else in the group. Sometimes it felt playful, other times people crossed lines. The added challenge now is that all of it is kept forever in the archives of these messages. It feels unfair in my mind to read through these types of group chats and make assumptions about the deep nuances that you miss in texts. Of course, any serious cyberbullying aspect needs to be addressed."*

Similar to 5-year-olds getting a little buzz from the reactions they elicit when they use "potty talk," preteens get a buzz from using "forbidden words." It makes them feel older, cooler and, best of all perhaps, it separates them from their parents. The primary drive, of course, is that it's a way to fit in with their peers who also are using this language.

Being strategic is the best approach to discussing this issue, because if we lecture our kids or if we use an overly concerned tone, they will likely tune us out. One way to decrease defensiveness and pushback is to bring up the science around swearing.

In one scientific experiment, researchers found a possible upside to why an individual might use harsh words in a difficult situation.[17] In the study, the people who swore while submerging a hand in ice water were able to keep their hands in the ice much longer than those who didn't curse. The researchers theorize that using harsh words activates the flight-or-fight adrenal response and interferes with the link between fearing and perceiving pain, so subjects who swore could tolerate more pain.

There are downsides to swearing that warrant discussion also. For example, using harsh words can make the people around you feel uncomfortable. And specifically online, the meaning and context of your words may be misunderstood.

Of course, it's key that kids know that any online conversation can be brought to the attention of school administrators, and serious consequences can follow. After you bring up the science I've mentioned, here is an approach to further talking about this:

- Tell your kids that you understand that swearing is common online and in person
- Ask them what swear words and harsh language they see and hear online
- Calmly explain why you are not a fan of crude words, what some of your concerns are and that you know they are navigating a complex social world and have to sort it all out
- Finally, you might consider a consequence for swearing at home — when my kids were younger, anyone who swore had to do 15 pushups

We can't control our kids' and teens' language. If we try and say things like, "Never, ever swear online," good luck. But we can help make them more mindful as they think moment-to-moment about what they will write online and say in person. Talking calmly about all of this increases the chance that they will come to us if social cruelty becomes a real problem. The good news is that for most teens, online and in-person swearing decreases after those early tween/teen years. The online social cruelty lessens as well.

IDEAS TO GET THE CONVERSATION STARTED:

1. What do you think are the evolutionary reasons that cause people to use extreme language sometimes?
2. Can you think of problems with swearing?
3. Do you have any creative workarounds to swearing — like replacing swear words with other random words? (My friend uses "peanut butter" or "fig" when she is frustrated.)
4. When people swear, does it ever affect your perception of that person?

· · ·

To Track or Not To Track

GPS and cellphone technology has made it possible to follow our kids' every move. Just because we can, is it OK to do it? The most recent data shows that among parents of teens who are 14 to 17 years old, 25% of parents track their kids' locations, but only 15% of teens actually think their parents do so.[18]

The argument for tracking is knowing where our kids are in this wild world. Proof of our kids' whereabouts in the form of a little dot on a screen provides the peace of mind some parents want. Tracking is also a surefire way to know whether kids are exactly where they say they are or are supposed to be.

The main argument against tracking is that it can undermine the desire to build trust between parents and kids. Some say it is important to give youth the freedom to make the right choice without following them. If they know we are tracking them, it can weaken their obligation to be responsible.

With my teens, I have always preferred not to use tracking, but to rely on our communication with each other. They tell my husband or me where they are. We have discussed with them that we want to know where they are if they go out at night, and they text us to let us know (or ask permission) when they want to change plans. Does that mean they have told us every change of location? During the day, definitely not, and we do not require that of them. They are living their lives, and we know that if we have to reach them, they will usually answer the phone unless there is a reason not to. For instance, they may not answer if their battery dies or they are not in cell range. For my teens, it has worked well to rely on discussing the plans in advance and then stay in touch about changes.

I realize this approach may not work for all families. Each family needs to make their own decisions about how they handle tracking. However, I feel strongly that when parents don't tell their kids they are tracking them, relationships can be damaged. That goes for monitoring any type of behavior. Using deceptive ways to monitor can cause serious rifts in relationships that can be daunting to repair.

There are many reasons that parents decide to use tracking. Commonly, they do it because they are concerned about their youth's safety. For example, if they cannot reach their child, they want to be able to see where they are.

I have never felt that being able to see their location will make them safer. Because I grew up in a high-crime neighborhood, I have raised my children to be very savvy about safety and I trust that they will rely on such skills to stay away from unsafe situations. That said, I realize that some parents just feel a lot better about being able to actually see where their kids are when they have doubts.

Another reason people like to track is to decrease the talks about logistics and instead rely more on tech for sorting out the location of everyone in the family. This is one way tech can really be helpful.

As we all know from recent news stories, concerns about tracking and maintaining privacy go well beyond the family unit. When we use GPS services, we implicitly agree that our movements will be followed by the various companies that provide these services. We know that the information about our whereabouts can get sold to other companies. It's important to understand that using GPS services always comes with a tradeoff regarding your privacy (or that of your child).

IDEAS FOR CONVERSATION STARTERS:

1. How do you imagine families managed logistics before cellphones?
2. What are the upsides of tracking? Downsides?
3. What do you think of the study results that show teens underestimating how often parents track teens' locations?

Chapter Eight:

Screens in Schools and Homework

A major reason I started filming *Screenagers* was that as my kids approached their teen years, I saw that more homework was moving to computers. I thought: "Wow, being a kid or teen trying to stay on task when the tech world is so entertaining. How will that work?"

As much as I feel for kids and teens, I also feel for us parents. It's really painful to think about how our teens are switching tabs when they should be on task.

Tech arrived in schools like a tsunami over the past decade — from more computers used in classes, one-to-one programs where students are provided iPads or Chromebooks for the year, to the ubiquitous presence of smartphones in kids' pockets.

How does tech work best in school? In 2018, Education Week Research Center published "School Leaders and Technology," a survey of 500 principals, assistant principals and school deans.[1] They were asked for their opinions on the use of technology both in and out of schools. Of those surveyed, 56% said they believed that paper and pencil are better for learning new math skills. And 88% said that screens are best used for conducting research and investigating a new subject. What do your kids and students think?

Now that homework is often assigned via online portals and usually requires computers, our kids and teens are constantly being challenged with all sorts of digital distractions while trying to study. Technology is just too tempting for them (and for all of us). It's so easy to click on a funny YouTube video or check Instagram between moments of concentration.

Meanwhile, many schools are struggling with what to do about smartphones. In just the few years it took to film *Screenagers*, I was shocked to see how kids with access to smartphones were just getting younger and younger. When I visited middle schools and asked people if the school had a policy on cell phones and information on policies, so often I would get the same response from teachers, staff, and students — one of confusion. They would start to scratch their head and try to recall if they had heard of any such policy and so often replied with something like, "Gosh, I really don't know if we have a policy or what it is if we do."

Having the "world" at their fingertips comes at the cost of constant distraction. I liken this to trying to ignore a plate of freshly baked chocolate chip cookies by my side. Entirely resisting is just not going to happen.

This chapter will look at tech's impact on learning and at solutions, like how to help with "homework hygiene" — which is when parents help their children develop effective practices around homework.

Many schools incorporate screen time via one-to-one programs or borrowed devices for certain classes. The question is not, "Should computers be in schools?" Instead, the question should be for what use, how often and how much?

Clearly, there are lots of ways students use computers in schools — such as doing research, designing the school newspaper and creating presentations. What components of technology do your kids and students find most useful, interesting and impactful when it comes to education? When I ask students about the on-screen things they do in class that they find most interesting, they often tell me about the videos they watch in the classroom. They also tell me about using Quizlet and searching on Google.

. . .

When Computers Replace Textbooks, How Do We Optimize Benefits and Decrease Downsides?

Many technological tools are used positively in the classroom. For instance, smartboards allow for interactive engagement. Students use computers to do research. There are classes on coding. In a one-to-one program, students may have their own device that they bring to each class and use to write papers, take notes, work on PowerPoint presentations and more. The onslaught of technology in the classroom came on fast and hard. Is it better for learning?

While making *Screenagers,* I learned that the Los Angeles Unified School District was launching one-to-one technology programs in many schools, which entailed loaning iPads to students that would be used at school and at home for schoolwork.

In 2013, LA Unified bought 43,261 iPads and curriculum from Pearson, an educational publishing company.[2] Fast forward three years. The LA Times reports that "the $1.3 billion iPad effort ... faltered almost immediately." One of the main problems the district reported came from the learning software purchased from Pearson.

I wanted to understand more about what was happening with tech in LA, so I flew down and spoke with teachers, administrators and families. One of the families ultimately ended up being in *Screenagers.*

I met the very kind 16-year-old Excel at her home. She told me:

> *"When I was smaller I would love building Legos or have, like, books and build, like, a utopian society for my dolls or something. Like, I would love building houses instead of actually playing with the Barbie itself. I want to be an engineer for NASA. Then the school gave me the Chromebook. Hours spent on social media affects my grades a lot."*

Excel's mom said:
> *"She has got Cs and Ds lately. From a straight-A student, she started failing in certain classes."*

Excel's younger sister said:
> *"She got a D in Spanish again and the other one was on something else, but definitely not math, because we're all good at math."*

Excel told me:
> *"I hope to decrease my social media usage, but it's there. It's conveniently there. How can I not use it?"*

I was so moved by this family and the mother, who was a single mom with four kids. I spent a full day at their home and saw the mom involved in so many loving interactions with her kids.

When I returned to Seattle, I met with the University of Washington professor Jacob Vigdor, Ph.D., who has done research on the impact of the introduction of computers into the home.

> Vigdor said:
>
> *"There had been an assumption out there that giving kids access to computers at home would make a big difference for them academically. We wanted to figure out if the evidence actually supported this. We had access to a database that covered hundreds of thousands of students in elementary and middle schools over a period of several years.*
>
> *"What we found is that when a computer arrives in a kid's home, their test scores in reading and math actually decrease, and the largest decreases we found were actually amongst the poorest kids. What we think is going on is that the computer in the home is actually taking time away from homework. It's taking time away from learning, particularly in families where there isn't a parent around to monitor what the child is doing.*
>
> *"There's a difference in the way kids use computers without that monitoring. It's more likely that the kid is going to the computer to go chat with their friends, play games — do things other than homework."*

So from a big-picture perspective, has the tech revolution really revolutionized how our students learn? Researchers have not been able to measure any increased overall academic performance since tech has been introduced into schools. For example, test scores in this country are not considerably higher, and schools with one-to-one programs do not show higher learning levels compared to similarly matched schools without one-to-one programs.

Researchers have found that teacher-student relationships and collective teacher efficacy has a higher impact on learning than tech. Education expert John Hattie explains collective teacher efficacy in this way:

"It is teachers working together to have appropriately high, challenging expectations of a year's growth for a year's input fit with the evidence of impact ... It is not just ra-ra thinking ... It is the combined belief that it is us that causes learning, it's not students from different backgrounds [or other reasons]."[3]

We must also keep in mind Jason's research about computers in the home offering so many distractions that some students, regardless of their socio-economic background, will really struggle to get homework done. As a society, we must work to provide plenty of support to these students and their caretakers by providing alternatives to screen time that aid tech balance, like after-school sports and arts programs.

Making kids aware of the time they spend on technology at school and getting them to think about how they feel about this built-in screen time will help them see the overall picture of their screen habits. It will also show them the huge part screens play in their lives and in turn, it will help them seek a healthy balance in their relationship with technology.

IDEAS FOR CONVERSATION STARTERS:

1. Name some of the ways computers help improve learning.
2. Can you think of ways that do not yet exist that computers would be able to help with learning?
3. What parts of the school day, including class time, would you want to make sure were not being replaced by screen time?
4. How much time do you think kids should spend on screens in school each day?
5. The Maryland legislature passed a bill requiring the Department of Education and the Health Department to develop best practices for the safe use of digital devices in schools.

    Maryland is considering having students take breaks from the computer every 20 minutes or so and requiring that their devices be left in the classrooms during breaks. What do you think about these ideas?

• • •

Addressing Cellphones in Middle Schools

As I was visiting schools while filming for *Screenagers*, I noticed more and more students on their phones in the hallways in middle schools. I was puzzled. I knew that high school students often had phones at school, but now kids in middle schools did too.

What were the cellphone policies in middle schools? It was amazing to me that when I would ask teachers and students in the schools this question, they would often have the same answer: "I am not really sure."

In terms of the overall landscape of policies in the country, or even just in school districts, I looked for data but was shocked that I could not find anything.

So my team and I decided to do our own survey. We reached out to the many parents who were on our mailing list. More than 1,200 middle school parents in the United States responded. On December 22, 2017, CNN.com reported our findings.[4]

While we recognize that parents who are on our email list and who responded to the survey may be more concerned about their kids' cellphone use than the general parent population, two particularly striking findings emerged.

1. 55% of the parents who responded to our survey said their children's middle schools now allowed cellphone use, and public schools were more likely than private schools to allow it.
2. More than 80% of parents who responded did not want their kids to use cellphones during school.

THE PROBLEMS WITH PHONES IN MIDDLE SCHOOLS

And it's not only parents who support "away for the day" policies — which require students to leave their phones out of reach — but science does too.

The frontal lobe, the part of the brain responsible for impulse control, is not fully developed in middle school-aged children. When we expect kids to learn how to handle phone use in places like classrooms, we are setting many of them up for failure.

Students, teachers and administrators whom we spoke to for the film said many students get in trouble at school for being on their phones during class when they're not supposed to be.

It is extremely disappointing that research specific to cellphone impact on middle schoolers' academics is almost nonexistent, but there is worrisome data about other school levels. For example, a 2013 study showed that college students who interact with their cellphones in the classroom perform worse on tests — often by a full letter grade or more.[5]

In fact, just having phones within reach can cause academic performance to decline, whether they're being used or not. In a 2017 study, participants completely turned off and silenced their phones. While they performed memory tasks, some were allowed to keep their phone and some were told to put it in the other room. Those who had the phone with them did significantly worse.[6]

The mere presence of smartphones reduced available cognitive capacity. In other words, the attention and energy it takes *not* to check a phone seems to cause "brain drain."

Visit any middle school where cellphones are allowed at lunch or break and everywhere you look, you will see kids with their heads down. Kids I've met through *Screenagers* tell me how they retreat into their phones to avoid feeling anxious while socializing.

While cyberbullying gets a lot of attention, the majority of students face micro-emotional hits when they get left out of group chats or see photos of people that they compare themselves to, feeling inferior. When this happens during the school day, it can make it very difficult to focus on school work.

THE UPSIDES OF PUTTING PHONES AWAY FOR THE DAY

Importantly, it's been found that face-to-face time with friends strongly correlates with less feelings of depression. Creating environments where kids disconnect from their devices and interact in person would be a smart public health move.

Schools that changed their policy from allowing cellphones to prohibiting them saw student test scores improve by 6.41%, according to a 2015 study from the United Kingdom.[1]

I have just listed off many concerns about student cellphone use in middle schools, but of course, one can also argue in favor of access to smartphones for things like learning apps like Quizlet (which works like flashcards for memorization) or the calculator app. My response to this viewpoint is when the teacher says, "OK, you can use your phone for Quizlet right now," how does the teacher know that this is really what the students are doing on their phones? How fair is it to expect a 12-year-old to not respond to texts that came in during the morning or to be sidetracked by other fun things?

Let's see what our kids think about the potential upsides and downsides of cellphone use in middle school. You might even consider playing a debate game to have this conversation. How about you take the side of pro-cellphones being in students' pockets for easy access and your child argues the anti-side?

IDEAS FOR CONVERSATION STARTERS:

1. What are the possible upsides of letting students use cellphones in middle school during class?
2. What are the possible downsides of phone use in class?
3. What are the upsides of letting students be on phones at break and lunch?
4. What are the downsides of letting students be on phones at break and lunch?

· · · ·

Empowering Parents With Our "Away For The Day" Campaign

By weighing the pros and cons of phone use in middle schools, my team and I felt strongly that something needed to be done to create "Away for the Day" policies. And from our survey of parents, we knew we were not alone. Not only did the majority of parents agree with us, but many were also asking us what they could do to try and make changes in their schools.

Some parents' kids were at schools that had wishy-washy policies — if any — and they wanted to be proactive and solidify healthy policies. Others wanted to reverse policies already in place. It wasn't just parents who wanted to do something, but also heads of schools, teachers, counselors and others too.

Some schools and parents were particularly activated when they read from our survey that private schools were twice as likely to have policies that require kids to put their cellphones away during the school day. Parents of public school kids saw this as a question of fairness — all students should get support to be undistracted against the pull of cellphones, not just the kids in private schools.

In response to all of these factors, my team and I decided to start the campaign "Away For The Day," which has been going strong for two and a half years thus far. For the campaign, my co-producer, Lisa Tabb, and I created the Away for the Day website providing research, video testimonials, examples of policies that are working in schools and much more.

Parents and others started to go to their schools with the tools we provided through our campaign, and we heard about several wins! Here is an example of the many emails we received. Matthew Burnham, a middle school principal in El Cerrito, California, told us, "When we took the phones away, we had very little pushback from the kids, and all of those distractions and problems went away."

While we have primarily received positive feedback, sometimes there is pushback from administrators. To help advocates, we created a list of pushbacks and responses. And I want to share them here because this is yet another good discussion generator for conversations with your kids, even if they are in college! Ask them, "What policies on cellphone use would you have if you were the principal of a middle school?"

1. **Pushback:** Schools do not want to shoulder the enforcement burden.

   Response: The reality is that when solid systems are in place, middle schools are not overburdened. We have heard from dozens of schools that have changed their policies that when they are clear and direct, there seems to be little pushback. One principal said she implemented an Away For The Day policy with clear consequences, but she told the students that they would simply get a warning for the first month. Once they got more accustomed to the new rules, the consequences would set in. Habit building takes time and this is a nice way to ease into a new policy.

2. **Pushback:** Parents want to reach their kids in the event of a school lockdown.

   Response: An NPR story entitled, "Should The Parkland Shooter Change How We Think About Phones, Schools and Safety?" provided many reasons on why putting phones away is safer.[8] Here is an excerpt from the story:

   "Ken Trump, the security expert, says phones can actually make us less safe in a crisis such as the one in Parkland. He ticks off several reasons:

   - *Using phones can distract people from the actions they need to be taking in the moment, such as running, hiding, and listening to directions from first responders.*
   - *The sound of the phone, whether ringing or on vibrate, could alert an assailant to a hiding place.*
   - *The shooter could be monitoring the event themselves on social media and find more victims or elude capture that way.*
   - *Victims and worried family members trying to get through can jam communications, interfering with first responders."*

3. **Pushback:** Schools believe that parents want to be able to contact their children all day.

   Response: Our data shows this is not the case. More than 80% of parents do not want their kids to use cellphones during school. When parents help their kids plan their days without text messages, they help them to develop valuable executive-functioning skills.

4. **Pushback:** Schools want their students to use their phones as a computer.

   Response: It is better to just let them use a computer than to have a phone because the apps and notifications on the phone will constantly distract them. Also, non-sanctioned screen time is much easier to sneak on phones than on a computer. Studies show that kids' academic performance actually goes down with the mere presence of a phone in class.

5. **Pushback:** Some people believe it is a nice tool for introverted kids.

   Response: When kids who are struggling with being social are allowed to retreat into their devices between classes, they never get the ability to work on their communication skills.

6. **Pushback:** Some people believe that students should just control their impulses to check their phones during the school day, so why do we have to take it away from them?

   Response: We know that the control center for impulse control, the frontal lobe, is not fully developed in middle school-aged children. When we say, "Kids just need to learn how to handle phone use in places like classrooms," we are setting many kids up for failure. We will help them more by giving them self-control challenges in which they can succeed.

Exploring the upsides and downsides of having access to their phones during the school day can help your middle schooler see that having an Away For The Day policy is actually one of the ways adults can support them.

IDEAS FOR CONVERSATIONS STARTERS:

1. What do you think of the cellphone policy at your school?
2. Do you sometimes wish you could check your phone during the school day? Or do you spend a lot of time checking your cellphone during the day?
3. Do you agree that, sometimes, when adults make decisions for you, it can make life less stressful? By having an Away For The Day policy, you don't even have to worry about checking your phone!

.   .   .

High Schools Get Students to Put Their Phones Away

Originally our Away For The Day initiative was about encouraging middle schools to have students store their phones in lockers or backpacks for the whole day. We did not explicitly discuss high schools very much on the website. That has now been changed and high schools are being included in this initiative by using what we are now calling a "Modified Away for the Day" policy.

Let me explain. Some high schools employ the full Away for the Day policy, in which they require that phones be out of reach for the entire day (such as kept in a locker). We have seen this more commonly among private schools, but in some instances, public high schools also have this policy.

Meanwhile, many other high schools have a "Modified Away For The Day" policy, in which phones are entirely away in a hanging phone pocket organizer or in a backpack during class periods. Then, students retrieve their phones at the end of the period and are allowed to use them between class periods and at lunch.

We believe that "Away For The Day" and "Modified Away For The Day" policies both benefit students and school climates overall, so we have explicitly changed the mission of Away for the Day to include all schools — elementary through high schools.

Many administrators are taking control and banning cellphones in their schools. Some school districts are banning cellphones in all of their schools at the district level. Forest Hills School District in Grand Rapids, Michigan, serves about 10,000 students. Recently, Superintendent Dan Behm instituted a phone Away For The Day policy in all schools, including the high schools. The rule states that students cannot use their phones during passing periods or lunch. Behm told Grand Rapids' online newspaper, MLive, "We see this as a way to strengthen the positive aspects of social and emotional learning."

Recently, I was at a local café near a high school in a suburb of Chicago where they were hosting a *Screenagers NEXT CHAPTER* event later that day. As students came into the cafe at lunch and after school, I talked to them about their high school phone policy. Many told me that several of their teachers try to get the kids to put their phones away, but often they remain visible on desks and in hands. Some teachers don't say anything about putting phones away, and in those classes, phone use runs rampant.

One student (who told me she was on social media "24 hours a day") said that she sees cellphones out a lot. When I asked her, "If you were the teacher, what policy would you have?" she answered, "I think I would have everyone put their phone in a basket during class."

Then I went to the screening. Before it started, a teacher wanted to tell me how frustrated he was about the phone policy in his school and how much time he spends reminding kids to put their devices away. His policy was to have them put away, while other teachers were more lax about phones being out. When I asked why he thought his school did not do what many high schools have done — which is to have phones put into shoe bags during class — he said he suspected a fear that the phones would get stolen.

The reality is that we do not hear about theft when it comes to the clear plastic pocket hangers teachers have in their classrooms for student cellphones. Phones are password-protected, many are trackable and teachers know the students in their class, so a student is unlikely to be able to take someone else's phone from under the teacher's nose.

At a public high school that has a one-to-one laptop program, a teacher told me:

> *"We still have the issue of students being distracted on the tablet even if we have phones put away, but having one less distraction is huge! Don't discount it. cellphones are offering so many tempting distractions, connections and entertainment. Taking that away is important. Any way you can decrease distraction is a win."*

A new study in JAMA Network Open sent surveys to a total of 210 middle and high schools.[2] The response rate was low, at 18.4 % but keeping that in mind let me mention a few of the interesting results. One finding, that is not at all surprising to me, is that 80% of the principals that responded believe that cell phone use during school has negative social and academic impact. Another important finding is that of the schools that responded, 33% of highschools said that they did restrict cell phone use during lunch and breaks.

The study's authors, Dr. Pooja Tandon, child health and development physician and researcher, said in the paper:

> *"Just like schools are encouraged to help students achieve the recommended 60 minutes per day of physical activity, they have a role to play in helping children limit their screen time exposure."*

If you want to change the cellphone policies in your school, we have a toolkit to help you get started at www.awayfortheday.org.

IDEAS FOR CONVERSATION STARTERS:

1. Do you think a school district's school board should be able to make phone policies that apply to all high schools in that district? Or should each high school decide for themself?

2. If you had the authority to decide the cellphone policy for the high school in your town, what would you choose?

• • •

Hold That Text

Your kid is at school and something you want to tell them pops into your head. Dinner plans have changed. The carpool has switched. Tomorrow's doctor's appointment is confirmed. You love them, etc. Should you send the text right when the thought comes or hold off?

Our survey of middle school parents regarding cellphone policies found that more than 80% of parents do not want their kids to use cellphones during school. That is a large majority and as discussed, the data we have shows that the risks of allowing phones outweigh the benefits.

We don't want them to have their phones at school, but at the same time, are we texting them whenever we have a thought we want to share with them? I have started to change my practice around this. A while back, I was more apt to text right away.

Tessa's school began working hard to get teens to be present, with teachers doing an excellent job of requiring phones to be put away in classes. So even though many students can check devices at lunch and in between classes, I realized that I no longer wanted to add to the list of things Tessa needed to think about or respond to in between her classes.

Also, I am a big believer in working hard to become a better planner, and I want my kids to work toward this too. The less we rely on the phone as an escape route for changing plans, the more we work together to get our plans organized outside of school time.

So I have started to "HOLD THAT TEXT."

This idea is especially important in schools that have 100% Away for the Day policies, where phones are put in lockers or backpacks for the whole day. A text sent during the school day implies we want them to see it, even if we don't expect them to see it until after school. Why give them these mixed messages?

HOLD THAT TEXT is not only applicable when kids are at school. After a talk I gave at a conference of health care providers, a woman with joint custody of her kids approached me, explaining that her time with her kids is that much more precious to her. She ensures she gets at least one hour of alone time per week with each of them by taking them out for ice cream. Her kids know that during this time, she will only answer texts and calls from the other kids. The kids also know that since they don't like it when their own time is interrupted, they try not to text their mom during the time she spends with their siblings. They are learning to HOLD THAT TEXT.

I must confess the hardest part of HOLD THAT TEXT is losing the thought if I do not send it quickly. Instead, I use the notes app on my phone to dictate the idea I have at the moment, and then I set an alarm to go off after school hours to remind me to send my text. I know, this seems like a lot of work versus just sending Tessa the text, but holding the text feels good each time I do it. There are also some apps that will schedule texts to be sent at assigned times.

IDEAS FOR CONVERSATION STARTERS:

1. When you have a thought or a question for someone, do you ever decide to wait to send it, thinking about that person's schedule?
2. Is it hard for you if you can't respond to a text right away?
3. Do you find it distracting to receive a text when you are in a situation where you cannot respond at that moment?

Multitasking: When is it Effective and When is it Not?

If you were to ask my family, they would tell you I am the most multi-tasking person they know. I am the first to say it — I love multitasking. I am happy when I cook, research a film, email and stretch essentially all at the same time. But then the happiness fades when I burn yet another pan (no joke) or I can't recall anything from some research I just read or I realize my stretching was half-hearted.

But now let's turn to the real topic at hand — our kids. Fights are breaking out in homes all over the country due to parents' fears that our kids are not doing "their best," given all the device and tab-switching we see them do when they should be doing homework. Sound familiar?

According to psychologist Larry Rosen's study published in ScienceDirect, "Facebook and texting made me do it: Media-induced task-switching while studying," middle school, high school and university students focus for six minutes on average before they switch off of homework to a technological distraction.[10]

I have little doubt that if you have ever talked to your child about multitasking, there is a good chance they have responded with something like, "You don't get it, I am a good multitasker, it is not a problem."

To their credit, they have nimble brains and we want to let them know that we get it — they have a huge learning capacity in those wonderful brains. It is important to start conversations about multitasking like this because most youth are barraged with the message, "Don't multitask," and they feel defensive because they don't see a problem with it and feel misunderstood.

An interesting lab experiment shows that the peak age for doing multiple things at once are the early 20s.[11] Researchers Larry Rosen and Adam Gazzly did an experiment that looked at people ages 8 through 70. The subjects played a computer driving game where they had to respond to different signposts and ignore others while continuing to drive. The 10-year-olds were not very skilled at this, but for each year they got older, they got better at the task. They peaked in their 20s. After their 20s, each year of aging caused their multitasking skills to decline. Interestingly, by 50, adults did worse on the experiment than the 10-year-olds, and this decline continued through age 70.

While the word "multitasking" is often used, it can mean two different things. One definition being truly doing more than one thing at the same time, which of course, we are biologically doing all the time — we breathe while our eyes move while we talk. There is multitasking involved when we talk and walk at the same time. That works extremely well, since the act of walking is not engaging much of the prefrontal cortex, where talking resides. Yet if a person is having a conversation with someone while also thinking about a math equation, that is of course impossible. The brain actually shifts from one task to another. This is referred to as "multitasking," but is actually task-shifting.

Two things that require cognitive control and attention cannot be performed at the same time. So when I began by talking about how I love multitasking, I really should have used the term task-shifting. Moving forward, I will use the term multitasking, but really I am talking about task-shifting.

For example, try answering two people talking to you at the same time, or write a paper while processing information that is coming to you over a Zoom call. These things feel close to impossible.

Let's explore the upsides and downsides of multitasking with our kids.

EXAMPLES OF THE UPSIDES OF MULTITASKING

So what are the upsides? Some teens say they like being able to go on their phone or to go on YouTube because it "energizes them," and they can go back to studying. They also tell me that laughing at TikTok videos lifts their mood, and then they can go back to their studies with more energy.

Here are some examples of downsides:

Homework takes longer

Yes, it takes longer to do your work when you are multitasking because the time spent on doing other things, such as scrolling through TikTok, still takes away from the time spent on work. There is something called a "lag time," which is when you shift attention from one task to the other. So, if a child is working on a paper and then switches over to Snapchat, it will take their brain a lot of time to return to the paper and catch up to where they were before, in order to start processing information again at full speed.

To drive home this idea of lag time, try this exercise with your child.

- Ask everyone at the table to count backward from 10 down to 1, and note how quickly they can do it

- Then do the same for A, B, C ... and see how quickly they can go through the alphabet
- Then ask them to say this sequence: 10, A, 9, B, 8, C ... and note the amount of time it takes to complete
- Talk about how speed slows down as the brain shifts from one thing to the other

Taxes the brain

One experiment looked to see if forcing the brain to process a lot of information quickly would have implications for little kids. In this setting, instead of switching between different tasks, the kids were engaged in a task that required the brain to process a lot of rapid information that forced the brain to switch course often.

In the experiment, children either watched a very rapidly-sequenced TV show, a slowly-sequenced one or they played with crayons. Right after, their cognitive ability was tested. The researchers discovered that the children who watched the rapidly-paced program performed poorer than the other two. It appears that this rapid stimulation tired the children's brains, and they tended not to function as well.[12]

IT IS INTERESTING HOW PEOPLE RATE
HOW TAXING IT IS TO PAY ATTENTION

There was a study done on light versus heavy-multitasking media users that looked at these two groups' ability to stay on task.[13] The heavy-multitasking media users performed significantly worse at staying on task than did the light multitaskers. Here though, is the real clincher: individuals who rank themselves as being good at multitasking actually perform worse on laboratory tests of multitasking on average.

IDEAS FOR CONVERSATION STARTERS:

1. When does multitasking work well for you?
2. When does it not work so well?
3. What tricks do you employ to stay on task when you need to (such as put your phone in the other room)?

• • •

Tips for Improving Study Time
That Work During and Post Covid-19

Over the years, the varying approaches with which youth take to school and homework has amazed me — some are just so wired to follow the path and do the work without question, while others go through rough patches and find very little enjoyment in academics. These students struggle to muster up the motivation to do even the bare minimum.

It goes without saying that we, parents, love our kids so much (I've always told my kids, "I love you to the moon and back a trillion times"). It is from this place of love that we want our kids to enjoy schoolwork and learning. It can be emotional for us when schoolwork pains our kids. My heart goes out to parents in these situations, as I have been there as well. I also, of course, feel such empathy for the kids struggling. And our kids have the extra challenge of trying to resist a million "goodies" just a click away.

I have some suggestions for improving study habits. I must add that as parents, we are so eager to help, but we must remind ourselves that while we can try to help, we can only do so much. The key is to tell our kids that we love them unconditionally, regardless of how they do in school. And also to remind them that even if they are not feeling motivated now, we do not doubt that they will find things they will love to learn about in the future.

As I mentioned before, Larry Rosen's study, "Facebook and texting made me do it: Media-induced task-switching while studying," indicated that middle school, high school and university students focus for about six minutes on homework before switching to a technological distraction. If you share this stat with your child, make sure they know this is just an average and that there are many young people who stay on task for longer than six minutes. Make sure they know that you are well aware that often, they stay focused for longer than six minutes.

I have some suggestions for improving study habits that I call "homework hygiene." Sleep hygiene is something we talk a lot about in medicine because sleep problems, particularly insomnia, are so common and so debilitating. We help people set up practices and habits to increase chances of a good night's sleep, such as going to bed at the same time each night, setting the alarm for earlier wake-up times to reset their internal clock and other techniques. Homework hygiene is meant to help kids develop effective practices around homework such as writing to-do lists, developing the habit of prioritizing the list and checking things off as they go.

DELVE INTO "SELF-AWARENESS"

Gosh, even just writing that, I am aware of how mushy it sounds but wait, hear me out. I was just talking with Nicholas Martino, who was awarded "teacher of the year," announced in The Washington Post. He told me that one of the first things he does with his students is have them reflect on their strengths and the areas they want to improve. Nicholas said that building self-awareness among his students is one of the most important things he does as an educator. Let's help our kids think about their long life as learners.

I suggest asking them any of these types of questions (it can be effective to include yourself in the discussion and, of course, to be as non-judgemental as possible when kids give their answers):

- "What do you find you are pretty good at in group projects?"
- "What is hard for you during group projects, and is there anything you would like to improve?"
- "When it comes to learning via lectures online with platforms like Zoom, what helps you stay focused? What pulls you away?"
- "With all that is going on in the greater world and your own world right now, are there any topics that you have found particularly interesting that you want to learn more about someday?"

EXPLAIN THE SCIENCE OF PROCRASTINATION AND WHY JUMPING INTO THE HARD STUFF FIRST CAN HELP

During my son's senior year in high school, he came across an online course called "Learning How to Learn," where he discovered that the brain experiences physical pain from simply the thought of doing work it does not want to do.[14] He told me how that rang true for him. He learned that is why it feels relieving at the moment to distract oneself with something else — known as procrastination. But just a few minutes into the feared task, that sensation of pain dissipates. He said that learning all of this helped him get better at jumping into a hard mental task rather than avoiding it.

If your kid tends to avoid hard homework — i.e., if you have a normal kid — suggest this little experiment. Have them say how much they are dreading doing their work on a scale of one to 10, 10 being extreme dread and one being mild dread. Then, have them do the assignment for five minutes. Then, an hour later, have them revisit the one to 10 scale and see if their dread has gone down. Hopefully, it will be closer to one than before. If your teen does not want to do this, then you can always do the experiment yourself and share your own results in real time with them. With my teens, this is an approach I often take because I know how much they don't want me to pressure them into doing something, but they will engage with me about the things I am testing out on myself.

EMPATHIZE

Let them know you realize how hard it must be to do homework during this time when everything is essentially "homework." You understand that after hours of Zoom school, it is challenging to do repetitive or hard work. Validate that having to do homework can feel torturous at times — and now, with distractions at our fingertips, there is a new and unprecedented level of challenge. If things have been really tense in your home around study time issues, this could be a great activity for you to consider doing — just spending one or two days focused on being more empathic. I know when I get stressed with my kids and I consciously switch my focus to what I can be working on, my stress level lowers, which in turn lowers everyone else's stress levels.

HELP THEM DEVISE A PLAN TO FIGHT BACK AGAINST THEIR BIGGEST "TIME WASTERS"

Teens tell me over and over that TikTok in particular causes them to "waste" the most time. They explain that even when they mean to just go on the app for a few minutes, they lose track of time and suddenly 90 minutes have gone by and they are mad. One teen noted that the app is designed to hide the time while it is running, so you literally can't see the time on the phone while watching TikTok videos. She realized how this is an intentional feature, designed to make users lose track of time. She also mentioned how she has realized that the algorithm of TikTok is amazing at delivering content that exactly fits what she likes. For other youth, maybe it is Snapchat or Instagram that grabs their attention and keeps it there way longer than they would like.

How can we fight back? Discuss ideas such as using an app like Moment to measure time spent on the app. Another approach might be to delete the app every other day. What ideas does your child have?

ASK THEM TO REFLECT ON THEIR STRATEGIES FOR STUDYING

Calmly ask your child to tell you about their school work strategies and habits in general. What has worked for them? What has not? Try focusing on the big picture and stop the conversation there. Try not to end by saying something like, "Well, so what are you going to get done tonight?"

DISCUSS THE DIFFERENCE BETWEEN EXTERNAL DISTRACTIONS VERSUS INTERNAL DISTRACTIONS

How often do they experience external distractions, i.e., their phone pinging? How often do they experience internal distractions, i.e., sensing the need to check social media or switching to a favorite website?

PHYSICAL ACTIVITY

Experiments have shown that after physical activity, one's ability to do academic work, particularly the ability to focus, is increased. Helping youth see this for themselves is ideal. Before having to be home due to Covid-19, had they ever noticed that they could concentrate better after recess? After dance or sports? Now at home, your family could come up with a little experiment. What if everyone had an assignment to sit and read an article on the computer for 10 minutes and then rate how easy it was to concentrate? Then the next day, everyone could do a certain amount of exercises — such as 20 jumping jacks, a few pushups or some sit-ups — and then try to read a new article. Now, how would they rate their focus?

PREVENT LATE NIGHTS OF STUDYING WITH A TECH CURFEW

One of the things I repeatedly hear from parents is that when they try to have their teens unplug for the night, the teen says they still have homework. To prevent this, psychologists recommend that parents consider setting a "tech-off time" and encourage their kids to plan accordingly. They will have to adjust their entertainment/social media time on screens so that they can get their schoolwork done at whatever shutdown time is agreed on — be it 9, 10 or 11, as every home has a different situation. Will there be exceptions? Of course, effective parenting is all about this. Listening to our kids and respecting and honoring when there are exceptions to the rule, like finals week or other issues that require them to work past the designated time, is important. If exceptions occur a few times a month, no problem. But if they occur more than that, then more discussion and problem-solving needs to happen.

PUT THE PHONE OUT OF SITE FOR PERIODS OF TIME

If they typically have a smartphone by their side while doing schoolwork, talk about the benefits of putting it in the other room for extended periods of time — say, like 20 minutes — and then taking a "phone break." You can propose an experiment with them. Have them keep their phone nearby while they study for 15 minutes, and then have them put the phone in another room for while they study for another 15 minutes. Then, talk about the experience. When I talk with teens about their study habits, many of them tell me they study without their phones because they know that they really impede their concentration.

EXPERIMENT WITH A TIMER

This can be very effective. An old-fashioned egg timer or an hourglass timer, where one sees the sand falling, are both ideal. They even make sets of hourglass timers in multiple time increments. Have your child set a goal for an uninterrupted amount of study time spent on a subject — for example, 10 minutes. A set study interval lets the brain know that an end is coming. This can help increase motivation to delve into a subject.

CONSIDER USING TECH TOOLS TO HELP LIMIT TECH DISTRACTIONS

There are many parent control apps and systems, such as Apple's Screen Time, that can limit the time kids spend on phones. Systems like Circle can turn off WiFi at scheduled times. Something like Circle can set the tech curfew I mentioned above automatically.

IDEAS FOR CONVERSATION STARTERS:

Remember, I always suggest starting a conversation about tech with everyone saying something positive about tech in their lives. This lets our kids know that we "get it" and can also see the positives about screen time. This helps them to be less defensive and more open to conversations on tech balance. Also, try not to make this all about their answers. Instead, talk about your own challenges and solutions.

1. Do you find it easier to concentrate after you have done a type of physical activity?
2. Which screen time activities make you completely lose track of time these days?
3. Do you feel like you are struggling more with external or internal distractions these days while studying?
4. How long do you think you can engage in effective, focused studying at one time? 15 minutes? 30 minutes?
5. Might an old-fashioned egg timer help?

Chapter Nine:

Fostering Human Bonds

When computers first entered our medical practice, we used them to look up information, but we still used paper for charting. Eventually, charting became entirely electronic and there was a move to put computers in clinic rooms with the expectation that the doctor would enter data into the computer while talking with the patient. I could never fathom doing that, and to this day I have never done it. I always bring paper to jot down a few notes when I am talking to a patient in the clinic, but my focus is on them. Seeing that they have my focus makes them feel comfortable and through eye contact and mannerisms, I can really process their body language, words and mood in order to adjust my interactions with them accordingly. My goal is that my undistracted focus will put them at ease and they will come to trust me.

While I was at UC San Francisco Medical Center, I did research on the science of interpersonal communication in health care settings. Using actors, I created two doctor-patient scenarios. In the first one, the doctor was paternalistic. In the next scenario, using the same actors, the doctor was a more active listener and less directive. Then, we recruited people to watch and say which doctor they would prefer seeing. We found that 30% of the respondents preferred the more paternalistic doctor. That percentage was higher than we had expected and was exactly why we did the study. Why this outcome? It turns out that people's preference when it comes to communication style varies greatly. The key is to understand what form of communication will work with a specific patient. As health professionals, we will be much more impactful if we can read the patient and adjust our approach based on what we gather from their reactions. It also helps to ask directly at times.

As much as technology has helped us become a global village — I can ping my dear friend in India in an instant via WhatsApp — it has also allowed us to be insular. In a Common Sense Media study, 54% of teens today agree that using social media "distracts me when I should be paying attention to the people I'm with." This percentage has gone up since 2012, when it was 44%.[1]

It is easy to forget that it takes practice to connect with other people. Because we're all so harried, we often let our digital devices slip between us and the human bonds we need to develop our emotional intelligence and strength.This goes for our children too.

I had a challenging childhood, that is for sure. But there are parts of my childhood that I am incredibly thankful for, including the many opportunities I had to get to know people from different worlds and the opportunity to build relationships that led to many wonderful adult mentors.

I was an only child living with my mom. Her emotional health was not always strong, and we struggled with emotional and financial hardships. But of course, there were positive things too, and one of them was my mom's weekly Middle Eastern dance class. This was Berkeley, California in the early 1970s, and Middle Eastern dancing was very popular. She brought me along to her classes with the idea that I would watch. However, sitting was never easy for me, and definitely not in such an exciting environment. Eventually, I was invited to join the class. By age 6, I performed alongside the adults in their shows. I remember the pride I felt the first time I had a solo. More importantly, though, was experiencing the warmth and support of all the women in the class week after week.

My father had schizophrenia that began before I was born. He did not live with us, but I saw him regularly. It was often very stressful being with my dad. He loved me very much, and he tried his best to show me the world. He would take me to poetry readings, bohemian cafes, horse races and parks known for their chess players (and he taught me to play). My dad's dream was to be a professor, and we would spend hours walking around the UC Berkeley campus. It was there that he met my mom, who was studying English (and later became a school teacher), and he was in the English Graduate department. When my dad wrote a novel, it was hard to follow because he was suffering from schizophrenia during the time he spent writing it. Even though the plot is impossible to follow, the prose is gorgeous nonetheless.

I got such a rich exposure to unusual and fascinating people in all of these instances. Most profoundly, I got to really talk with these people and interact with them. It gave me a deep acceptance, curiosity and respect for the variety of people on this planet.

I became so interested in people from all over the world that by age 11, I decided I wanted to learn French so I could visit France one day. Eventually, I learned to speak four foreign languages well enough to have meaningful conversations with people in their own tongue. I love the joy on people's faces when I try to speak their language, and they get to smile and laugh at my funny pronunciations.

Meeting people from many economic backgrounds helped me see how similar we all are as humans and how some of us are just dealt a bad hand. I also learned that all people have interesting life stories. I find that when you ask questions, you often get to the more emotional elements of a person's story.

I started working when I was 12, and it was the first time I had a mentor who was also a mom figure. I worked for a wonderful woman who made clothes, and she would have me come and help her at the Renaissance and Charles Dickens Holiday Faires. I loved the work, but more importantly, I loved having this woman who cared about me in my life. There were many more "mentor moms" throughout my childhood and adolescence who made a world of difference to me. If things weren't going well at home or socially, having people I could turn to was wonderful.

These and other experiences made me passionate about helping youth find opportunities to connect with all sorts of interesting and supportive people as they grow up. It is so important because so many youth do not have this naturally. For example, in the State of Washington, a survey is given out every two years to high schoolers. The 2018 results found that 11% of eighth graders reported that if they were feeling sad or hopeless, they had no adult that they could turn to.

This chapter is about how we build stronger bonds in our homes. I start out by admitting how I need to be more proactive in this realm at times.

• • •

Expanding Their Connections With Humanity

Some of our best moments as parents come from exposing our kids to the wonders of the world — like when they're infants, and they discover the warmth of human skin or the soft cotton of their baby blanket. A toddler is thrilled by a garbage truck or fire engine driving by.

As they get older, it can be the workings of a musical instrument or the bounce of a soccer ball.

It is such an honor and privilege — and our job — to introduce our children to all sorts of different objects, places, cultures and experiences while they grow up.

Since my kids were young, I would bring them on many different kinds of outings where they were often the only young people around. These include talks given by members of Congress, rallies, improv shows, lectures on science, art exhibits and volunteer projects, such as removing invasive plants in city parks.

I purposely started this when they were young so that they would be less self-conscious around adults when they hit the self-conscious years. I also did not give them a screen so that they would learn to be comfortable with just sitting and being able to tolerate some boredom at times — although I was never looking for boring things to expose them to.

They weren't always excited to go on these adult outings, but with some compromises on my part — like promising that they would get to choose the next thing we did together that day or promising that we could leave early — they generally would agree to come along. We certainly have had our duds, and when this happened I would sheepishly whisper to them that we could leave at the intermission.

But more often than not, we got something from these experiences — in part because I would do homework before presenting my suggestions to them. My kids, now older, tell me that they are happy that we took them to many types of events as well as introduced them to many types of people, even if they were self-conscious at times. They have expressed that it was always worth it. The other day, Chase brought up two talks he particularly liked that we took him to. One was a retired Navy SEAL who spoke about resiliency, and the other was the author Simon Sinek who spoke about what it means to be a leader.

Tessa told me she most vividly remembers her meetings with Leon. Leon was a man I got to know who lived under the freeway in our neighborhood. When I jogged by him, I would stop to talk with him. He had schizophrenia and while his thought processes were disorganized, he was such a kind person. He made me smile and always wanted to give me little gifts. Since I spent years working with homeless people and people suffering from severe mental illness, I felt at ease with him. I had a heavy heart because even though I tried to help by calling city services to get him treatment and housing, I couldn't make it happen. A few times, I brought food to Leon and brought my kids to meet him too. He was so friendly and gave them little gifts that to this day, Chase still has. Just the other day, Tessa wondered where Leon might be all these years later.

It meant a lot to me that I could introduce Leon to my kids. I wanted to open their hearts in the way that Leon — and all the Leons I have met — opened mine. Research has shown that the number one way to decrease prejudice against people with mental illness is to spend time with them.

When we involve young people in more adult-focused activities, we show them that we value and respect their insights. We want to hear their reactions to important issues. We are also conveying that we know they have creative leadership qualities, and we want to give them examples of how they can employ such traits as adults.

With free time often equaling screen time for both kids and adults, how do we ensure we take the time to expose our kids to people of different backgrounds, to people on different career paths, to people who are creating art, or people who are working to improve the world?

The goal, of course, is not just to expose our kids, but to help them engage with others. I have told my kids over the years how much adults love it when young people show interest in them. I have spent much of my career teaching medical students and residents, as well as many students who help me in filmmaking. I am incredibly touched when these people ask me questions about my life and views.

Recently, I had one of those deeply rewarding moments when I learned that my kids "got" something I have worked so hard to convey to them. Tessa has been doing a lot of babysitting for a family and one evening, we were talking about how it was going. Tessa said the mom always worked in her office, but that she was not sure what she did in there. She then looked at me and said, " I will ask her tomorrow because, I know, I know ... adults love when we want to know about them." I smiled at her.

HERE ARE FOUR SUGGESTIONS TO ENSURE THOSE IN-PERSON ENCOUNTERS TAKE PLACE

1. Winter, spring and summer breaks are a great time to put some activities on the calendar for the upcoming months and to ensure that they actually happen and are not passed over by the convenience of yet another Netflix movie. Is there a dance performance or recital in your area? Is a speaker coming to town?

2. Talk with other parents to plan an event. My friend gets people to donate $5 to $10 a week, and then hires a yoga teacher to come to a house and lead some adults and teens through a class. Plan to see a talk together. Or have a few parents organize food preparation at someone's home with the kids — perhaps an apple pie, simple sushi or dumplings. These are hands-on recipes that allow time for chatting and jokes that everyone can help out with.

3. Give kids a say in things. For example, if you want to take them to a museum but they moan and groan about the plan, tell them that if they decide they want to leave after 20 minutes, you will be perfectly fine with that decision — and if they want to stay, that will be even better! Have you considered bringing them to a city council meeting? If you are bringing them to an art outing, share this little story: When Facebook asked us to show *Screenagers* at their headquarters, I found they are filled from floor to ceiling with pieces of art! Facebook works with many kinds of artists because they know how important it is that their employees think outside of the box, and art can inspire that sort of thinking.

4. Consider house policies that inspire connections with guests. For example, when we invite families with kids to come for dinner, I email the parents beforehand to say that we love having screen-free visits. That way, everyone knows in advance that personal devices are to be kept out of sight. The great thing is that after the night, I often get emails about how much the kids appreciated that devices were away.

IDEAS FOR CONVERSATION STARTERS:

1. Have you been to events, talks, etc. where there were not many other kids? How was that experience?
2. What experiences might be good to commit to in the near future to learn more about people and the world?

· · ·

Siblings and Screen Time

One night, a good friend of mine came over with his kids. We were chatting when he turned to my son and said, "Don't take for granted your relationship with your sister." I asked him where this heartfelt advice came from. He said that something we were talking about reminded him of the time years ago he and his older brother had a falling out. He said:

> *"My brother told my parents something I didn't want them to know. I remember my brother getting real joy out of seeing me get in trouble. We haven't been close since then."*

Then there is the flip side: siblings who are exceptionally close. I really enjoyed an interview I heard on Terry Gross' radio show, Fresh Air, with the filmmakers Mark Duplass and his older brother Jay.[2] They talked about a time when Jay went to college and felt alone and unsettled, and how it really helped him when Mark would come and spend weekends with him. Terry asked the brothers if people thought it was strange that this college guy was hanging out with his 14-year-old brother. They both said they never thought about what others might be thinking; they were just happy to be together.

The brothers started making films together in their mid 20s and have been doing so for over 20 years. Talk about a close relationship!

How does this relate to screen time? When I went into homes to film, I would often see siblings in parallel worlds for hours at a time, each in their own personal screen silos. I remember when 12-year-old Chris, who is in *Screenagers*, told me, "The only time my sister talks to me is when she bangs on the bathroom door telling me to get out."

Chris and his sister told me about the funny dress-up activities they used to do and family gatherings they had in the past. However, since he started playing video games and she started constantly interacting with her smartphone, that had all gone away.

I didn't have a brother or sister growing up — but boy, did I want one. I have always been fascinated with sibling relationships, especially now, seeing how the tech revolution is impacting them. I know tech can enable sweet interactions, like when my kids send thoughtful texts to each other — like photos or an inside joke. Siblings may love playing video games or watching movies together, but I also know that lots of times, they are in their own screen worlds and not interacting.

In talking with teens, I have heard different examples of the ways tech time will both connect and disconnect siblings. For example:

> "One thing I can think of are views and beliefs, because every-one is filled and given all their ideas and beliefs through social media platforms and ideas that I receive may be different than hers. I'm not super happy because nowadays, everything pretty much has to do with technology. So if she's home, we sometimes never hangout and are just cooped up on our screens." — Tye, 15-year-old boy.

> "I have one sister who is turning 22 next month, so she is four and a half years older than I am — I'm 17. We're a really close family and my sister and I are also best friends. TV definitely brings us closer, since we have special shows that the two of us

watch. Recently, we've been watching the Bachelor/Bachelorette and we love talking about it and "hate watching" it together. I guess when we are both on our phones doing stuff on our own it isn't making us closer, but we're not very phone obsessed, so it doesn't cause any problems between us. I'm really happy that we can use screens, such as TV, to find common interests. I wouldn't really change anything about our relationship, except wishing that she liked some other things that I like, such as playing sports in our yard. " — Ali, 17-year-old girl.

"I have a sister named Chloe who is 13 and graduating eighth grade this year. I am three years older and two school grades ahead of Chloe. The screen brings us together because we love to watch movies and TV shows with each other and talk about them. Sometimes we show each other funny things from TikTok or memes, etc., and it brings us closer. In quarantine, we started a tradition where we eat ice cream and watch a movie together. Our favorite was "Breakfast Club." Right now, we laugh a lot about "The Office." Although the screen does bring us together, sometimes we don't talk to each other in person as much because we're on our phones or watching movies." — Andy, 15-year-old boy.

"I have two older brothers. Watching movies and shows together is something that helps us spend time together. Recently, one of them was teaching me to play video games because quarantine boredom was getting to me. Also talking about things we've all seen on the internet or shows we watch is something that often starts bigger conversations. But screen time also gets in the way of us spending time together. Sometimes we all go off on our own screens separately when we could be spending time together. Everyone is in different places watching shows, on YouTube, playing video games or something else. I'd want more time spent hanging out all together off of screens." — Isabel, 15-year-old girl.

Here are some suggestions of how to approach things.

TALK ABOUT THE COMPLEXITIES OF SIBLING RELATIONSHIPS

All too often, there is this unwritten expectation that having conflicts in relationships is somehow the failing of parties involved. I often think the reverse, in that every individual is so different from any other being that it is amazing to see people get along as well as they do. Talk about how different everyone is in the family, and think of all the ways you do get along so much of the time despite these differences.

NORMALIZE THE INTENSE RANGE OF EMOTIONS THAT A SIBLING CAN HAVE IN RELATION TO ANOTHER SIBLING

As an adult, part of the wisdom we gain is a realization that it is normal to have a host of feeling toward someone we care about — such as jealousy or anger. We forget that kids can often feel shame for having feelings like jealousy or spite toward a sibling. I have found that it can help my kids form deeper emotional intelligence when I say things like: "As humans, it is wacky and frustrating that we can't control our feelings more. For instance, we can't always avoid being jealous about something someone has, like a brother or sister."

NEVER UNDERESTIMATE THE POWER OF FAMILY GAME TIME

When our kids were little, we had much more success when we said, "Hey, go and play with your sibling — I need more time to work." Bam, they would start playing together — not always, but most of the time. Once they hit teen years, they really don't want us telling them to go play with their siblings.

I have found that it is productive to play family games to get my two kids to engage in some positive, connected time.

My family has several board games that we love. Wits and Wagers is my all-time favorite game for the family, particularly when my kids were between 10 and 16 years old. In the game, you try to get closest to the correct answer. An example is, "How many pounds does the Oscar statuette weigh?" As a family, we have made up our own questions based on cities we have lived in, such as, "How many Starbucks stores are there in Seattle?" Now, when we play with our made-up cards, we laugh a lot.

My second favorite would be Apples to Apples. During a recent Thanksgiving break, I was jazzed to walk downstairs to find my high school daughter playing the game with her 23 and 18-year-old cousins. Another of our family favorites is Boggle, where cubes are painted with one letter per side and are shaken up and displayed on a grid. Players come up with as many words as they can before time runs out. Finally, Code Names is a blast. You work with a partner and you give them clues to help them identify cards.

IDEAS FOR CONVERSATION STARTERS:

1. When does technology bring you closer to another person?
2. When does technology pull you and other people apart?
3. What are some of the best times you have had with your siblings or friends, and how can you ensure that you will have more?

• • •

Building Communication Skills Via Jobs

The blog I wrote about ways to manage screen time in the summer was so popular that it motivated me to write about the positives of jobs (and tasks) for our kids in this screen-saturated world. People often tell me that they worry that youth are losing their ability to communicate face-to-face. What particularly concerns me about this is how some youth may not get as much face-to-face communication time with adults as they once were able to.

There was a time not long ago when a child would go to a friend's home, and communicate with the parents like they were an adult. Now, when kids and teens go into other people's homes, often everyone — the kids and adults — are looking at a phone or another screen.

One incredible antidote for this is having jobs or volunteering, so that our children have built-in interactions with adults. These early working experiences provide preteens and teens communication and negotiation skills with people who are older than them. Examples include babysitting, working in a frozen yogurt shop, a clothing store, a movie theater or volunteering at a day camp. One of my jobs in high school was working in the clothing store on Telegraph Avenue in Berkeley, where I gained experience interacting with adults. The store manager, Kathleen, became a "mentor mom" to me. I knew she had respect for me and boy, was that a wonderful feeling.

I had other mentor moms growing up — some from other jobs, but also a couple who were my girlfriends' parents. I am still close with those moms today. I would define a "mentor mom" as a woman who fully cared about me as a person and who would take the time to really listen to me and help me see different perspectives. They also believed in my abilities and encouraged me to think bigger.

I once was talking with a girlfriend who has kids about this idea of mentor moms, and she said to me: "I wish I had some mentor moms growing up. I didn't, but I really try to be one for my kids' friends."

The reality is that jobs are hard to find in many parts of the United States for young people, and for adults too. Particularly now with Covid-19, we are going through very hard economic times. To find jobs, youth need to be thinking outside of the box even more so then they did pre Covid-19. Jobs can include all sorts of things, like helping a neighbor out regularly, setting up car washes or volunteering at a retirement center to help residents with technical issues like setting up Skype (Tessa did this in ninth grade). It is great when youth come up with ideas themselves, but adults can also play a key role.

My neighbor, a middle-aged dental hygienist who lives alone, came over to borrow some cooking oil, which I excitedly gave her because neighbors so rarely pop over. Two days later, she left a bag of cookies for my teens with this note:

> "I need help with a few jobs ... price negotiable per job! Thanks, Tessa and Chase. P.S., You may also bid the job. All pay well and fair. Thanks, we'll have fun together."

I LOVED THIS. How great that my neighbor reached out in this way. Tessa texted her to say she was interested, but was in the middle of finals and would contact her right after. I was so jazzed that Tessa would be able to both help out and have regular conversations with my neighbor — more time talking with adults!

I am also conscious of trying to find tasks for neighborhood kids. For example, when we got a dog, a 12-year-old neighbor asked to walk him. She does this for us now and then, and when she comes by, I always stop what I am doing to talk with her.

Besides all the wonderful face-to-face time that jobs provide, they also provide kids with opportunities to build feelings of self-efficacy. It helps them have thoughts like, "I am a good worker," "I am responsible," "I can negotiate" or "I asked questions, even though it made me feel uncomfortable."

Another wonderful plus of jobs is that it can expose youth to employment tracks that they might get excited about. For example, youth can have jobs in construction, restaurants, car repair, working with kids and the list goes on.

In the 1980s, 70% of teens (ages 16 to 19) had summer jobs.[3] This number has declined yearly, and in 2010, it reached 43% and has stayed about the same since.

They help prevent screen time overload and have many other upsides — remember, even occasional small jobs count.

Here are some suggestions:

- It takes a lot of grit and resourcefulness to find a job — if your kid takes the lead on this, that's a great and wonderful learning experience for them. If they need a little help, it's also fine to help brainstorm and give them some leads.
- Other parents are great resources to check in with about work opportunities for your child.
- Remind your kids that their school counselor is a resource for job ideas.
- One of the best resources are their friends. For example, Tessa told a neighbor friend about her job at a cafe that might have extra hours, and that friend started working there.

IDEAS FOR CONVERSATION STARTERS:

1. What jobs look fun to you at this time in your life?
2. Have everyone in the family talk about jobs they have had in the past and what they learned from those experiences.
3. What adults in your life do you think of as mentors?
4. How has our tech revolution helped with communication?

. . .

The Art of Asking People to Put Their Phone Away

In 2016, when actress Jennifer Lawrence was talking to the press after winning a Golden Globe for her performance in the movie "Joy," she told a reporter to put his phone away. She said: "You can't live your whole life behind your phone, bro. You can't do that, you know. You have to live in the now."

The reporter responded by saying, "Sorry, sorry, sorry."

Studies have shown that the mere presence of a cellphone puts our brains on alert for potential distractions, making cognitive functioning and connecting in person more difficult.[4] So why aren't we asking people more often to give us their full attention and put their phone away?

There is an art to asking people to do this. The way you approach the ask is key to the get. I have asked dozens of middle and high schoolers whether they have ever asked friends to put their phones away. About 80% of them tell me they have. When I inquire about their tactic, many say what works for them is to just be straightforward and say something like, "Hey, can you please put your phone away?"

Tessa and I often talk about how people ask for phones to be put away. One day, I was driving her somewhere and she was checking her phone.

"Hey, what are you doing?" I asked, because she knows we have a no-phone-in-the-car rule.

She laughed and said, "That's how you always ask me to put my phone away — 'Hey, what are you doing?'" She was right: That is typically my go-to for the family.

But let's think of situations not involving family, such as when you are trying to have a conversation with a friend at school or at work who is clearly preoccupied with their phone.

Could you see yourself ever saying any of the following?

- "You seem really busy. Should we shoot for another time together instead of now?"
- "It would be great to have your attention. I know many others want it right now too. What are your thoughts?"
- "Would you mind waiting until we are done to use your phone?"

One helpful approach is to try to get ahead of the situation. In *Screenagers*, there is a scene where a group of teenagers is out at a restaurant and they all put their phones in the middle of the table. The first one to check their phone pays the bill. How about trying this with your family, but in this case, the first one to check their phone has to do the dishes.

Elaine Giolando, who writes for Fast Company, decided enough was enough and began asking people to put their phones down.[5] In 2018, she wrote:

> *"It's an experiment in doing something pretty unthinkable these days: asking for someone's full attention. It takes some vulnerability to speak up, but I've found it's also provoked worthwhile conversations about the importance of being present."*

Undistracted presence fosters connection and trust in a relationship. There is nothing wrong with asking the person you are with to put their phone down. But how we do it is important.

Google these fun videos on this very subject: "Adam Levine of Maroon 5 asking the crowd to put their phones away for his next song." Or the rap video, "Put Your Phone Down," from Fog and Smog Films (an adapted version of this song appeared in *Screenagers*).

IDEAS FOR CONVERSATION STARTERS:

1. Have you heard people ask others to put their phones away? Have you done this?
2. What are "wrong" or rude ways of asking? What are effective ways to ask?
3. What approaches do some teachers have that you find respectful and effective?
4. How can we do better at asking each other for undistracted attention?

Why Talk to the Cashier?

The other day, a mom told me this funny/not-so-funny story. She had sent her son to the butcher and got a text from him:

> **Son:** *"Mom, do I have to talk with the butcher?"*
> **Mom:** *"Yes! Yes, you do!!!"*
> **Son:** *"Mom, why are you freaking out?"*
> **Mom:** *"Because you are 16, you should be able to talk with the butcher!"*

There is no doubt that all of us want our kids to grow up feeling comfortable talking with people in all sorts of settings — whether a butcher, a cashier or someone on a tram in the airport.

Today, I was talking with a 12-year-old about social media and self-confidence and he told me that posting pictures of himself doing cool things can boost his confidence. He then added, "But I feel like most of my confidence comes from actually talking to people in person because it is a lot harder."

Since my kids were toddlers, I encouraged them to ask questions, make comments, ask for directions, make requests, give compliments and order food from people who are new to them (in safe settings, of course). I am not using the word "stranger" because it has taken on such negative connotations.

Many of us now look down at devices when we are out in the world rather than interacting with others. We need to ask ourselves, at what cost? What are we missing out on when we forfeit these small interactions with others?

Psychologists Juliana Schroeder and Nicholas Epley wanted to understand why strangers near one another seldom interact, so they embarked on a study of Chicago subway commuters to compare those who talked with the people around them on the train to those who did not.

First, they asked participants if they thought they would be happier talking with strangers or less happy talking with strangers. The majority said they would be less happy and less productive. Statistically however, it turned out that the participants who interacted with their fellow commuters actually felt happier than those who were not randomized to do so.

So why don't people naturally talk to others more often? One hypothesis is that many of us assume that strangers don't want to talk to us. But actually, they found the opposite was true. Furthermore, the people who were spoken to by the participants in the study were also asked how that interaction made them feel. They too reported feeling happier.

"The pleasure of connection seems contagious," Schroeder and Epley wrote in their study, "Mistakenly Seeking Solitude," which was published in the Journal of Experimental Psychology.[6] They wrote:

> *"This research broadly suggests that people could improve their own momentary well-being — and that of others — by simply being more social with strangers, trying to create connections where one might otherwise choose isolation."*

Sadly, there are many people who are experiencing loneliness on a regular basis.

As former Surgeon General Vivek Murthy wrote in his article, "Work and the Loneliness Epidemic," which was published in The Harvard Business Review, "During my years caring for patients, the most common pathology I saw was not heart disease or diabetes; it was loneliness."[7]

In a Forbes interview about the study, Murthy said:

> *"Loneliness and weak social connections are associated with a reduction in lifespan similar to that caused by smoking 15 cigarettes a day — and even greater than that associated with obesity. Loneliness is also associated with a greater risk of cardiovascular disease, dementia, depression and anxiety."*

It is so common for people who are living alone when they are in their 70s or older to come to my clinic and say they feel isolated. It is a gift we can give when we are present, even for a short moment, to engage with the people around us.

Meanwhile, as we shop online more often, opportunities for real-time relating dwindles. When I learned that JCPenny had filed for bankruptcy and was closing 2,300 stores, I not only thought about all the lost jobs, but also the fun of shopping for my first pair of bell-bottom jeans as a tween at JCPenny.

Modeling behavior that I want my kids to mirror is always on my mind. One thing I'm consciously working on is making sure to be off the phone when I get to the front of the line at the grocery store. I don't want to miss the opportunity to connect with the cashier. I'm not perfect, and there have been times when I am on a call for a medical emergency and can't jump off the phone. In these situations, I apologize to the cashier right as soon as I get off the phone.

IDEAS FOR CONVERSATION STARTERS:

1. Can you think of someone you got to know just by striking up a conversation?
2. How easy is it for you to talk to strangers?
3. When was your last conversation with someone you did not know and how did it make you feel?
4. Let's all agree to talk (such as make a kind comment or ask a question) to five people we don't know this week. This could be a staff member at school, a person at the grocery store, someone at our jobs, someone walking their dog, etc.

Building Good In-Person Digital Etiquette

Our kids learn a lot about how to behave by watching us. When we listen and don't interrupt someone, smile at a cashier or embrace a friend, they are watching. When we are out in the world with a smartphone in our hand, what are we teaching them about digital etiquette? How do we nurture relationships in the face of mobile technology?

It's not easy, but I have some ideas to share:

WHEN EVERYONE HAS A PHONE BUT YOU DON'T

Once, I gave a talk for a school district in Coppell, Texas and a girl who appeared to be about 12 years old came to the microphone during the Q&A and said:

> *"At my middle school kids can use their phones. We only get one break, and that is lunch. Well, all my friends are on their phones. I don't have one, and I wish they would talk with me."*

My heart sank a bit but I smiled and I asked her what she had tried. She didn't have an answer, so we brainstormed some ideas, including asking her friends if they could try to put their phones away perhaps one day a week or for a time at the end of lunch.

I encourage parents to teach their children to put phones away when they are in a group with kids who do not have a phone. Maybe they won't do it, but they are hearing from us what we think is a kind thing to do.

GIVE A HEADS UP

If you are with someone and you decide you need to check your phone, use some digital etiquette such as, "My apologies, but I have to check my phone for a second." Or, "Can you excuse me, I just have to do this one thing quickly."

Years ago, I worked with my family to establish this etiquette so that when we were out together, and someone had to check their phone (which we try not to do), we gave a quick heads up beforehand. I had a strong motivation to do this because when someone would turn to a phone, I never knew if they were disappearing for a while into their phone or if it was just going to be a quick thing. Not knowing meant that I often snapped at them — they didn't like it when I did that, and I didn't like it when I did that either.

Don't get me wrong, we are not some family in a Jane Eyre novel who constantly asks for permission, apologizes and sips tea. We often don't give warnings. But we are all aware and we try to.

KEEP DEVICES OFF AND AWAY FOR MEALS

My family does not have devices out when we eat a meal together. The visual reminder of the device on the table can create pressure. Also, the desire to check messages and notifications takes our attention away from those who are right in front of us.

I teach my teens about the benefits of putting away smartphones when they are eating with friends. For example, they know the study, "The iPhone Effect: The Quality of In-Person Social Interactions in the Presence of Mobile Devices." They know that the mere presence of a smartphone at the table increases the chance that conversations will be more superficial.[8] Now, when they are with their friends, they can joke about the "iPhone effect" and subtly impart this knowledge. I hope this results in more phones off of tables and in pockets.

Digital etiquette is a topic that is rich for discussion. It is a constantly-changing landscape, and I love how kids often tell me things that I hadn't considered — such as how groups navigate sharing video game controllers.

IDEAS FOR CONVERSATION STARTERS:

1. Have you seen anyone be particularly respectful when it comes to tech and social situations?
2. What digital etiquette do you try to follow?
3. How do you feel when you are talking to someone, and they take their phone out in the middle of your conversation?

• • •

Raising Helpers Starts at Home

Providing alternatives to screen time is our job, joy, burden — all of the above. I am constantly thinking of new alternatives, particularly those that build a sense of the "can do" spirit in my kids, as well as a "can give" sensibility.

Being a "house helper" or "home helper," if you live in an apartment, is something I want my kids to do all of their lives. This will help lay the groundwork for a lifetime of good habits. For instance, if they eat at a friend's home, they will automatically help clear the table. If they are living in a dorm and the inside sprinklers are accidently set off, (this happened in my son's dorm last year) they will start stuffing towels into the cracks of doors of as many dorm rooms as possible before they run outside. The instinct to help is one that is definitely nurtured by our parenting.

Long ago, I stopped using the word "chores" and started using the phrase "house help" to describe the tasks that keep a home running. On the weekends, my kids are expected to do about 20 minutes of house help — things like sweeping, cleaning bathrooms and doing some laundry. During the week, there are a couple of tasks they are responsible for, like cleaning up after dinner.

A while back, I realized I wanted to start changing weekend activities in order to give them more practice with ways to help in the household. I also wanted to make sure they were gaining mastery in more skills, which leads to building more self-confidence.

To get more buy-in from my teens, I've had to be thoughtful about my approach. For starters, I often ask if there is anything they want to help with during the weekend. I've also tried putting the tasks I want to be completed on a board, allowing them to sort out who will do what. Finally, I gave them some options to choose from.

But of course, as parents we know we must always be prepared for our kids to gripe about doing chores. But that's OK. As Tammy Fisher Huson, Ph.D., and author of "Fearless Parenting" said to me: "I do the dishes, and I don't have a smile on my face — we can't expect that from our kids." She went on to tell me that the key is that we give them positive recognition when they complete the task. You get more of what you name — and just because they "had " to do a task, it still is something we can express gratitude toward.

I loved hearing this from Tammy because I must confess, I was always a bit confused about how much to thank my kids for doing tasks that were expected of them. It always felt a bit odd, sort of like if a teacher thanked her kids for coming to class that day. Of course I would say thank you at times, but now I make sure to always thank them for doing house help.

Tammy taught me that honest recognition is the goal, so I have learned to say phrases such as,

"I know you really weren't excited to mop the kitchen, but I have to say, the floor looks amazing and I am so appreciative." Or: "I know that it is a pain to clean windows, but they look great. Thank you so much." And, "It is so wonderful not having all the grime on the cabinet doors, and I really can't thank you enough."

A common trap I find myself in is that I am aware my kids have a lot of homework and I find myself thinking that I shouldn't bother them with any house help, so as to allow them to focus on their work. Later on, my rational brain kicks in and I realize that they found plenty of time for unproductive screen time!

I want my kids to be helpers, and I know they also feel better knowing they are helping in the home. I know that asking them to help in new ways increases their self-efficacy — all good things. So, I catch myself when I have silly thoughts about school work, and I push those aside. The truth is, they have time to help in the house, and there are plenty of new skills to learn in doing so.

Here are some ideas of house-help activities you might have your kids do:

- Straighten books on a shelf and find a few to donate.

- Do some outside watering or pruning. It is a great one to do with them so you can talk about what plants do in various seasons, which plants hibernate, which are evergreen and so on.

- Clean the refrigerator. This is a good skill to have when living with others.

- Wash windows. A YouTube video beforehand can really help because it can take real skill to do this well.

- Have them make homemade granola — bonus points if they make it lower in sugar than store-bought granola. My favorite recipe is apple cinnamon. It's easy: mix several cups of regular oats with apple or orange juice until it's moist. Add a quarter cup of canola oil (or not), a little brown sugar or honey, and some cinnamon. Mix it all together and spread it out on two cookie sheets lined with tin foil or sprayed with cooking oil. Bake at 325 for about 20 minutes. Once it is out, add some raisins and nuts, if desired.

- Are there any small sewing tasks needed? I remember when my mother-in-law had all her grandkids sit in a circle so she could teach them how to sew on a button. She lovingly explained that sewing is an essential skill and that she wanted to make sure they knew how to do it. Now my teens know how to do small sewing repairs.

IDEAS FOR CONVERSATION STARTERS:

1. Have you ever shared with your kids what house help you did as a kid? If so, ask if they remember what that was. If not, talk about that with them now.
2. What are house-help activities that your kids might have time to learn? How about tuning up a bike, discussing how to change a tire or checking the oil in a car?
3. You might not feel happy about doing house help while you are doing it, but do you think that, eventually, you will feel good knowing you are contributing?

. . .

Confessions of a Distracted Parent (i.e., Me)

Recently, I felt a serious pang of remorse. My son Chase called me from college. Frankly, I assumed it was a quick check-in or perhaps an ask of some sort. I was editing footage at the time, and I kept editing while we talked. At some point during that call, I realized he had called intending to have a solid conversation. But by the time I realized it, the call was ending.

When we hung up, I had a pit in my stomach. I realized I was only half listening. On top of that, it was pretty obvious I was not fully present by the tone of my voice and the cadence of my responses. It was strange, but my mind started playing back my exact halfhearted responses and my delayed "yeahs."

I missed him and I kicked myself for not having pushed aside the computer mouse to focus totally on him. I wanted to call him right back to apologize. That tends to be my usual response when I wish I had spoken or acted differently.

Instead, I thought I would just sit with the feeling of remorse and use it to remind myself to stop when I started to do that again. If I could turn back time, I would push my chair back from my editing system, put my feet up on the desk and indulge in the interchange.

That said, I don't believe that we have to drop everything all the time for our kids. I also don't believe that we must never be distracted or that we always have to model perfect screen time use. As adults, our work is often on screens, so our use of screens is very different from our kids'.

Still, we can work on modeling certain behaviors as best we can. For instance, rather than being half present, try saying things like, "I am on a tight deadline, can I call you back later tonight?" Or, "Hey, so glad you called, let me put my computer to sleep so I won't be distracted." I wish I had said that second line to Chase when he called, but there's always next time.

In an international survey of more than 6,000 youth, ages 8 to 13, 32% reported feeling "unimportant" when parents used their cellphones during meals, conversations or family time.[9] Meanwhile, we adults can also feel dissed when the young people in our lives go on a device when we are with them. We may feel that they are ignoring us or are distracted, like I was with my son.

In *Screenagers NEXT CHAPTER*, there's a funny moment when an elementary school boy tells us how he doesn't want to come down to dinner when his mom calls him because he is too engaged in his game. He says:

> *"When you click on a game, you can't take your eyes off the screen. When your mom calls you for dinner, and you're like, 'one second.' And then she keeps on calling and calling you, but you just don't go. You just keep playing because it's so interesting. More interesting than you having dinner or helping your mom."*

Not long ago, I listened to a great episode of the podcast, "Like a Sponge," which looked at screen time and youth.[10] In the episode, a preschool teacher named Tara tells the host that during the first week of school, she always asks parents to stay for a couple of hours. She asks them to engage with their kids in order to help their children begin their journey into schooling.

Tara says that in the past, parents would really engage, but something has changed over the past five years. Now, most of the parents sit near their kids and focus on their cellphones or laptops instead. Tara's concern is that the parents weren't engaging with each other or the teachers and that the parents' disengagement signaled to the toddlers that school is not interesting.

That made me sad. And yet there is another way to look at the situation. Perhaps it is ideal for kids to see their parents doing their own thing so that children get the message that this is THEIR new place. They need to discover the toys and friends, and their parents are close by if they need them.

Still, I worry that the signal to the toddlers is more negative than positive. It would be ideal to have studies that look at how those toddlers did in school a few months later compared to toddlers whose parents were not on their phones during that first week.

I learned about an app development class where fourth through seventh graders were asked to define a problem and come up with an app that offers a solution. Students brought up the issue that they often felt ignored by parents who were distracted by their screens. The kids suggested that a voice recognition app that would freeze parents' phones whenever the child's voice was detected could solve this issue.

So often we want our children to get off of their phones. But what if our kids want US to get off of our phones too? I'm sure you've heard, "Mom, mom, mom," while you're reading an email, checking a text or reading an article. Our phones have become such a part of our daily lives that we often don't realize how much we use them. But our kids know.

IDEAS FOR CONVERSATION STARTERS:

1. What are some of the best ways I give you my attention?
2. Do you find that I'm on my phone, tablet or laptop when you want my attention?
3. What are the ways you can tell that I am only half paying attention?

· · ·

The Power of Helping Others and Feeling Needed

Kids and teens get so many positive emotions when they feel that they matter and that they are making a difference in someone's life or a situation. Resilience is fostered when they can take action to support and help others. When shelter-in-place began, I felt it was so important that we help kids, teens and college-age youth figure out ways to safely help others via tech and non-tech means. Some of the ideas below came directly from youth themselves.

TECH ENABLED WAYS YOUR CHILD CAN HELP OTHERS

Using tech to create uplifting gifts

GarageBand is a fun way to create a song. Maybe you can create a song based on a memory of a grandparent and then send it to them. Or maybe create an opening melody and put it at the front of an audio card.

Consider creating a video montage to make others smile. How about a video to educate others — as some young people did regarding Covid-19? Maybe create an online photo album by using some of your favorite photos and including captions.

Using tech to find ways to help the community

Learn how to help in your neighborhood by using an app. Recently, my college-age son, Chase, learned that he could help at the local food bank through Nextdoor. When he went to volunteer, he really enjoyed it.

Using tech to find ways to make donations

Consider making small financial donations, even if it's just $5. Very small online cash donations actually make a difference for several reasons. One is that all small donations add up. Also, when people donate, they are also more likely to spread the word to others which helps generate more donations. Finally, organizations want to be able to tell others about their campaigns, contact foundations that might fund them and track the number of people who have made donations, irrespective of the dollar amount.

Rachel Kisela, a University of Washington student who helped in the making of *Screenagers NEXT CHAPTER*, wrote this:

> *"I know one thing that has made me feel helpful during this time is using the internet to find places to donate money. A lot of my favorite social media influencers are directing their viewers to donate to various charities, and donating even a little has made me feel helpful during this time."*

CONSIDER NON-FINANCIAL DONATIONS

The Internet is a wonderful way to find places that need non-financial donations, such as food banks that are trying to get more items to distribute to those in need. Rachel, the UW student I mentioned above, said, "Also, posting on social media about looking in your garage for spare masks to donate to local hospitals and offering to pick them up to donate them."

NON-TECH WAYS TO HELP OTHERS

Brighten up your neighborhood

Consider creating art. The other day I got such a smile from walking past a young girl who was drawing beautiful chalk art. I have since seen the art in more places, and know that many teens are doing this all around the country. My family had an artist outline a mural on our garage, and we had friends help us paint it this past summer.

Consider creating smiles

When it comes to taking walks in the neighborhood, so often smiles and greetings are lacking. Consider trying this challenge: smile and say "hi" or wave to people when you go on a walk and see how many of them smile or wave back. No matter if they respond to your kind gesture, you can feel good knowing that you are spreading good cheer. And then you can see if on another day you get more waves back.

Another important step to take is to think of those who live alone in your neighborhood that are at risk of feeling isolated. Consider writing a note as a family and putting it in their mailbox explaining that your family would love to be in contact just to say hi, and to help in any way.

Surprise friends with snail mail

Consider sending cards to friends in the mail. In February, I sent friendship-themed cards to several of my closest girlfriends. I told them it was Valentine's Month, and it was such fun to think about my dear friends (and to eat chocolate). My friends all texted or called me to say how excited they were to get something fun in the mail.

Consider random acts of kindness for a family member

Help your child create a funny costume for a younger sibling's stuffed animal, help them make a sibling breakfast in bed or have them make their bed ... the list goes on. Think of new ways to help around the home. One sixth grader wrote me the following:

> *"I have been helping my parents with yard work. Last week I spread out 90 bags of mulch and cut my whole yard. I have also been helping the older neighbors with their yard work since they haven't been outside as much."*

Consider spreading the gift of appreciation

When Covid-19 hit and school campuses were closed, I was moved by the number of students who wrote letters to their teachers to say how much they appreciated them and how much they missed their in-person classes.

As a teacher myself (to medical students and residents), I have told my teens that it makes us feel so good when we hear appreciation from our students.

A local newspaper in Marin Country published a letter a student wrote them about her teacher. Here's an excerpt:

> *"I am currently a junior at Drake High School and a student of Kendall Galli. After seeing her [Mrs Galli's] comments in an article published ... regarding school closures, I felt inspired to write to my teacher thanking her ... While online school is far better than nothing at all, it is simply not the same."*

The list above was just a tiny drop in the ocean of goodness youth are doing day in and day out.

IDEAS FOR CONVERSATION STARTERS:
1. What have your friends been doing to help others?
2. What have others done that have helped you?
3. Have you hit a low spot during this hard time?

Chapter Ten:

Cultivating Creativity, Insight and Focus

I am of the mindset that we are all born with not only the capacity to be creative, but also the need to be creative. We are creative all day long in at least very basic ways — thinking of how to respond to a person takes creativity!

When I was a kid, screen time was not too appealing — after all, there were only so many "Gilligan's Island" or "Brady Bunch" reruns I wanted to watch.

Instead, I spent a fair amount of time on creative endeavors, such as painting flowers with watercolors, making up a dance to Stevie Wonder's album or beading bracelets.

Nowadays, there are so many things that can pull at our kids' attention, providing them with less time off screens to create. And it turns out a lot of on-screen time is not creative time. Common Sense Media's 2019 Census: "Media Use by Tweens and Teens" asked 8 to 18-year-olds how they spend their time on computers, smartphones and tablets.[1] The number one category selected was "passive," which included watching videos and TV shows, reading and listening to music. This made up 39% of all screen time consumption. Communication — think social media — made up 16% of the time. Video games and scrolling the internet made up 30% of the time. Only 3% of the time was spent creating digital art or music. Only 3%!

Having many opportunities to be creative — to think up original ideas, experiment with building and designing, etc. — is all key for our youth. When young people create things, they get to experience important feelings of self-efficacy, pride and grit since so often, creation is full of frustrations that need to be overcome.

Another key component of creativity is the courage it takes to put one's ideas and creativity out into the world to be seen by others. The notion of the self-critic starts somewhere around 10 years old and introduces feelings of doubt and fear when it comes to putting things out that will be seen by others. Around this time, youth start to opt out of creating in fear of negative judgment from others and themselves. This is exactly the time when parents want to give kids more chances to overcome the false-negative narratives and practice taking feedback — learning to ignore some and improve from others.

This chapter contains ideas for redirecting kids and teens toward creative online endeavors, such as composing music or writing a story — all made easier by technological tools. One might provide an aspiring young writer with a software such as Scrivener, which lays out how to build a movie manuscript or write a nonfiction book.

In conjunction with creativity, this chapter also offers ideas of how to promote greater insight and focus. What do we learn about ourselves and our tech habits when we shake things up by changing our physical spaces or our tech screens? In our hyper-paced culture, what are the upsides of slowing down and checking in?

. . .

Fostering Creativity
in Their Online and Offline Lives

When we presented *Screenagers* to employees at Pixar Animation Studios, I talked with Guido Quaroni, VP of Software R&D and the voice of Guido in "Cars," about Pixar's recruitment efforts. I said to him, "It must be hard to find good software coders for your many projects." He responded:

> *"No, it is not too hard — yes, we compete with Google down the way, but that's OK because frankly, we are a bit cooler. The real challenge is finding the creatives ... the people to write the stories, to do the animation, to create the set designs."*

That surprised me. I mean, who doesn't want to have a creative job at Pixar?

I suppose this is not so surprising after all. It's hard work to be creative, and entertainment seduces the brain into relaxation. It's not just teens either. The iconic American novelist Norman Mailer once said of the hard work of writing, "Every one of my books killed me a little more."

Perhaps the key is to tease your kids into creativity until it's no longer hard work.

I've been shocked that my kids' teachers never give homework that involves using technology to create something. I'd love to see homework that requires listening to music tied to history or trying to compose a funny jingle using GarageBand. Students have so much homework on the computer, why not have it focus on creativity?

A while back, a team at Facebook's headquarters in Menlo Park asked me to show *Screenagers* and give a talk. When I brought up a study that found that content creation only accounts for 3% of the time teens spend online, one of the VPs argued that social media exercises their creative muscles.

It so happens that the interior of Facebook was covered with art installations. Our host said, "We have great internships where we invite artists because it is so key that all our employees be reminded to think outside the box."

We all want young people to be thinking outside the box and executing their original ideas. I think back to a screening where I spoke with two teen girls about their phone use, and one said, "Everything is OK I guess, but I am bummed that I don't do any of the art projects that I used to do."

That's where parents come in. We need to help our kids find creative things to do online and off. If you are tired of barking at them to get offline, here are some ideas to redirect them toward engaging in something more creative online. And by the way, this can be a great opportunity to create alongside them. If there is a creative tool they already know and love, ask them to teach it to you — who doesn't love witnessing their excitement when they get to teach us new things?

HERE ARE SOME SUGGESTIONS TO GET YOUR KIDS
TO BE MORE CREATIVE WHILE ONLINE:

- Code a video game (Code.org, CodeAcademy, Code Avengers all have free resources).
- Create a movie on a phone using one of the many editing apps. The iMovie app is way easier to use on a phone than on a desktop.
- Work on a piece of music. They can make it offline and then record it online, and if they are inspired to share it with others, they can upload it to SoundCloud.
- Mix some music. Tell them what a mixtape was back in your day.
- Make a podcast. They can use their phone to do interviews; GarageBand has a podcasting feature. PodBean, Anchor and Buzzsprout are easy and fun.
- Have them listen to any of these family-friendly podcasts for inspiration: "Planet Money," the "Ted Radio Hour," "How I Built This with Guy Raz," "Hidden Brain" or "Revisionist History."
- Draw on a tablet.

AND HERE ARE SOME OFFLINE SUGGESTIONS FOR CREATIVITY:

- Write a script for a scene in a movie and if they create a part for the parent, have a family script reading — or better yet, truly act it out.
- Prick a hole in an egg, blow out the inside and use sharpies to make beautifully decorated shells.
- Create a scavenger hunt with their friends.
- Go to a museum and sketch an art piece.
- Build a sculpture from recycled materials.
- Bead — it was and still is one of my favorite artistic pastimes.
- Build something from wood.

IDEAS FOR CONVERSATION STARTERS:

1. What are all the things you do online that you would categorize as creative?
2. Are Snapchat stories, TikTok, Facebook Live or Instagram filters forms of creativity?
3. Can you estimate how much time you spend online passively viewing other people's creations?
4. How much of the time spent online do you actually use to create something?
5. Read the list of ideas above and see if any of them appeals to you. Do you have some ideas for something new and creative you might want to try?

* * *

Creating Via Tech to Make a Difference

When I ask a young person about how they might solve a major societal problem, they often start talking about an app-based solution. Thinking about the apps that people develop for social good is a great topic to discuss with our kids and students. The more we can help them think of tech as a tool rather than just as an entertainment and social center, the better.

I hear of many ways that youth use tech tools to help others. For example, the app Garage Band allows people to create music, and I know some have used it to create and send funny songs to others to brighten up their mood.

Being able to make videos to bring joy is another great tool. A 16-year-old boy named Andy recently wrote this to me: "My girlfriend's mom is the administrator of an assisted living center, and she asked us to do something to bring some happiness to the residents." Andy made a funny video of his dog and put it to music that he thought the residents would like. He told me: "Our idea is to have the residents come up with a song list and our plan going forward is to give our friends with dogs a song, so that we will have a whole playlist for the residents with a variety of dogs."

My son Chase excitedly told me about meeting Andrew, a guy in his mid 20s who, alongside his friend Miraj, got the idea to create the app Harness. One day, Andrew and Miraj were driving when Miraj had to hit the brakes suddenly, causing the loose change in his cup holder to spill onto the floor.

"What a waste," Miraj said, referring to all the change that had just been thrown around. A few minutes later, Andrew and Miraj noticed how almost all the billboards they were passing were asking for donations for various causes. They started talking about how they could harness the digital revolution to get the spare change floating around in people's lives to those who could really use it.

From this idea, the app was born. With Harness, people can donate a little change to good causes by rounding up their online purchases.

Here are some other examples of creative technology that benefits communities. I purposely included ones started by adults, and not just teens. The last thing any of us want is yet another dispatch that implies that a "successful" teen should have already started a foundation, created two apps, taken 10 AP courses, etc.

Kiva.org was started in 2005 by Matt Flannery and Jessica Jackley. They were inspired by a talk they saw during graduate school. Kiva is a microfinance company that enables people to give a small loan to others using the power of the internet. People can lend as little as $25 to help a borrower start or grow a business, go to school, access clean energy or realize their potential in some way.

As of April 2019, $1.3 billion has been lent through Kiva, with a 97% repayment rate. Tessa and I got involved with Kiva and find it inspiring to read stories about what people are doing all over the world. And being able to make loans to them is rewarding as well.

Astra Labs was developed by Amanda Southworth, a teenager suffering from anxiety and depression who turned to coding to find relief. The app has games and exercises to help a person get through a panic attack. It also uses a person's location to suggest local resources so that the person can find help.

IDEAS FOR CONVERSATION STARTERS:

1. When was the last time you created something via tech to bring joy to someone else?
2. What issues are dear to your heart? Are there any that you would like to get involved with one day?
3. How might an app and the internet help with that cause?
4. How can you help offline?

. . .

Unplugging — Restful or Stressful?

Many people have ways to digitally detox — even our country has a National Day of Unplugging. This day occurs in March, starting on a Friday night at sunset and ending at sundown on Saturday. The National Day of Unplugging started about a decade ago. The project is an outgrowth of the Sabbath Manifesto — an adaptation of the ritual of carving out one day per week to unwind, unplug, relax, reflect, get outdoors and connect with loved ones.

WHY UNPLUG?

One reason to unplug is to "break free of automaticity." I came up with this line thinking about National Day of Unplugging because one gains a lot of insight from stepping out of habits. Noticing urges — like the urge to check a phone or laptop or the urge to pick up a video game controller — can be educational. Thoughts may emerge, like, "I never thought how many times I go to do this or that," or "Wow, I never knew it would be so hard to resist the urge to … ," or "It felt great knowing it was not an option for me to default to a screen during that period."

Your family's "why" may be to reclaim a sense of relaxation. In a 2017 American Psychology Association survey of parents, 45% reported they felt disconnected from their families even when they were together because of technology.

I just learned about the app lilspace, which matches business sponsors with people who unplug. In response to a person not using their phone for a certain amount of time, a business will donate to a designated charity or nonprofit. For example, a sock manufacturer gave new pairs of socks to people living in homeless shelters based on people taking phone breaks, which were recorded and measured by the app.

Schools, or even individual classes, can consider an unplugged day. Creating opportunities to rock the status quo is the perfect way to spark thoughtful discussions on how tech helps us learn, how it hinders us, how it affects student-teacher time and how it impacts peer-to-peer time. Framing an unplugged day at school as an "Experiment in Digital Citizenship" could be cool.

WILL IT BE RESTFUL OR STRESSFUL?

Some people welcome unplugging as a time of freedom from the constant mental pull of devices. Shutting down all tech for a period of time can allow for focus on more present matters. Others may react with a flood of anxious feelings.

The MIT Review wrote about professor Ron Srigley's work with his students. In 2015, Srigley asked his students to try spending several days without using their cellphones. In 2019, he again asked students to do the same thing. Each year, many students signed up for the challenge. Students from both years reported upsides and downsides of their experiences.

Some students reflected on the positives of not having a phone. They reported that it was easier to complete school work. One said: "Writing a paper and not having a phone boosted productivity at least twice as much. You are concentrating on one task and not worrying about anything else."

Some students gained essential insights during the challenge. A student wrote: "Having a cellphone has actually affected my personal code of morals and this scares me … I regret to admit that I have texted in class this year, something I swore to myself in high school that I would never do …"

Not surprisingly, in 2019, the students were more dependent on their phones. It was harder for them to go without their phones and all of the tools that they rely on, like the bus schedule or payment apps.

HOW CAN WE UNPLUG?

If you decide to unplug, how can you increase the chance that it is a restful experience? One way is to plan for it. For instance, I realized that I was bringing my laptop into my bedroom and working on it while lying in bed before falling asleep. This was not what I had wanted to do, as I really loved keeping my area of the bedroom screen free (my husband sometimes reads the news on his phone while in bed). So I decided I wanted to take action and get back to a screen free nighttime ritual. The first thing I did was place a paperback book and a highlighter by my bed (I love highlighting my books). Arranging my bedside table helped me no longer bring my laptop into my bedroom (I now do so about once every two weeks, which I am fine with).

You might suggest a card game in place of a video game or perhaps an outdoor scavenger hunt. Or, if you are driving with your kids somewhere, maybe suggest the car games we used to play in the "olden days," where we looked for license plates from different states.

IDEAS FOR CONVERSATION STARTERS:

1. If you were to unplug for the day, what do you expect would be the best parts of the day? What would be the worst parts?
2. What are some ways you would set up your day to lessen the pull of your devices?
3. Do you think you could gather a group of friends to unplug for 24 hours or a different amount of time?

. . .

Phone and Device-Free Vacations — Possible?

What might be the upsides of leaving devices behind for a family vacation, whether it be a smartphone or a game-filled iPad? Maybe it is for the weekend, or maybe it is a rare vacation of several weeks. My co-producer Lisa Tabb discussed this with her 13- year-old daughter before they left the country for two weeks.

Her daughter, Meleah, is a highly social teen. Lisa wrote about her daughter's decision to leave her smartphone behind. This would be great to read to your kids in order to start a discussion about vacations and phones.

Meleah really likes to talk to her friends via Snapchat, FaceTime and Instagram. A week before they left, Meleah said, "Mom, I think I'm going to leave my iPhone at home." Lisa played it cool and just asked why. Meleah said she needed a break, so they went "old school." Meleah brought along a Kindle (which can only download books), an iPod Nano (no screen, just a music clip-on), a digital camera and a flip phone.

Results:
1. She used the flip phone once
2. She read five books in three weeks
3. She listened to music and podcasts daily
4. She took photos, but no selfies
5. She was present, fun and inquisitive daily
6. She was NOT looking forward to returning home and had a dream the night before she returned that her friends were mad at her for not communicating. (The opposite was true. She returned to people texting and Snapping her about how much they missed her, which made her feel appreciated as a friend.)
7. When Meleah started up her iPhone, she had 500 texts, 15 Snapchat threads (which means that was about 100 actual Snaps — remember she wasn't engaging; had she been home, this number would have been 20 times higher) and an untold number of Instagram notifications

When she returned from the trip, she ignored everything that had been sent while she was gone and started fresh. For the first week, Lisa noticed she was spending less time online than before. And there were some notifications that she never re-enabled, which helped decrease the time she spent on her phone overall.

Tessa also decided to leave her phone at home during some of our trips. During those trips, she would sometimes use our phones to log onto her Instagram or Snapchat accounts. It was wonderful to not have her reaching for her own device. Chase was older when he got his smartphone and he tended to want to bring his phone with him on trips.

The key has been talking about our expectations around tech time before trips and making sure to check in during trips. There are definitely times of frustration when someone is on a screen too much or is using a phone in a place where we agreed we would not be on devices.

IDEAS FOR CONVERSATION STARTERS:

1. How do you think you would feel about leaving your smartphone at home?
2. How would you feel about being unreachable and out of touch?
3. What would you miss the most?
4. Do you think your friends would be mad at you, or understanding?

• • •

Gaining Insights Through Hack Challenges

We are all making choices all the time, consciously and subconsciously, of where to put our attention, what we want to do and what we want to say. So much of those decisions are about what motivates us and what our incentives are. When we stop and think about our behaviors around screen time, we get to see how much we might be elevating screen time above other things, how we feel about balance and if it would make sense to shake things up a bit.

In an effort to fire your insight neurons, ask your family how much money it would take for them to ditch their main mobile device for an entire year?

A few years ago, Vitaminwater announced it would award $100,000 to someone who was willing to give up their smartphone for a year.[2] People entered the challenge by declaring what they would do with the time they would save by eliminating the smartphone from their lives. The winner — a young-adult fantasy novelist — would get $10,000 if she made it past the six-month mark, and the full $100,000 if she went for a whole year. She made it.

30-year-old Elana Mugdan won the Vitaminwater challenge. "I've always had a love-hate relationship with the phone," Mugdan said in a CNBC interview.[3] "Like many millennials, I'm attached to it; it comes everywhere with me."

This was a relatively cheap way for Vitaminwater to get a lot of free advertising. (By the way, don't let them trick you into thinking that just because they have the word "vitamin" in their name, that their product is a healthy beverage. There is a large amount of sugar in these drinks.)

You don't have to enter contests to gain insight into your relationship with screen time. Let's look at some "hack challenges" that are ways you can experiment and change things up with your child when it comes to screen time. See what you can learn about each other and yourself at the same time.

Here are some hack challenges to consider. Who doesn't like a challenge?

Reorganize your home screen

Putting all your favorite apps on your home screen can be quite tempting. Try removing all the tempting apps and replacing them with just your calendar, your clock and your calculator. Lisa, my co-producer, removed Facebook and Twitter from her home screen and it has significantly decreased the amount of time she spends on social media.

Delete certain apps

When it seems a particular app is taking up too much of your time, the best thing to do is delete it. Many teens have video game apps (I was amazed to see how many ads they get on Instagram for additional games). Perhaps your teen will take the challenge to remove a game app for 72 hours.

Use blocking software
A Pew Research Center survey found that 45% of teens say that they are online "nearly constantly."[4] Apps like Freedom and Self Control aim to help people minimize this. They work by blocking social media, online shopping and any other online features that distract you for whatever amount of time you designate.

Time control apps
On an iPhone, you can set a Screen Time limit, which designates a specific amount of time during which you can use particular apps. Android phones have something on their Digital Wellbeing dashboard called App Timers, which allow you to set specific time limits for each app.

Turn off autoplay on YouTube
It is rumored by tech reporters that about 70% of videos watched on YouTube are videos that YouTube has put on the screen as a suggestion to you. These algorithms are so smart already, and it is disconcerting to think how much better they are yet to become with the rate of investment in AI development and Big Data analysis. Meanwhile, more automatic yet is what I call, "living by default" — just letting the autoplay do its thing and voila, one Youtube video right after another — no decisions required.

Here is something that is technically simple that can fight against autoplay. Go into your settings of YouTube and choose to "stop autoplay."

Limit notifications
One study found that the average person receives about 63 1/2 notifications each day.[5] This is distracting and can lead a person down a rabbit hole of scrolling. You'll be amazed at how much time you can save by turning off your notifications — limiting them to only those you need. I have set up my phone so that the only notifications I get are alerts for flights, notifications from rideshare apps and texts — but even for texts, I have an app that lets people know that I will not receive their message

until I stop my car if I am driving when they send it. People who know me well call me if it's urgent.

Take ads and other distractions off your pages

You might have noticed that some websites are cluttered with multitudes of distractions like autoplay videos, pop-up ads and sidebars that make it difficult to concentrate on one thing. There are several browser extensions that allow you to remove ads and other distractions from your webpages, leaving you a clean page of just text and images. Mercury Reader, a Chrome extension, is a popular one. If the ad blocker does not allow you to access something you need, it usually gives you the option to turn it off just for that page. You just look at the top of your screen for a notification.

Make your phone only perform in black and white

Try making your phone screen grayscale. The colors on your screen are like candy to your brain, and changing your phone to black and white is less rewarding to your cerebrum, so you may be inclined to spend less time scrolling. The red notifications — signifying that you have emails and messages waiting — can cause stress and are difficult to ignore.

Unfollow a few people you know whose posts bother you

Young people tell me how they "curate" their social media accounts to unfollow or block people that make them feel low in some way.

Unfollow influencers who don't make you feel great

My friend's daughter, who is in high school, told me that when she started unfollowing models, she was surprised by how much better she felt on social media.

IDEAS FOR CONVERSATION STARTERS:

1. When you realize that you have spent too much time on your screen, what gives you the power to stop?
2. Let's all pick one of the ideas above to try. But first, let's measure how much time we spend on our screens now. Then, compare that to the amount we will spend when we try one of these hacks.

3. After trying one of these hacks, consider the insights it gave you about yourself. Did you realize that you had lots of apps that you never used? Did you choose to delete some of these? Did you realize that getting notifications was controlling your behaviors more than you thought?

· · ·

How To Improve Mental Focus in Our Kids and Ourselves

How do we achieve maximal mental focus in an overly-wired and wireless world? Georgetown University professor, author and father, Cal Newport, addresses this in his book, "Digital Minimalism."[6] He writes about ways to prune your digital life, getting it down to the technologies that truly help us to think deeper.

I often talk about new strategies to help our kids focus during this tech revolution, whether that's enforcing a no-cellphone rule at school or finding ways to stay on task while doing homework. So, I am always excited to get ideas from others about helpful approaches that foster deep thinking.

Discussing this topic gives us a chance to share with our kids some of the strategies that we use to focus. When I talk with youth, they often complain about how distracted adults are on their devices — yes, true, we are often doing work on our devices. So, subtly reinforcing the point that we are working is key to making sure that we share how we stay on task.

In "Digital Minimalism," Newport argues that we should be much more selective about the technologies we adopt in our personal lives, in order to "radically reduce the time you spend online, focusing on a small number of activities chosen because they support things you deeply value, and then happily miss out on everything else."

Newport adds: "Technology is intrinsically neither good nor bad. The key is using it to support your goals and values, rather than letting it use you."

In an interview in the New York Times, Newport discusses with writer Tim Herrera how to achieve "deep work."[7] Here are some of the main points:

GIVE UP TECH TEMPORARILY TO GET BACK USEFUL TECH

He suggests the radical idea of giving up all things tech — like apps and social media — for a month to help reflect on your values, and then mindfully add back only the ones that will help you to achieve those values. The basic idea is that people need to be more intentional and selective about what apps and services they allow into their digital lives. I find it interesting that when embarking on the research for "Digital Minimalism," Newport asked his newsletter subscribers whether any of them wanted to try this idea. He thought just a handful of people would do it, but in fact, 1,600 responded.

I'm not proposing you go this far, but I do think that the more we talk to our kids about our values, their values and everyone's goals, the more it becomes clear that too much screen time can get in the way of one's values and goals.

CONSCIOUSLY CARVING OUT DEEP WORK TIME SLOTS

Newport tells Herrera, "You cannot just wait until you find yourself with lots of free time and in the mood to concentrate. You have to actively fight to incorporate this into your schedule. It helps, for example, to include deep work blocks on your calendar, like meetings or appointments, and then protect them as you would a meeting or appointment."(You may be interested in a book written by Daniel Pink called "When: The Scientific Secrets of Perfect Timing" that looks at the times of day that are more productive for certain tasks.)

EMBRACING BOREDOM FACILITATES DEEP THOUGHT

Newport says to Herrera:
"The ability to concentrate is a skill that you have to train if you expect to do it well ... If you always whip out your phone and

> *bathe yourself in novel stimuli at the slightest hint of boredom, your brain will build a Pavlovian connection between boredom and stimuli, which means that when it comes time to think deeply about something, (a boring task, at least in the sense that it lacks moment-to-moment novelty) your brain won't tolerate it."*

While I do not agree with how Newport equates thinking deeply with boredom, I agree that if one continually interrupts brain flow, new connections and mental breakthroughs can be hampered. (That's my excuse, at least, when my creativity falls short.)

Here are three examples of things I do to help create times of undistracted thinking:

1. I have no notifications on my phone other than for texts. For a long time, I didn't even have a sound notification for texts and instead, I told people who might genuinely need my attention to call in such cases. I have since turned back on the sound alert for my texts, but I am contemplating going back to the old way.

2. I often go to nearby cafes to do deep thinking, such as intensive research and writing. For a good chunk of time that I spend at the cafe, I turn off my WiFi so I will not reflexively keep checking my email.

3. I almost always keep a notebook at the side of my computer, so when thoughts pop up about things I want or need to do — such as check something online, sending a text or making a call — I write the task down so I will remember it later. Case in point: this is happening right this moment. I have the urge to go online and find the showtimes of the improv theater near my home. Instead, I will quickly write these thoughts down in my notebook and stay focused on writing this book.

IDEAS FOR CONVERSATION STARTERS:

1. What strategies have you tried in order to create sacred time free of distractions?

2. If suddenly, screens disappeared in the world and you were able to choose three screen-dependent activities/tools/apps that you could have back, which would you pick?
3. Do you agree or disagree with this sentence, "To be able to think deeply, one needs to be able to tolerate and even embrace moments of boredom"?

$$\cdots$$

Building Brain Attention Skills With Mindfulness

For most of my life, I had no interest in meditation or anything like it. Perhaps because I grew up in Berkeley, California — a mecca of hippie culture — or maybe it was because I grew up with intense adversity in my home. For whatever reason, I always steered away from things that felt "new age-y."

Meanwhile, I thought mindfulness meditation — which I will just refer to as meditation — was all about being able to clear thoughts from one's mind. I figured, why even try? It seemed impossible.

It was my son who got me thinking that I should look into meditation. In 10th grade, Chase started to use an app called Calm that helped him with relaxation techniques. He told me several times how much it really helped him relax.

With his input, and with mindfulness becoming all the rage, I looked into meditation. I was relieved to learn that mindfulness meditation does not tout the goal of clearing one's mind. Our brains are mega-processors that are constantly scanning the environment and continually generating thoughts. There is no "off" button for that, no matter how long you sit and breathe and try.

So many people, including youth, find it useful to gain control of their focus, deal with stress and help with screen time issues and even more. I am now one of those people. About two years ago, I began using apps such as Headspace and Ten Percent Happier to do about 10 minutes of meditation five times a week.

Let's explore some of the upsides people talk about regarding meditation. But let me be clear, meditation does not offer an overnight change. The changes are subtle. One of the upsides is actually just knowing you are practicing it. When I first started doing meditation, I remember telling a few friends: "Most days I sit and practice putting my thoughts where I tell them to go. Who knows how much it helps, but I am proud of myself for sticking with this."

BUILDING UP ONE'S ATTENTION MUSCLE

One main goal of a meditation practice is to learn how to pay attention to what you want to pay attention to, rather than being pulled by random thoughts. This practice helps build your "attention" muscle. It helps you get more insight into your patterns of thinking and learning in order to direct attention to more helpful thoughts.

In *Screenagers NEXT CHAPTER*, we visit a classroom in my daughter Tessa's high school, where for a few minutes on Tuesdays, they have quiet time. Some teachers lead a guided mindfulness meditation, and students choose whether or not to participate — no one is ever forced to close their eyes and partake.

I filmed one teacher as she led the class and said these words: "The invitation this week is to notice when you're starting to be critical of yourself. And just notice, can I shift what I'm focusing on away from that?"

DEVELOPING NEW WAYS TO HANDLE
PHYSICAL AND EMOTIONAL PAIN

When Chase was in 10th grade, he sustained a major concussion, which led to more than four years of chronic pain. He had medical workups for many symptoms that he had on and off over the years. There were months when he felt discouraged, angry and sad that he had so many unexplained physical problems that kept him from being physically active. It was so hard to see him so sad.

Eventually, Chase started using apps to teach himself mindfulness meditation. He particularly loved learning from George Mumford, who teaches meditation to professional athletes such as Michael Jordan.

In *Screenagers NEXT CHAPTER*, we see Chase listening to Mumford on an app. Then Chase talks about how learning mindfulness meditation has helped him deal with his chronic pain. He says:

> "There's the sensation of pain, but then I add the stress of being in pain and the emotional baggage of the history of the pain and the uncertainty of the future of the pain. And I recognize that I actually have a lot more control over this than I thought. So in my day-to-day, when I'm in physical or emotional pain, I can be mindful of the negative layers that are building up on top of it and intervene before they themselves cause unnecessary suffering."

During a gap year before college, Chase took a 10-day silent meditation retreat. For that week and a half, the participants did not speak and they meditated 10 hours a day. He said it was the hardest thing he ever did, but that he was happy he did it. In an article he posted on Medium he wrote:

> "The elation of making it to the end of the ten days was unlike any I had ever experienced. Throughout the week, the heaviness of boredom, pain and loneliness nearly convinced me to leave, as over a quarter of the attendees did. But I had overcome my reaction to these sensations. I had learned an invaluable skill to beat a debilitating enemy. ... Meditation has been a powerful tool for my chronic pain, and it is still a work in progress. While the Vipassana course was not much different in concept than the fifteen-minute sits I had done at home with meditation apps, the repetitive act of training my mind to get back up and let each sensation pass in its own time has taken hard work. While I still 'live in pain,' meaning painful and complicated sensations are constantly arising in my neck, head, and back, I continue to let go of my aversion to the narratives that give them power. I'm also less attached to a 'pain-free' state."

STRENGTHENING ONE'S ABILITY TO PUSH THE PAUSE BUTTON

Meditation can help people get better at being able to consciously stop for a split second to notice what is happening, and decide how to act before reacting. For example, when a person is sitting at a table with friends and has an urge to check their phone, they may get better at noticing the urge, choosing not to respond to it and letting it pass. In that moment of consciousness (mindfulness, attention, awareness), the person can then respond with a choice of:

> *"Do I want to give the signal to my friends that I am not genuinely engaging with them? Do I want to leave where I am virtually? Or, do I want to stay focused on my friends and take a big breath, letting the urge to check my phone pass?"*

Kids and teens may have said something during a video game they regretted or posted a comment they later wished they hadn't. Talking to them about getting better at pressing a mental pause button is definitely a good discussion topic.

GETTING TO A RELAXED STATE

When we meditate, we relax and breathe calmly, activating our parasympathetic nervous system, which is our body's stress-reduction system. When I speak to students at schools where mindfulness is incorporated into classrooms, they talk about how they appreciate that the breathing exercises help them handle stress better.

While working as a physician in an ER, I helped ease the misery of many people experiencing panic attacks. I use the word "misery" because people having a panic attack feel horrible and sometimes genuinely believe they are having a heart attack or are experiencing some other lethal event. Part of the treatment is to gently guide the person to breathe more calmly, so as to activate their parasympathetic system.

Since learning more about mindfulness meditation, I am much more likely to bring it up with certain adolescents and adults in my clinic when I think it might benefit them. It is wonderful that I can give them information about apps and YouTube videos.

PERMISSION TO "BEGIN AGAIN"

Something I love about mindfulness is the frequently used term "begin again." Many meditation teachers use this phrase. It is the idea that when you pick a focus point — it could be your breath, the feeling of your feet on the floor, or the sound of birds — your mind will soon start to wander. When your mind wanders, you just begin again. The cool thing is the viewing of the need to begin again as a win rather than as a failure because it is impressive to realize that your mind was wandering and to use your brain to redirect to your focus point.

Recognizing when we are off course and then gently bringing the focus back can help in real life. When we set up goals and then digress, it's easy to completely give up rather than calmly reminding ourselves to "begin again."

We can use the same skill to prevent getting overly frustrated when we express ourselves in ways we wish we hadn't. When I unintentionally bark at my son for being on his phone, I apologize for my tone and I tell myself, "begin again." Or, when I stop writing (my current attention spot), and start checking email, I catch myself. Instead of saying, "You're a loser, you will never finish your book," I non-judgmentally go back to writing, beginning again.

FINAL WORD OF ADVICE

Pushing our kids or teens, even gently, to try something like meditation can very often turn them off from it. One of the times I've failed is featured in *Screenagers NEXT CHAPTER*. Tessa was talking to me about why she started going to a weekly teen group and said, " ... because you didn't get involved ... unlike when you emailed the debate club, and I won't go back."

Tessa rarely practices mindfulness meditation, but I am glad that she overhears the little lessons and short guided meditations that I listen to. It is also cool that she does it in her high school. Someday in her life, she might decide to do it more, but until then, I generally bite my tongue and try not to suggest that she do a lesson with me. About every two months, however, I do find myself asking. And about 50% of the time, she agrees.

For kids and teens who are interested, there are many many apps and YouTube videos that provide little lessons in meditation. The short lessons that precede the sessions on the Headspace app are fun, designed with animation and explain the basic concepts well.

IDEAS FOR CONVERSATION STARTERS:

1. When you think about the words "mindfulness" and "meditation," what comes to mind?
2. Have you ever learned anything about mindfulness or breathing exercises in school?
3. Does your mind focus on negative thoughts more than you want? And if so, do you think it is possible to get better at redirecting your thoughts toward more pleasant ones?
4. Do you think people can get better at stopping before doing something, like hitting send on a picture they might regret or sending a harsh text?

NOTES

Chapter 1 Social Media

1. Lauricella, A. R., Cingel, D. P., Beaudoin-Ryan, L., Robb, M. B., Saphir, M., & Wartella, E. A. (2016). The Common Sense Census: Plugged-In Parents of Tweens and Teens. (p. 24). San Francisco, CA: Common Sense Media. Retrieved from https://www.commonsensemedia.org/sites/default/files/uploads/research/common-sense-parent-census_whitepaper_new-for-web.pdf.

2. Cain, S. (Producer). (2016, March 3). Episode 5: How Young Introverts Can Thrive on Social Media [Audio podcast]. Retrieved from https://www.quietrev.com/wp-content/uploads/2016/03/Quiet-The-Power-of-Introverts-with-Susan-Cain-Episode-5-Transcript.pdf

3. Twenge, J. M., Spitzberg, B. H., & Campbell, W. K. (2019). Less in-person social interaction with peers among U.S. adolescents in the 21st century and links to loneliness. Journal of Social and Personal Relationships, 36(6), 1892–1913. doi:10.1177/0265407519836170.

4. 25 Myths about Bullying and Cyberbullying: Englander, Elizabeth K.: 9781118736500: Amazon.com: Books. (2020). Retrieved July 6, 2020, from https://www.amazon.com/25-Myths-about-Bullying-Cyberbullying/dp/1118736508

5. Rideout, V., & Robb, M. B. (2018). Social Media, Social Life: Teens Reveal Their Experiences (p. 26). San Francisco, CA: Common Sense Media. Retrieved from https://www.commonsensemedia.org/sites/default/files/uploads/research/2018_cs_socialmediasociallife_fullreport-final-release_2_lowres.pdf.

6. Fang, T. (2019, December 21). We asked teenagers what adults are missing about technology. This was the best response. Retrieved July 6, 2020, from https://www.technologyreview.com/2019/12/21/131163/youth-essay-contest-adults-dont-understand-kid-technology/

7. Lorenz, T. (2019, November/December). Here's What's Happening in the American Teenage Bedroom. The New York Times. Retrieved from https://www.nytimes.com/2019/11/29/style/the-clout.html.

8. Cohen, R., Shah, P., Kwerel, L., Lu, T., & Schmidt, J. (Producers), & Vedantam, S. (Director). (2019, September 9). *Online Behavior, Real-Life Consequences: The Unfolding Of A Social Media Scandal* [Video file]. Retrieved from https://www.npr.org/2019/09/06/758281834/you-cant-hit-unsend-how-a-social-media-scandal-unfolded-at-harvard

9. Gilbert, B. (2019, December 07). There might be another reason Instagram is testing hiding 'likes': To get you to post more. Retrieved from https://www.businessinsider.com/instagram-removing-likes-to-get-users-to-post-more-report-2019-12.

10. Loren, T. (2020, January 13). Hidden Likes on Instagram: The Ultimate Guide to Likes Disappearing. Retrieved from https://later.com/blog/hidden-likes-instagram.

11. CBS News. (2019, November 11). Instagram's decision to hide "likes" is getting dislikes. Retrieved July 6, 2020, from https://www.cbsnews.com/news/instagram-decision-to-make-likes-private-getting-dislikes/

Chapter 2 Video Games

1. Rideout, V., & Robb, M. B. (2019). The Common Sense Census: Media Use by Tweens and Teens (p. 37). San Francisco, CA: Common Sense Media. Retrieved from https://www.commonsensemedia.org/research/the-common-sense-census-media-use-by-tweens-and-teens-2019#:~:text=The%20Common%20Sense%20Census%3A%20Media%20Use%20by%20Tweens%20and%20Teens%2C%202019,-Kids'%20media%20preferences&text=This%20large%2Dscale%20study%20explores,and%20what%20they%20enjoy%20most.

2. Flatow, I., & McGonigal, J. (2011, February 18). Could Gaming Be Good For You? NPR. Retrieved from https://www.npr.org/2011/02/18/133870801/could-gaming-be-good-for-you.

3. Reilly, C. (2009). Gaming and the Public Health, Part 1 (p. 3). National Center for Responsible Gaming. Retrieved from https://www.icrg.org/sites/default/files/uploads/docs/faq/ncrg_monograph_vol3.pdf.

4. Leslie, I. (2016, October/November). The Scientists Who Make Apps Addictive. 1843. Retrieved from https://www.1843magazine.com/features/the-scientists-who-make-apps-addictive.

5. Schüll, N. D. (2014). Addiction by Design: Machine Gambling in Las Vegas. Princeton, NJ: Princeton University Press. doi:10.1515/9781400834655.

6. Wakefield, J. (2019, April 4). Fortnite: Is Prince Harry right to want game banned? BBC News. Retrieved from https://www.bbc.com/news/technology-47813894

7. Wijman, T. (2019, June 18). The Global Games Market Will Generate $152.1 Billion in 2019 as the U.S. Overtakes China as the Biggest Market. Retrieved from https://newzoo.com/insights/articles/the-global-games-market-will-generate-152-1-billion-in-2019-as-the-u-s-overtakes-china-as-the-biggest-market.

8. Pembroke parent gets $8K Xbox bill after son racks up charges. (2016, January 12). Retrieved July 6, 2020, from https://www.cbc.ca/news/canada/ottawa/pembroke-xbox-bill-8000-1.3397534

9. Video game loot boxes declared illegal under Belgium gambling laws. (2018, April 26). BBC News. Retrieved from https://www.bbc.com/news/technology-43906306

10. Senator Hassan Statement on Announcement that Major Video Game Manufacturers Will Make Loot Box Odds More Transparent | U.S. Senator Maggie Hassan of New Hampshire. (2019, August 7). Retrieved from https://www.hassan.senate.gov/news/press-releases/senator-hassan-statement-on-announcement-that-major-video-game-manufacturers-will-make-loot-box-odds-more-transparent

11. Fung, B. (2018, November 28). U.S. consumer watchdog to investigate video game loot boxes. The Washington Post. Retrieved from https://www.washingtonpost.com/technology/2018/11/28/us-consumer-watchdog-investigate-video-game-loot-boxes/.

12. Anderson, C. A., & Bushman, B. J. (2001). Effects of Violent Video Games on Aggressive Behavior, Aggressive Cognition, Aggressive Affect, Physiological Arousal, and Prosocial Behavior: A Meta-Analytic Review of the Scientific Literature (5th ed., Vol. 12, pp. 353-359). doi:10.1111/1467-9280.00366.

13. Violent Video Games and Aggression | National Center for Health Research. (2018, March 27). Retrieved from http://www.center4research.org/violent-video-games-can-increase-aggression/

14. Sussman, C. J., Harper, J. M., Stahl, J. L., & Weigle, P. (2018). Internet and Video Game Addictions: Diagnosis, Epidemiology, and Neurobiology (2nd ed., Vol. 27, pp. 307-326). Child and Adolescent Psychiatric Clinics of North America. doi:10.1016/j.chc.2017.11.015

15. *The Making of Eterna* [Video file]. (2014). United States: PBS NOVA Labs. Retrieved 2020, from https://www.pbs.org/wgbh/nova/labs/video_popup/4/29/.

16. Miltenberger, R. G. (2008). *Behavior Modification: Principles and Procedures* (4th ed.). Belmont, CA: Thomson Learning. Retrieved from http://rehabilitationpsychologist.org/resources/[Raymond_G._Miltenberger]_Behaviour_Modification_(BookFi.org).pdf

17. Gaming Disorder. (2018, September 14). *World Health Organization*. Retrieved 2020, from https://www.who.int/news-room/q-a-detail/gaming-disorder

18. Weinstein, A., & Lejoyeux, M. (2015). *New Developments on the Neurobiological and Pharmaco–Genetic Mechanisms Underlying Internet and Videogame Addiction* (Vol. 24, pp. 117-125). The American Journal on Addictions. doi:10.1111/ajad.12110.

19. Gentile, P. (2019). *Video Game Addiction Questionnaire* [PDF]. Horsham, PA: Be a Part of the Conversation. Retrieved from https://conversation.zone/wp-content/uploads/2019/05/Video-Game-Questionnaire.pdf.

20. Adair, C. (2019, December 18). Video Game Addiction Articles and Resources. Retrieved July 06, 2020, from https://gamequitters.com/blog/

Chapter 3 Mental Health

1. Rideout, V., Fox, S., & Well Being Trust. (2018). Digital Health Practices, Social Media Use, and Mental Well-Being Among Teens and Young Adults in the U.S. Retrieved from https://digitalcommons.psjhealth.org/publications/1093/

2. Richards, J. M., & Gross, J. J. (2000). Emotion regulation and memory: The cognitive costs of keeping one's cool. Journal of Personality and Social Psychology, 79(3), 410–424. https://doi.org/10.1037/0022-3514.79.3.410

3. My Age of Anxiety: Fear, Hope, Dread, and the Search for Peace of Mind: Stossel, Scott: 9780307390608: Amazon.com: Books. (2020). Retrieved July 6, 2020, from https://www.amazon.com/dp/0307390608/ref=dp-kindle-redirect?_encoding=UTF8&btkr=1

4. Washington State Department of Health. (2013). Washington State Healthy Youth Survey. Retrieved from https://www.doh.wa.gov/DataandStatisticalReports/DataSystems/HealthyYouthSurvey

5. Duffy, M. E., Twenge, J. M., & Joiner, T. E. (2019). *Trends in Mood and Anxiety Symptoms and Suicide-Related Outcomes Among U.S. Undergraduates, 2007–2018: Evidence From Two National Surveys* (5th ed., Vol. 65, pp. 590-598). Journal of Adolescent Health. doi:10.1016/j.jadohealth.2019.04.033

6. Merikangas, K. R., He, J., Burstein, M., Swanson, S. A., Avenevoli, S., Cui, L., ... Swendsen, J. (2010). Lifetime Prevalence of Mental Disorders in U.S. Adolescents: Results from the National Comorbidity Survey Replication–Adolescent Supplement (NCS-A). Journal of the American Academy of Child & Adolescent Psychiatry, 49(10), 980–989. https://doi.org/10.1016/j.jaac.2010.05.017

7. Learn more about mental health | NAMI: National Alliance on Mental Illness. (2020). Retrieved from https://www.nami.org/About-Mental-Illness

8. Parent Match Program. (2016). Retrieved from https://www.naminycmetro.org/parent-match-program/

9. Mental Health Resource Center - The Jed Foundation (JED). (2020, May 5). Retrieved from https://www.jedfoundation.org/mental-health-resource-center/

10. (2020). Seize the Awkward. Retrieved from https://seizetheawkward.org/

11. Topics A-Z | Child Mind Institute. (2019, June 19). Retrieved from https://child-mind.org/topics-a-z/

12. Take A Course - Mental Health First Aid. (2013, October 18). Retrieved from https://www.mentalhealthfirstaid.org/take-a-course/

13. Finding Help. (2020). Retrieved from https://www.mhanational.org/finding-help

14. Crisis Text Line | Text HOME To 741741 free, 24/7 Crisis Counseling. (2020). Retrieved from https://www.crisistextline.org/

Chapter 4 Sleep

1. iGen: Why Today's Super-Connected Kids Are Growing Up Less Rebellious, More Tolerant, Less Happy--and Completely Unprepared for Adulthood--and What That Means for the Rest of Us (9781501152016): Twenge, Jean M.: Books. (2020). Retrieved from https://www.amazon.com/dp/1501152017/ref=dp-kindle-redirect?_encoding=UTF8&btkr=1

2. Recharge with sleep: Pediatric sleep recommendations promoting optimal health - American Academy of Sleep Medicine – Association for Sleep Clinicians and Researchers. (2016, June 12). Retrieved July 6, 2020, from https://aasm.org/recharge-with-sleep-pediatric-sleep-recommendations-promoting-optimal-health/

3. Nelson, E., Leibenluft, E., McClure, E., & Pine, D. (2005). The social re-orientation of adolescence: A neuroscience perspective on the process and its relation to psychopathology. Psychological Medicine, 35(2), 163-174. doi:10.1017/S0033291704003915

4. Telzer, E. H., Goldenberg, D., Fuligni, A. J., Lieberman, M. D., & Gálvan, A. (2015). Sleep variability in adolescence is associated with altered brain development (Vol. 14, 1878-9293, pp. 16-22, Rep.). Developmental Cognitive Neuroscience. doi:10.1016/j.dcn.2015.05.007

5. Kirk, M. (2017, March 23). Suburban Sprawl Stole Your Kids' Sleep. Retrieved from https://www.bloomberg.com/news/articles/2017-03-23/urban-sprawl-affects-school-start-times-for-sleepy-teens

6. Carter B., Rees P., Hale L., Bhattacharjee D., Paradkar M. S. Association Between Portable Screen-Based Media Device Access or Use and Sleep Outcomes: A Systematic Review and Meta-analysis. JAMA Pediatr. 2016;170(12):1202–1208. doi:10.1001/jamapediatrics.2016.2341

7. Rideout, V., & Robb, M. B. (2019). The Common Sense Census: Media Use by Tweens and Teens (p. 37). San Francisco, CA: Common Sense Media. Retrieved from https://www.commonsensemedia.org/research/the-common-sense-census-media-use-by-tweens-and-teens-2019#:~:text=The%20Common%20Sense%20Census%3A%20Media%20Use%20by%20Tweens%20and%20Teens%2C%202019,-Kids'%20media%20preferences&text=This%20large%2Dscale%20study%20explores,and%20what%20they%20enjoy%20most.

8. Cooper, A. (2018, December 9). Screen time kids study: Groundbreaking study examines effects of screen time on kids - 60 Minutes. Retrieved from https://www.cbsnews.com/news/groundbreaking-study-examines-effects-of-screen-time-on-kids-60-minutes/

9. Munzer, T. G., Miller, A. L., Weeks, H. M., Kaciroti, N., & Radesky, J. (2019). Differences in Parent-Toddler Interactions With Electronic Versus Print Books (4th ed., Vol. 143, E20182012). Pediatrics. doi:10.1542/peds.2018-2012

Chapter 5 Essential Preparation For Screen Related Conversations

1. Worley, B. (2018, February 28). 48-hour screen-time experiment: What happens when kids have no limits. Retrieved from https://abcnews.go.com/GMA/Family/48-hour-screen-time-experiment-kids-limits/story?id=53410728

2. Ciciolla L., Curlee A.S., Karageorge J., Luthar S.S. When Mothers and Fathers Are Seen as Disproportionately Valuing Achievements: Implications for Adjustment Among Upper Middle Class Youth. *J Youth Adolesc.* 2017;46(5):1057-1075. doi:10.1007/s10964-016-0596-x

3. Handheld screen time linked with speech delays in young children. (2017, May 04). *American Academy of Pediatrics News.* Retrieved from https://www.aappublications.org/news/2017/05/04/PASScreenTime050417

4. Madigan S., Browne D., Racine N., Mori C., Tough S. Association Between Screen Time and Children's Performance on a Developmental Screening Test. JAMA Pediatr. 2019;173(3):244–250. doi:10.1001/jamapediatrics.2018.5056

5. Delaney Ruston. (2012). INDIA'S FIRST KIDS FLASH MOB DANCE - WORLD TB DAY [YouTube Video]. Retrieved from https://www.youtube.com/watch?v=6tynGqZV1Ao

6. Jiang, J. (2018). *How Teens and Parents Navigate Screen Time and Device Distractions.* Pew Research Center. Retrieved from https://www.pewresearch.org/internet/2018/08/22/how-teens-and-parents-navigate-screen-time-and-device-distractions/

7. Neal, D. T., Wood, W., Wu, M., & Kurlander, D. (2011). The Pull of the Past: When Do Habits Persist Despite Conflict With Motives? (11th ed., Vol. 37, 1428–1437). Society for Personality and Social Psychology. doi:10.1177/0146167211419863

8. Rideout, V., & Robb, M. B. (2018). Social Media, Social Life: Teens Reveal Their Experiences (p. 26). San Francisco, CA: Common Sense Media. Retrieved from https://www.commonsensemedia.org/sites/default/files/uploads/research/2018_cs_socialmediasociallife_fullreport-final-release_2_lowres.pdf.

9. Bryan C. J., Yeager D. S., Hinojosa C. P., et al. Harnessing adolescent values to motivate healthier eating. *Proc Natl Acad Sci USA.* 2016;113(39):10830-10835. doi:10.1073/pnas.1604586113

10. Davis, K. C., Nonnemaker, J. M., & Farrelly, M. C. (2007). *Association Between National Smoking Prevention Campaigns and Perceived Smoking Prevalence Among Youth in the United States* (5th ed., Vol. 41, pp. 430-436). Journal of Adolescent Health. doi:10.1016/j.jadohealth.2007.05.008

11. American Psychological Association, Ethics Committee. (1992). Ethical Principles of Psychologists and Code of Conduct. American Psychologist, 47(12), 1597–1611. https://doi.org/10.1037/0003-066X.47.12.1597

Chapter 6 Contracts and Family Rules

1. Worley, B. (2018, February 28). What happens when kids have no limits on their screen time. Retrieved from https://www.goodmorningamerica.com/family/story/48-hour-screen-time-experiment-kids-limits-53410728

2. Carlson, S. A., Fulton, J. E., Lee, S. M., Foley, J. T., Heitzler, C., & Huhman, M. (2010). Influence of Limit-Setting and Participation in Physical Activity on Youth Screen Time (1st ed., Vol. 126, E89-e96). Pediatrics. doi:10.1542/peds.2009-3374

3. Price, A. (2017). Is It Good to Fight With Your Teen? Retrieved from https://www.psychologytoday.com/us/blog/the-unmotivated-teen/201707/is-it-good-fight-your-teen

4. AVG Technologies. (2015). The AVG 2015 digital diaries. Retrieved from http://now.avg.com/digital-diaries-the-battle-forour-attention-press-kit/.

Chapter 7 Challenging Conversations

1. Lenhart, A., Smith, A., & Anderson, M. (2015, October). Teens, Technology and Romantic Relationships. Retrieved from https://www.pewresearch.org/internet/2015/10/01/teens-technology-and-romantic-relationships/

2. TAG Counseling. (2018). Street Drugs Available on Social Media?! Retrieved from https://tagcounseling.com/whats-new/page/5/

3. Dwoskin, E. (2018, September 25). Instagram has a drug problem. Its algorithms make it worse. The Washington Post. Retrieved from https://www.washingtonpost.com/business/economy/instagram-has-a-drug-problem-its-algorithms-make-it-worse/2018/09/25/c45bf730-bdbf-11e8-b7d2-0773aa1e33da_story.html?noredirect=on

4. Bickert, M. (2018, September 26). How We Enforce Against Illicit Drug Sales. Retrieved from https://about.fb.com/news/2018/09/enforcing-against-drug-sales/

5. Nash, S. G., McQueen, A., & Bray, J. H. (2005). *Pathways to adolescent alcohol use: Family environment, peer influence, and parental expectations* (1st ed., Vol. 37, pp. 19-28). Journal of Adolescent Health. doi:10.1016/j.jadohealth.2004.06.004

6. Martino S. C., Setodji C. M., Collins R. L., et al. Persistence of Shifts in Beliefs Associated With Exposure to Alcohol Advertising Among Adolescents. *J Stud Alcohol Drugs*. 2018;79(3):399-407. doi:10.15288/jsad.2018.79.399

7. Rimal, R.N. and Real, K. (2003), Understanding the Influence of Perceived Norms on Behaviors. Communication Theory, 13: 184-203. doi:10.1111/j.1468-2885.2003.tb00288.x

8. Linkenbach, J. W., Bengtson, P. L., Brandon, J. M. et al. Reduction of Youth Monthly Alcohol Use Using the Positive Community Norms Approach. *Child Adolesc Soc Work J* (2020). https://doi.org/10.1007/s10560-020-00666-4

9. Madigan S., Ly A., Rash C. L., Van Ouytsel J., Temple J. R. Prevalence of Multiple Forms of Sexting Behavior Among Youth: A Systematic Review and Meta-analysis. JAMA Pediatr. 2018;172(4):327–335. doi:10.1001/jamapediatrics.2017.5314

10. Statistic Brain. (2017, April 25). Sexting Statistics. Retrieved from https://www.statisticbrain.com/sexting-statistics/

11. Powell, L. (2015, September 8). Teen "Sexting" Is a Problem, But Is It a Crime? Retrieved from https://nccriminallaw.sog.unc.edu/teen-sexting-is-a-problem-but-is-it-a-crime/

12. Sex Etc. (2020). I have a naked picture of my partner. Can I get in trouble? Retrieved from https://sexetc.org/info-center/post/my-partner-is-17-and-im-18-i-have-a-naked-picture-my-partner-sent-to-me-on-my-phone-my-friend-told-me-that-if-someone-else-sees-it-i-can-be-charged-with-having-child-pornography-is-this-t/

13. Orenstein, P. (2020). Boys & Sex: Young Men on Hookups, Love, Porn, Consent, and Navigating the New Masculinity eBook: Orenstein, Peggy: Kindle Store. Retrieved from https://www.amazon.com/Boys-Sex-Hookups-Navigating-Masculinity-ebook/dp/B07RFLTCD8

14. Smith, C. E., & Rizzo, M. T. (2017). *Children's confession- and lying-related emotion expectancies: Developmental differences and connections to parent-reported confession behavior* (Vol. 156, pp. 113-128). Journal of Experimental Child Psychology. doi:10.1016/j.jecp.2016.12.002

15. Lee, K., Talwar, V., McCarthy, A., Ross, I., Evans, A., & Arruda, C. (2014). Can Classic Moral Stories Promote Honesty in Children? Psychological Science, 25(8), 1630–1636. https://doi.org/10.1177/0956797614536401

16. Bronson, P., & Merryman, A. (2020). NurtureShock: New Thinking About Children. Retrieved from https://www.amazon.com/NurtureShock-New-Thinking-About-Children/dp/0446504130

17. Keele University. (2009, July 13). Swearing Can Actually Increase Pain Tolerance. ScienceDaily. Retrieved from www.sciencedaily.com/releases/2009/07/090713085453.htm

18. Common Sense and SurveyMonkey Release Survey of Parents and Teens on Social Media Concerns | SurveyMonkey. (2017). Retrieved from https://www.surveymonkey.com/newsroom/common-sense-and-surveymonkey-release-survey-of-parents-and-teens-on-social-media-concerns/

Chapter 8 Screens in Schools and Homework

1. Kurtz, H., Lloyd, S., Harwin, A., & Osher, M. (2018). School Leaders and Technology: Results From a National Survey. Editorial Projects in Education. Retrieved from https://www.edweek.org/media/school-leaders-and-technology-education-week-research.pdf.

2. Blume, H. (2015, April 16). L.A. school district demands iPad refund from Apple. Retrieved from https://www.latimes.com/local/lanow/la-me-ln-ipad-curriculum-refund-20150415-story.html

3. Visible Learning. (2018, March 7). Collective Teacher Efficacy (CTE) according to John Hattie - VISIBLE LEARNING. Retrieved from https://visible-learning.org/2018/03/collective-teacher-efficacy-hattie/

4. Delaney Ruston. (2017, December 22). Smartphones: the new teen mental health crisis? Retrieved from https://www.cnn.com/2017/12/22/opinions/smartphones-middle-school-opinion-ruston/index.html

5. Kuznekoff, J. H., & Titsworth, S. (2013). *The Impact of Mobile Phone Usage on Student Learning* (3rd ed., Vol. 62, pp. 233-252). Communication Education. doi:10.1080/03634523.2013.767917

6. Ward, A. F., Duke, K., Gneezy, A., & Bos, M. W. (2017). Brain Drain: The Mere Presence of One's Own Smartphone Reduces Available Cognitive Capacity (2nd ed., Vol. 2, pp. 140-154). Journal of the Association for Consumer Research. doi:1086/691462

7. Beland, L., & Murphy, R. (2016). Ill Communication: Technology, distraction & student performance (Vol. 41, pp. 61-76). Labour Economics. doi:10.1016/j.labeco.2016.04.004

8. Logan, E., & Kamenetz, A. (2018, February 17). Should The Parkland Shooting Change How We Think About Phones, Schools and Safety? Retrieved from

https://www.npr.org/sections/ed/2018/02/17/586534079/should-the-parkland-shooting-change-how-we-think-about-phones-schools-and-safety

9. Pooja S. Tandon et al. Cellphone Use Policies in US Middle and High Schools. *JAMA Netw Open*. 2020; 3(5):e205183. doi:10.1001/jamanetworkopen.2020.5183

10. Rosen, L. D., Carrier, L. M., & Cheever, N. A. (2013). Facebook and texting made me do it: Media-induced task-switching while studying. Elsevier. doi:10.1016/j.chb.2012.12.001

11. Gazzaley, A., & Rosen, L. D. (2016). *The Distracted Mind: Ancient Brains in a High-Tech World*. Cambridge, MA: MIT Press.

12. Peterson, J., & Lillard, A. S. (2011). *The Immediate Impact of Different Types of Television on Young Children's Executive Function* (4th ed., Vol. 128, pp. 644-649). Pediatrics. doi:10.1542/peds.2010-1919

13. Ophir, E., Nass, C., & Wagner, A. D. (2009). Cognitive control in media multi-taskers (37th ed., Vol. 106, 15583-15587). PNAS. doi:10.1073/pnas.0903620106

14. Oakley, B. (2018). Learning How to Learn: Powerful mental tools to help you master tough subjects. Retrieved from https://www.coursera.org/learn/learning-how-to-learn

Chapter 9 Fostering Human Bonds

1. Rideout, V., & Robb, M. B. (2018). Social Media, Social Life: Teens Reveal Their Experiences (p. 26). San Francisco, CA: Common Sense Media. Retrieved from https://www.commonsensemedia.org/sites/default/files/uploads/research/2018_cs_socialmediasociallife_fullreport-final-release_2_lowres.pdf.

2. Gross, T. (2018, May 8). Duplass Brothers On Working Together And Growing Apart: "We Are Ex-Soulmates." Retrieved from https://www.npr.org/2018/05/08/609349238/duplass-brothers-on-working-together-and-growing-apart-we-are-ex-soulmates

3. Morisi, T. L. (2017, February). *Teen labor force participation before and after the Great Recession and beyond*. doi:10.21916/mlr.2017.5

4. Ward, A. F., Duke, K., Gneezy, A., & Bos, M. W. (2017). Brain Drain: The Mere Presence of One's Own Smartphone Reduces Available Cognitive Capacity (2nd ed., Vol. 2, pp. 140-154). Journal of the Association for Consumer Research. doi:1086/691462

5. Giolando, E. (2018, May 9). How I've Learned To Get Someone To Put Down Their Phone And Listen. Retrieved from https://www.fastcompany.com/40568212/how-ive-learned-to-get-someone-to-put-down-their-phone-and-listen

6. Epley, N., & Schroeder, J. (2014). Mistakenly seeking solitude. Journal of Experimental Psychology. General, 143 5, 1980-99. doi: 10.1037/e578192014-009

7. Murthy, V. (2017, September 26). Work and the Loneliness Epidemic. Retrieved from https://hbr.org/cover-story/2017/09/work-and-the-loneliness-epidemic

8.   Misra, S., Cheng, L., Genevie, J., & Yuan, M. (2016). The iPhone Effect: The Quality of In-Person Social Interactions in the Presence of Mobile Devices. Environment and Behavior, 48(2), 275–298. https://doi.org/10.1177/0013916514539755

9. Kids Competing with Mobile Phones for Parents' Attention. (2015). Retrieved from https://now.avg.com/digital-diaries-kids-competing-with-mobile-phones-for-parents-attention

10. GreatSchools. (2017, September 6). Like a Sponge Podcast: Their Own Devices. Retrieved from https://www.greatschools.org/gk/articles/like-a-sponge-their-own-devices/

Chapter 10 Cultivating Insight, Creativity, and Focus

1. Rideout, V., & Robb, M. B. (2019). The Common Sense Census: Media Use by Tweens and Teens (p. 37). San Francisco, CA: Common Sense Media. Retrieved from https://www.commonsensemedia.org/research/the-common-sense-census-media-use-by-tweens-and-teens-2019#:~:text=The%20Common%20Sense%20Census%3A%20Media%20Use%20by%20Tweens%20and%20Teens%2C%202019,-Kids'%20media%20preferences&text=This%20large%2Dscale%20study%20explores,and%20what%20they%20enjoy%20most.

2. Bach, N. (2019, February 15). This Young Adult Author Is Giving Up Her Smartphone for a Year to Try Winning $100,000. Retrieved from https://fortune.com/2019/02/15/vitaminwater-smartphone-challenge-winner/

3. Leonhardt, M. (2019, February 15). This millennial will give up a smartphone for a year to win $100,000 in the Vitaminwater challenge. Retrieved from https://www.cnbc.com/2019/02/14/millennial-gives-up-smartphone-to-win-100000-dollars-in-vitaminwater-challenge.html

4. Anderson, M., & Jiang, J. (2018). Teens, Social Media & Technology 2018. Pew Research Center. Retrieved from https://www.pewresearch.org/ internet/2018/05/31/teens-social-media-technology-2018/.

5. Pielot, M., Church, K., & de Olivera, R. (2014). An in-situ study of mobile phone notifications | Proceedings of the 16th international conference on Human-computer interaction with mobile devices & services. Retrieved from Acm.org website: https://dl.acm.org/doi/10.1145/2628363.2628364

6. Newport, C. (2019, February 5). Digital Minimalism: Choosing a Focused Life in a Noisy World. Retrieved from https://www.amazon.com/ Digital-Minimalism-Choosing-Focused-Noisy/dp/0525536515

7. Herrera, T. (2019, January 13). How to Actually, Truly Focus on What You're Doing. Retrieved from https://www.nytimes.com/2019/01/13/smarter-living/how-to-actually-truly-focus-on-what-youre-doing.html

Acknowledgments

I am deeply appreciative of all those that have contributed to the creation of this book. My greatest thanks go to Lisa Tabb who has helped me brainstorm a myriad ideas. Not only is Lisa a brilliant thought partner, but she has also been instrumental in helping me express ideas in an organized and clear way.

I am incredibly grateful to Beth Duff-Brown, Gen Chase and Sam Silverstein for their masterful editing of this book, along with Logan Smith, who did such a stellar job in the final proofing. A special thanks to Manisha Khakoo for her meticulous work in verifying and collating all of the references. And thanks to Rachel Keisla who helped with the book's organization.

Thanks to Alan Hebel for his beautiful book design and to Ian Koviak, an extraordinarily talented artist, who created the book's cover. And I could not have been happier than with Starhouse Media for being my wonderful publisher, a non-stop source of ideas and encouragement throughout this whole process.

A major thank you goes to the *Screenagers* Community Engagement Team made up of Anna Simmons, Monica Bergman, Katherine Csizmadia, Kelsey Fernandez and Rebecca Tollen, for sharing their wonderful wisdom with me for all these years.

My thanks go out to the incredible researchers and thought leaders who I have had the privilege of interviewing along the way. Many of these scientists have become dear friends and I cherish the in-depth conversations we have had about so many topics. I must confess that I am particularly thankful for their unwavering availability to answer my ongoing questions.

The willingness of so many families and youth to share their experiences and perspectives with me has been instrumental in making this book so rich with examples and I am eternally grateful. In addition, I am grateful to the *Screenagers* Teen Advisory Council, and the countless other young people who have helped me see things from many different viewpoints.

I am blessed to be able to thank so many friends and family for providing essential critical feedback and loving support including, but not limited to, Jennifer Iverson, Debra Jarvis, Lynn Delaney, Parker and Natalie Small, Carla Small, Lisa Cox, Bezalel Dantz, Patricia Boiko, Deborah Wang, Laura Kastner, Tammy Huson Fisher, Katie Small and Janet Delaney.

It is with such love that I thank my kids Chase and Tessa for their willingness to be in this book, as well as the *Screenagers* movies. I have always made sure to get their approval before sharing things about them in any of my work and I feel so fortunate for the trust we have built over the years in this regard. Not only have they allowed the sharing of their lives and ideas, but have been so generous in sharing their perspectives on the digital lives of kids and teens in today's world.

And finally, I am beyond thankful to my husband, Peter Small, for being so patient with my hours and hours of writing and also allowing me to share stories from our home life. Writing this book was definitely made with many labor pains and to have Peter's enduring confidence in me along the way made all the difference.